Probing the Mind:
How does Consciousness Work?

DUKKYU CHOI

Probing the Mind: How does Consciousness Work? by Dukkyu Choi

ISBN 978-1-952027-12-3 (Paperback)
ISBN 978-1-952027-13-0 (Hardback)

This book is written to provide information and motivation to readers. Its purpose is not to render any type of psychological, legal, or professional advice of any kind. The content is the sole opinion and expression of the author, and not necessarily that of the publisher.

Copyright © 2020 by Dukkyu Choi

All rights reserved. No part of this book may be reproduced, transmitted, or distributed in any form by any means, including, but not limited to, recording, photocopying, or taking screenshots of parts of the book, without prior written permission from the author or the publisher. Brief quotations for noncommercial purposes, such as book reviews, permitted by Fair Use of the U.S. Copyright Law, are allowed without written permissions, as long as such quotations do not cause damage to the book's commercial value. For permissions, write to the publisher, whose address is stated below.

Printed in the United States of America.

New Leaf Media, LLC
175 S. 3rd Street, Suite 200
Columbus, OH 43215
www.thenewleafmedia.com

Table of Contents

Preface v

PART I: The Mind in Every Day Living 1

1. The Brain is Not as Smart as We Think 3
2. Five Sense Consciousnesses 11
3. Storage of Consciousness—Store Consciousness 17
4. A Sense Organ for Reading Consciousness Information—Mind 23
5. Fifty One Mental Activities (Caittas) 31
6. The Difference between Thinking and Memorizing 37
7. The Epitome of Thinking and Its Contamination 43
8. The Delusion of Thinking—Why Do We Not See the True Nature? 49
9. A Dog Has a Better Mind Organ than a Human 55
10. An Inanimate Being Has a Mind Organ 61
11. See Your Mind (I): See Your Mind Interactions (Mental Activities) 69
12. See Your Mind (II): How? 75
13. See Your Mind (III): See Your True Nature 81
14. Ways of Thinking in Oriental and Western Cultures ... 87
15. The Amalgamation of Oriental and Western Philosophies .. 93
16. Four Wisdoms through Consciousnesses 99
17. What Is Emptiness? 105

PART II: The Mind and the Dream World 113

18. The Mystery of Dreams—Dream Consciousness............115
19. A History of Dream Research............................121
20. Does the Brain Dream?—A Wrong Hypothesis...............127
21. How Is a Dream Made Up?—The Mechanism
    of Dream Consciousness 131
22. Why Is a Dream Illogical or Inconsistent? 137
23. Why Is It Difficult to Remember Dreams? 141
24. Thinking and Judgement in a Dream—Lucid Dreaming .147
25. How Does Dreaming Result in Revelations?...............153
26. A Dream Is Not a Mere Dream Any More...................161
27. More on the Mind Organ and Mind Information 165

PART III: The Mind After Death 173

28. The Unknown World of 'After-Death' 175
29. What Is Soul? 179
30. Mechanism of After-Death Consciousness 187
31. Communication with the Dead...........................193
32. Reincarnation and Samsara 199
33. Why Don't We Remember Previous Lives? 207
34. Impetus for Reincarnation—Karma 211
35. Nirvana—Eternal Life 219

Appendix—Summary of the Consciousness Only Theory......231
Bibliography.. 243

Preface

Which is primary, the *mind* or the *brain*? We can see an evolution of this topic as we go from the nature-oriented and mystical philosophies and traditions of pre-scientific thought through the scientific focus of the Renaissance and the Age of Reason, and then more recently into the realm of the Transcendentalists and modern philosophers buoyed by the psychologists and psychiatrists and their associates. It is in this context that the brain/mind question might lead to an increased depth of understanding of whatever spiritual or non-spiritual philosophy one might be considering.

Dukkyu Choi does an outstanding job of breaking this question into its relevance to various phases of our existence (awake, dreaming, and after-death) and helping us to understand each of these from the perspective of the Consciousness-Only Theory within Mahayana Buddhism, but the relevance of his exposition is far broader than just to Buddhism itself. The concepts presented herein may amplify or complement existing elements within your current belief system, or may provide the catalyst for an expansion or solidification of your beliefs. In any case, a consideration of these concepts will lead to a better understanding of what you believe and why you believe it, whether it incorporates or dismisses the concepts within this book.

As we consider this we are led to a related question: is there a continuation of existence after death. Does anything survive following the 'death' of the brain? There are modern scientists who say that when the brain dies there is nothing left of the previous person—no spirit or no other existence. The brain is all. The person is gone other than what memories or mementos might remain with family, friends, acquaintances, etc.

There are, on the other hand, a great number of scientists and non-scientists who posit the ongoing existence of another manifestation of the self—a continuation of the spiritual or higher being which had been incarnate in the body which is now deceased. These would say that the living energy which had been manifest in the living body is still extant, but it is now associated with a non-material form which may or may not continue to interact with people who continue to reside in the 'real' world of the material existence. These latter would envision a 'mind' or other essence which supersedes the brain and exists independent of it. Although the concepts may vary, for many of these the brain is simply an organ which enables the material body to serve as the manifestation of the 'mind.'

One question we might ask is whether we can put this into any kind of a historical context. We have written records of the past few thousand years, but what about early humankind in prehistory? Early rock art (both pictographs and petroglyphs) are open to interpretation and cannot provide any definitive data on the beliefs of the early people who made them other than to depict the life which they lived and the hunting and other methods which they used. We might say the same about all other evidence of their history, but I believe that we can make some educated inferences about their spiritual beliefs based upon their art and their burial sites as well as apparent ceremonial sites. If we do this, we should acknowledge that their spiritual beliefs could well reflect their concept of a continuing existence after the death of the physical body.

What evidence might we find in the burial practices of the prehistoric people which might provide clues as to their beliefs? Early humans led a nomadic lifestyle prior to learning farming techniques since the flora and fauna of an area would be depleted as they used it for their sustenance. This would require them to move on to another area which had not been recently 'harvested' and let the prior area recover and regrow for the next time they passed through. In many areas this amounted to following the migrating herds of animals as they followed the seasonal fluctuation of the grasslands or other food sources. During this period there would be isolated burial sites at best since the people were on the move. When they began to practice the art of cultivation, of farming, however, they formed settlements where multiple people inhabited an area for extended periods of time and we can find where they created burial grounds or cemeteries. It is at these burial grounds that we can discern patterns which might better reflect their beliefs.

There are some burial grounds where all of the bodies are laid out in a parallel fashion, commonly oriented east to west. Is this related to the movement of the sun from the east to the west, possibly as a symbol of the rebirth of the spirit/soul even as the sun is 'reborn' each day? We can't say for sure, but we do know that the ancients did study the heavens and honored or worshiped the solar and lunar cycles of the day, month and year. Other burial grounds had all of the bodies buried in a fetal position. Again, was this in preparation for a rebirth, or just to require a smaller hole to be dug? Other bodies were buried in caves, or suspended in woven baskets from cliffs. We cannot say definitively that these represent proof that these people believed in an afterlife, but is there more?

Many of the ancient graves had the decedent dressed in very good clothes with fancy headdresses and/or beads or other jewelry, and many with a very nice tools or weapons. It was also common to paint the dead with ochre or other colorings. Were these strictly out of respect for the one who had died, or were these to give them the things which would be needed in the next life? Again, we cannot say for sure, but can only try to make reasoned judgments as to the intent. We may get additional clarification as we move into the period of written history, however, and that would mostly support the concept of an afterlife. That would imply that something continues beyond the death of the brain.

The ancient Egyptians believed that each person had a soul, and after death that soul would split into two parts: the *Ba*, which represented all aspects of the deceased except for the physical body, would remain on the earth plane and look after the family which remained behind; and the *Ka*, which would return to the Egyptian heaven each day before returning to reunite with the Ba each night. The ancient Romans believed that the soul would be escorted to the River Styx upon the death of the body and would be ferried across the River by Charon upon payment of a token (which would be buried with the corpse). The soul would then face three judges who would determine where it was to go from there. The ancient Sumerians also believed in an afterlife, but it was in a fairly nondescript netherworld which was but a shadow of the earth without the physical bodies. In summary, it would appear that nearly all, if not all, ancient cultures believed in an afterlife. This would require the continued existence of the person after the death of the brain, and this would be consistent with the concept of a *mind* as the primary determinant of the personality as opposed to the brain as that determinant.

It would seem that the concept of an afterlife was an integral part of nearly all of the major belief systems throughout early human history. If this was so widely accepted, however, we might ask what might have happened that would cause the major shift in thought to proposing that a person died in his or her entirety (i.e., with no remaining spirit, or soul, or energy form) with the death of the brain? I would propose that this might have been a result of the transformation of our thinking as a result of the Renaissance. Prior to the Renaissance was an Age of Faith wherein the great philosophers and religious thinkers set the tone for the belief systems which were accepted and followed by the masses, but the Renaissance was the period of time during which science began to overtake philosophy in the Western world and initiated the Age of Science in Europe and the United States. This was the age of Copernicus, Galileo and Newton, the "Golden Age of Knowledge" which initiated the role of repeatable demonstrations as the hallmark of *truth*. Repeatedly demonstrable facts became the only mark of an acceptable scientific thesis or belief system.

Since the concept of an afterlife could not be demonstrated in a repeatable manner, what did this do to the concept of *something* surviving death? Most in the scientific community in the 'West' rejected spirituality and said "science is all," whereas many in the 'East,' or who were raised in an oriental or 'eastern' belief system retained the primacy of the spiritual system within which they found themselves and sought to fit science into that structure. There were also times when the concept of true knowledge coming through intuition, dreams, meditation or imagination became popular within the West and joined with those in the East to say that science is not the only path to knowledge. One of the best known examples of this school of philosophy would be the Transcendentalists of the early 1800s in the United States. This group included Henry David Thoreau, Nathaniel Hawthorne, Henry Wadsworth Longfellow and Walt Whitman among others, but in spite of the influence of men such as these the scientific method has largely remained the benchmark of *truth* in the West.

There have also been scientists who have said that they get some of their best ideas through dreams, or meditation and contemplation, or otherwise intuitively, then use the scientific methodology to bring them to a fuller state of understanding. In other words, intuition or non-scientific thought brings the concept into their consciousness where they can then amplify on it and prepare it for public scrutiny through the scientific process. One of the most famous of this type dream is a dream which Albert Einstein had. Einstein dreamed that he was hurtling down a mountainside faster and faster, and when he looked at the sky he saw that the appearance of the stars changed as he approached the speed of light. It was this realization that led him to develop the Theory of Relativity.

Another example would be Russian chemist and professor Dmitri Mendeleev who was obsessed with trying to visualize and present the chemical elements in a way that made sense. He wrote the characteristics of each element on a card and set about trying to arrange them in a way which would do that, and he later wrote "In a dream I saw a table where all the elements fell into place as required. Awakening, I immediately wrote it down on a piece of paper."

Likewise Elias Howe, the inventor of the sewing machine, had a dream in which he was being captured by a group of savages. He noticed that all of their spears had holes in the tip, and this provided the insight that by placing the hole at the tip of his needle the thread could be caught after piercing the cloth. This insight enabled him to design and build a sewing machine which worked.

The above examples tell us that some of the achievements of the scientific age still take advantage of a working of the mind which transcends the scientific method, a foray into the *transcendental* realm of knowledge evidenced by Thoreau and the others of that school of thought. The battle between those who do not believe in transcendental inspiration versus those who do continues to this day, and this seems to align quite well with the topic of this book. I will draw heavily below upon an unpublished manuscript by David Stang who teaches a continuing education course in Washington D.C. for some modern examples of ongoing controversies in the scientific community which characterize this difference in philosophies.

Peter Atkins, a highly prominent British professor of chemistry and author of the book *Galileo's Finger*[1] is a proponent of the view that the empiricist scientific method "is the only valid means of determining whether an idea, concept, theory, intuition or hypothesis is true or false ... because of its purported objectivity, reductive technique and replicability.... This belief is partly due to the fact that most scientists confine their attention almost completely to material objects and measurable forms of energy, and they believe there is no other reality." Therefore, these scientists tend to believe that every dimension of human consciousness orig-

---

1 Atkins, P. W. (2003). *Galileo's Finger: the Ten Great Ideas of Science.* Oxford; New York: Oxford University Press.

inates only in the brain, and that all non-empirical methods are useless and invalid.

If we consider the scientific method to be based on a three legged stool, of which the preceding paragraph presents the first leg, the second leg would be that any statement or assertion regarding subjective sensory perception must be based on interaction with a material object interacting with at least one of the five senses functioning in a normal mode; i.e., not in an extra-sensory modality. Thus, "for anyone to claim that he witnessed an object or event which occurred in non-material form would constitute a hallucination." ... The third major component of this [stool] is that after one's last breath, one's last heartbeat, one's last neuron to synapse firing, all that remains of the once incarnate being, other than a dead body, is an absence of the decedent's life-force energy."

"Accordingly, the materialist contends that a Near-Death Experience is not only an hallucination but it's impossible for it to occur while the person is flat lined or technically deceased, and can only occur while the brain is still functioning. Therefore the patient's so-called memory of an adventure in the afterlife realm is wholly hallucinatory and could not possibly be considered an objectively verifiable reality. It follows from that conclusion that there can be no afterlife because without the brain being able to function ... there is nothing to see and the cognitive functioning of the decedent has been permanently terminated.

"If we were to adopt this materialist epistemology as our own then we would deny any reality that is not material. Put another way—as physicalists perceive reality—inasmuch as they believe that all valid perceptions of external reality are achieved through our five senses and mediated and originated by the brain—for anything to be correctly perceived as real it must be material. Following this line of reasoning they would deny the existence of a soul, spirit, mind or afterlife because each of them are immaterial therefore not only not real, but any perception of them, on its face, would be considered to be conclusively hallucinatory."

When we set out to investigate a philosophy of the mind rather than that of the brain, however, it "leads us in two directions: Philosophy and Spirituality. To help point us in the former direction we have the benefit of a related pair of definitions from *The Oxford Dictionary of Philosophy* regarding 'Philosophy of Mind' and 'The Mind-Body Problem.' If the brain is not necessarily the cause of consciousness (which is contrary to what materialists and physicalists claim) then how is the cause of consciousness to be understood? Max Velmans and Yujin Nagasawa's article 'Introduction to Monist Alternatives to Physicalism'[2]... is an overview of seven papers published in a special issue of *The Journal of Consciousness Studies* which present 'monist' (meaning 'one,' and therefore non-dualistic) views of wider consciousness which they contend may be conceptually preferable to the physicalist perspective which holds that the brain itself—and no other agent—is what creates consciousness, mind, awareness, etc. Max Velmans is Emeritus Professor of Psychology, Goldsmiths, University of London, Visiting Professor in Consciousness Studies, University of Plymouth, and has been involved in consciousness studies for over thirty-five years. Yujin Nagasawa is Professor of Philosophy at the University of Birmingham. He is author of *God and Phenomenal Consciousness*.[3]

"There is a growing number of thinkers who—while still clearly in the minority—sense that since the speculations of William James over a century ago there has been developing the beginnings of a paradigm shift that when in full bloom will be recognized within our Western culture as being as profound as the paradigm shift nearly five centuries ago involving the death of the Ptolemaic perception and the birth of the Copernican understanding of the structure of our solar system and universe. [An issue of] *The Journal of Consciousness Studies* (JCS) set forth the arguments for still another apparent paradigm shift which is slowly

---

2   Velmans, M. N., Yujin. (2012). *Introduction to Monist Alternatives to Physicalism.* Journal of Consciousness Studies: Special Issue on Monist Alternatives to Physicalism, 19 (Number 9-10).

3   Nagasawa, Y. (2008). *God and phenomenal consciousness: a novel approach to knowledge arguments.* Cambridge; New York: Cambridge University Press.

emerging. Prof. Max Velmans, a monist—therefore not a physicalist—(and co-author of that special issue of the JCS), sponsored an international workshop entitled '*Explorations Around the Edges of Consciousness*' in April 2014 at Dartington Hall in Devon, England. Those invited to the workshop included most of the leading thinkers in the world from both Eastern and Western cultures on the nature of consciousness. Prof. Velmans summarized the contribution of each participant in that workshop in a special report in Volume 21, No. 11-12, 2014 of the JCS at pp.140-148. ...

"...one of the most brilliant minds in the history of psychology was certainly Carl Jung, who concluded science seems unable to probe meaningfully into the ethereal realities we are exploring .... Jung, in his essay 'New Paths in Psychology' (in *Two Essays on Analytical Psychology*[4]) stated that science is able to reveal little that is useful in coming to comprehend human spiritual nature: 'Anyone who wants to know the human psyche will learn next to nothing from experimental psychology [such as the behaviorists insist upon]. He would be better advised to abandon exact science, put away his scholar's gown, bid farewell to his study, and wander with human heart throughout the world.'

"There is a cognitive psychologist named Steven Pinker... who... has unrestrainedly adopted the physicalist-Darwinist view of how the mind functions. He is so convinced that the brain causes thought that he uses the terms 'brain' and 'mind' interchangeably in his classic text, *How The Mind Works*[5], published in 1997 and then republished with a new Forward in 2009. He asserts that all speculations about consciousness, will, self, and ethics, since they can't be proven by empirical criteria, are meaningless.

"Thomas Nagel's most recent book *Mind & Cosmos: Why The Materialist Neo-Darwinian Conception of Nature Is Almost Certainly*

---

4   Jung, C. G. (1966). *Two essays on analytical psychology* (2d ed.). New York: Pantheon.

5   Pinker, S. (1997, 2009). *How the mind works* (Norton pbk. ed.). New York: Norton.

False[6] ... has caused quite a foundation shaking stir within academia. Professor Nagel opens his book with this declaration: 'The aim of this book is to argue that the mind-body problem is not just a local problem, having to do with the relation between mind, brain, and behavior in living animal organisms, but that it invades our understanding of the entire cosmos and its history. The physical sciences and evolutionary biology cannot be kept insulated from it, and I believe a true appreciation of the difficulty of the problem must eventually change our conception of the place of the physical sciences in describing the natural order.'

"He stated that 'most practicing scientists may have no opinion about the overarching cosmological questions to which this materialist reductionism provides an answer...[b]ut among the scientists and philosophers who do express views about the natural order as a whole, reductive materialism is widely assumed to be the only serious possibility. The starting point for the argument is the failure of psychophysical reductionism, a position in the philosophy of mind that is largely motivated by the hope of showing how the physical sciences could in principle provide a theory of everything. If that hope is unrealizable, the question arises whether any other more or less unified understanding could take in the entire cosmos as we know it....It seems to me that as it is usually presented, the current orthodoxy about the cosmic order is the product of governing assumptions that are unsupported, and that it flies in the face of common sense.'

... "At the end of his book Professor Nagel suggests that 'It would be an advance if the secular theoretical establishment, and the contemporary enlightened culture which it dominates, could wean itself of the materialism and Darwinism of the gaps—to adopt one of its own pejorative tags. I have tried to show that this approach is incapable of providing an adequate account, either constitutive or historical, of our universe.... I have argued patiently

---

6   Nagel, T. (2012). *Mind and Cosmos: Why the Materialist Neo-Darwinian Conception of Nature Is Almost Certainly False.* New York: Oxford University Press.

against the prevailing form of naturalism, a reductive materialism that purports to capture life and mind through its neo-Darwinian extension. But to go back to my introductory remarks, I find this view antecedently unbelievable—a heroic triumph of ideological theory over common sense.'

"Professor David Gelernter came to Thomas Nagel's defense in an article that appeared in *Commentary* in early January, 2014. Professor Gelernter's piece is entitled 'The Closing of the Scientific Mind[7].' ... [Professor Gelernter] is a scientist, not a philosopher or a humanities professor. He is speaking as a scientist to his fellow scientists about what a nonscientific philosopher has to say to scientists that should, he believes, have considerable value to them. His major contention is 'The modern "mind fields" encompass artificial intelligence, cognitive psychology, and philosophy of mind. Researchers in these fields are profoundly split, and the chaos was on display in the ugliness occasioned by the publication of Thomas Nagel's *Mind and Cosmos* in 2012. Nagel is an eminent philosopher and professor at NYU [New York University]. In *Mind and Cosmos*, he shows with terse, meticulous thoroughness why mainstream thought on the workings of the mind is intellectually bankrupt. He explains why Darwinian evolution is insufficient to explain the emergence of consciousness—the capacity to feel or experience the world. He then offers his own ideas on consciousness, which are speculative, incomplete, tentative, and provocative—in the tradition of science and philosophy' [but worthy of being considered].

"Professor Gelernter stressed in his article that science needs to explore 'what subjectivity is and why it shares the Cosmos with objective reality.' This is an enormous undertaking indeed. You can learn more about what Professors Nagel and Gelernter had to say in his article 'The Closing of the Scientific Mind.'

"Another scientist, Dr. Rupert Sheldrake, is a world renowned British biologist who has done significant research in the UK and

---

7   Gelernter, D. (2014, January 2014). *The Closing of the Scientific Mind*. Commentary Magazine.

the US, as well as elsewhere throughout the world. He too shares David Gelernter's concerns about the closing of the scientific mind and the need to more adequately comprehend subjectivity and why it shares the cosmos with objective reality, but he is also equally committed to providing evidentiary documentation which supports hypotheses and theories challenging the more traditional scientific perspective.

"One book Dr. Sheldrake recently wrote was published simultaneously in England under the title *The Science Delusion: Freeing the Spirit of Enquiry* and more positively titled in the United States as *Science Set Free: 10 Paths to New Discovery*[8].... In *Science Set Free* Dr. Sheldrake identifies ten major components of traditional science and provides alternative scientific means for understanding the phenomena in question. ...[Two of the topics he addresses are]: 'Are Minds Confined to Brains?' and 'Are Psychic Phenomena Illusory?' His answer to both questions is an unequivocal 'No'. As you might infer, Rupert Sheldrake's *Science Set Free* was intended to help open more scientific minds.

"... [Dr. Jim B. Tucker, M.D.] in his *Return to Life*[9], suggested that 'Findings in physics over the last hundred years—particularly in quantum physics or quantum mechanics, the study of the universe's smallest particles—have shown that the physical universe is much more complicated than it appears. They strengthen my view that there is a consciousness that exists separate from the material world. I now believe that the physical grows out of the mental, meaning that the physical world is created out of something you can think of as Mind or consciousness or the spiritual. Our cases, and the possibility of children remembering past lives, then fit in nicely with a new understanding of existence....'

"It would not seem unreasonable to inquire how Dr. Tucker, who is a child psychiatrist, was able to reach that conclusion, and

---

8   Sheldrake, R. (2012). *Science set free: 10 paths to new discovery*. New York: Deepak Chopra Books.

9   Tucker, J. B. (2013). *Return to life: extraordinary cases of children who remember past lives* (First Edition. ed.). New York: St. Martin's Griffin.

one glance at his bibliography of over one hundred titles provides us with the answer. There are over a dozen titles featuring quantum physics and quantum mechanics and on their relationship to consciousness itself. Thus, volumes have already been published on these topics. It might therefore be useful to acquaint ourselves, at least superficially, with such matters. In addition to the discoverers of quantum physics and quantum mechanics, there are other scientists who understand physics and the history of science who have written authoritatively about this topic.

"One of these authoritative experts is Amit Goswami, professor of physics at the Institute of Theoretical Sciences at the University of Oregon who authored *The Self Aware Universe: how consciousness creates the material world*[10]. In an anthology entitled *Mind Before Matter: Visions of a New Science of Consciousness*[11] Professor Goswami outlines how all these complicated ideas fit together in his opening essay "From information to Transformation." ... The Introduction to *Mind Before Matter* summarizes his essay as follows:

> Physicist Goswami meditates on mental information processing, on mental and emotional intelligence, and describes the limitations. He argues for a greater use of what he referred to variously as 'transformational intelligence' or, citing Sri Aurobindo, 'supramental intelligence' [or F.W.H. Meyer's and Dean Radin's 'supernormal' consciousness]. This faculty allows a person to move 'in the domain of archetypes' and even to transcend physical laws—to literally perform miracles. He complains that a deterministic materialistic worldview skews our understanding, relegating consciousness to the mere epiphenomenon of matter, concluding this

---

10　Goswami, A., Reed, R. E., & Goswami, M. (1993). *The self-aware universe: how consciousness creates the material world*. New York: Putnam's Sons.

11　Goswami, A. (2007). *Mind Before Matter: Visions of a New Science of Consciousness* (J. E. M. a. P. D. Trish Pfeiffer Ed.). New Alresford, Hampshire, UK: IFF Books.

to be a 'faulty ideology'. He associates supramental intelligence with the principles of quantum physics, and claims that though we all naturally possess supramental intelligence we allow it to lie dormant for one reason or another....

"The operation of such supernormal consciousness or supramental intelligence manifests also in what is termed 'downward causation'. Mastering the use of such consciousness or intelligence leads to personal transformation of the person or persons who learn to access it or who are gifted with a capacity to access it. The term 'downward causation' means what appears to be a transmission from a greater non-local universal consciousness to an individual's consciousness. Professor Goswami explains that 'if we think of consciousness as [merely] brain epiphenomenon as materialists do, then there is a paradox, the quantum measurement paradox. The paradox is resolved by turning the materialist metaphysics upside down—recognizing that consciousness is the ground of all being, and matter, including the brain, are the epiphenomena.'

... "Dean Radin, PhD is ... a leading parapsychologist in the United States, if not the world, and properly believes himself to be a cautious and meticulous scientist. Dean Radin's *The Conscious Universe: The Scientific Truth of Psychic Phenomena*[12] discusses, as did Professor Goswami, the quantum principle of downward causation:

> [Downward causation] allows for all of the methodology and vigor of conventional science. But it also allows for the existence of effects that appear to be driven by higher purposes. It allows us to expect that events at higher levels of the hierarchy can cause effects at lower levels. It provides a way of thinking of how the placebo effect can work, how deep hypnosis can significantly alter body chem-

---

12 Radin, D. I. (1997). *The conscious universe: the scientific truth of psychic phenomena* (1st. ed.). New York, N.Y.: HarperEdge.

istry, and why something as ephemeral a goal as wishing might produce meaningful coincidences in the real world.

"Dean Radin, in his *Supernormal: Science, Yoga and the Evidence for Extraordinary Psychic Abilities*[13], suggests that there are extensive parallels between quantum physics and mysticism. He concluded that 'to go beyond [Newtonian-reductionist] physics [into quantum physics and quantum mechanics] is to head toward the metaphysical or mystical—and that is why so many of our pioneering physicists were mystics.'

[In an interview] ... "a physician, Larry Dossey M.D., discussed a frequent mystical experience he has while reading poetry. While working with his patients in his medical practice he frequently witnessed trans-rational phenomena which carried him and his patients into transcendental consciousness. Having authored numerous books and multitudes of scholarly papers pertaining to the beyond-rationality, possible supernormal consciousness of human beings, Dr. Dossey turned his attention to seeking to comprehend, or at least become more intimately familiar with, the Consciousness God of quantum physics and quantum mechanics whose Mind is connected so inextricably to our individual minds as a function of downward causation. That quest led him to entitle his latest book, *One Mind: How Our Individual Mind Is Part of a Greater Consciousness and Why It Matters*[14].

"In his Introduction he informs us that 'This book is about the concept of the One Mind—which, evidence suggests, is a collective, unitary domain of intelligence, of which all individual minds are a part. The One Mind is a dimension in which you and I meet as we are doing even now.... I have written this book

---

13   Radin, D. I. (2013). *Supernormal: science, yoga, and the path to extraordinary psychic abilities* (First edition. ed.) New York, Random House, Inc, Deepak Chopra Books

14   Dossey, L. (2013). *One Mind: How Our Individual Mind is Part of a Greater Consciousness and Why It Matters* (1st edition. ed.) Hay House, Inc.

because I believe the One Mind is a potential way out of the division, bitterness, selfishness, greed, and destruction that threaten to engulf our world—from which, beyond a certain point, there may be no escape. Identifying with the highest expressions of human consciousness can clear our vision, prevent the hardening of our moral and ethical arteries, and inspire us to action'.

"Dr. Dossey has turned every stone, looked in every nook and cranny, investigated every relevant academic discipline, meditated for many years, read many sacred texts (and philosophical ones to boot) in his quest to better come to know the One Mind. As a young man, even before he went to medical school, Larry Dossey was highly impressed by what the American transcendentalist philosopher Ralph Waldo Emerson had to say about the topic and provides us an Emersonian quotation:

> There is one mind common to all individual men. Every man is an inlet to the same and to all of the same. He that is once admitted to the right of reason is made a freeman of the whole estate. What Plato has thought, he may think; what a saint has felt, he may feel; what at any time has befallen any man, he can understand. Who hath access to this universal mind is a party to all that is or can be done, for this is the only and sovereign agent.

"Throughout his book Dr. Dossey shows us how others in the course of human history have shared a similar perception and it should be no surprise that many of these were the great mystics. Quoting from Chilton Pearce's book, *Evolution's End*[15], he ushers us into the realm of mysticism: 'To become whole all parts must be left behind, for a whole is not the sum of its parts but a different state entirely. [Meister] Eckhart spoke of "All named objects" being left behind when one enters the unknown. We must go beyond the

---

15 Pearce, J. C. (1992). *Evolution's end: claiming the potential of our intelligence* (1st ed.). San Francisco: HarperSanFrancisco.

fragmentation of parts and leave the world of diversity to discover the single unity from which all springs.'

"The mystic is able to transcend his or her limited little self by ascending to an awareness of an underlying and never-ending unity with the Whole. Dr. Dossey continues, 'In the One Mind, all possibilities, all configurations of information, appear to exist *in potentia*, all superimposed on one another, awaiting some prompt in order to transform into an actuality in our world of experience. This is an image that physicists would immediately recognize because it is the one they employ in quantum physics.'

"Just as Professor Goswami recognized that becoming experientially aware of the One Mind propels us into transcendence, so did Dr. Dossey: 'Science's great failure is that, having stripped life of self and soul, it has nothing to put in their place except the notion that humans should simply man up, live nobly, and go bravely into the night. Many people perceive this as inadequate advice. This is a reason why the evidence pointing to the One Mind is important. The inclusive One Mind, of which all individual minds partake, nourishes the human drive toward transcendence.'"

We could continue with many more examples of modern scientists and physicians, as well as religious and spiritual teachers who have come to know the One Mind, but it is better to let you become familiar with the much more in-depth and insightful presentation which Dukkyu Choi presents in this book. His presentation of this material is based on that which has been passed down through the Consciousness-Only school of the Buddhist tradition which we find is amazingly modern when considered in light of the current developments in the scientific and medical communities as they too debate these issues.

It is in the hope that you too find that this work serves as a catalyst for better understanding and growth in your journey that I wish you peace and blessings on your path.

Namasté,
Michael O'Dell

PART I

The Mind in Every Day Living

1

The Brain is Not as Smart as We Think

The brain is stupid. This statement can certainly elicit an emotional reaction rather than an intellectual consideration in many people, but it begins to make sense when we consider the concepts of the brain, of 'consciousness,' and of the overall functioning of the human system. Although traditional education in both Western and Oriental school systems teaches us that the brain thinks, we have not been able to produce any scientific evidence to support this. Rather, it remains merely a belief or a hypothesis, and may be one of the greatest errors which human beings have made from the dawn of human history.

For instance, a person who has enjoyed eating a sweet, juicy plum may find that they salivate or drool in the future when they think of the taste and the experience of eating the plum. Is this due to impulses from the brain? Medical science would tell us that this is a result of the parasympathetic nervous system (which includes the brain and the spinal cord) sending the impulses to activate the salivary glands and the rest of the digestive system. Given that activating the digestive system when there is nothing to digest is not only wasteful of the body's energies but is also totally without logic, one could surmise that the brain acts more like an automaton in this function rather than acting with intelligence. The brain is the controller who does not distinguish between an actual situation of eating plums and simply the thought of doing so. If the brain were truly intelligent and logical it would not activate the digestive system simply on the thought of eating, but would reserve the digestive processes for when there was food or drink to digest; to do otherwise is both unnecessary and inefficient. The above is an example of how the brain seems to react to a thought or a feeling and responds as a mere puppet to the external stimulus; it is not capable of thinking or judging by itself, but rather serves more like an idiotic automaton which serves at the behest of the thoughts and feelings which drive it.

Take another example: nearly all men have experienced wet dreams, 'an erotic dream culminating in orgasm and … ejaculation of semen.'[16] We certainly understand that sexual contact can result in the release of semen, and this was built into the human and animal nervous systems to provide for the survival of the species with pleasure as an incentive to ensure procreation. But in the instance of a wet dream, the brain does not differentiate the dream from reality and it initiates the ejaculation even though there is no partner to inseminate. Both this example and the one above show us that the brain does not do the thinking to evaluate the 'reality' of a situation, but instead acts as an automaton which does not think or judge for itself; in other words, it is our body's resident idiot.

We believe that the brain is a very important organ in the body—and like the eyes, the ears, the nose and so forth, it certainly is. We have however tended to overrate the brain up to now by crediting it with functions which it has not been proven to have, but for which we may not have other accepted theories. We consider the brain as the source of thinking whereas it is a thought-dependent organ which is operated by thoughts and feelings.

We tend to get one data point and then extrapolate from it to create generalizations. For instance, we believe that a student will

---

16 *Merriam-Webster's Collegiate Dictionary, Eleventh Edition*, Merriam-Webster Inc., Springfield, Massachusetts (2003)

do well in school if the brain is 'smart,' but it is wrong to believe that a student must have a high IQ in order to do well in school. If somebody has a high IQ we believe that he will have a good memory as well as good mental capabilities such as calculation, analysis, extrapolation, synthesis, creativity etc. We believe that the brain performs such mental activities by itself, but the brain does not in fact have such capability because it is an organ which is operated by the thoughts or feelings of the master. For example, everybody remembers his or her birthday, and most people remember the birthday of his or her parents or brothers or sisters. The memory will be different, however, in case of nephews or nieces or brothers in law. If it is not a special case it is not easy to remember the birthday; a special case means a special concern. If you agree with this you may realize that the memory has nothing to do with the brain. Memory depends on the level of concern, not on the brain, and the concern is a function of the mind. Consequently, the memory has a correlation with the mind but not with the brain.

Take another example. We learn the Pythagorean Theorem in school, which is an equation relating the lengths of the three sides of a right triangle: $a^2 + b^2 = c^2$. When we have a question relating to the equation, we have to remember the equation in order to determine the answer. If we cannot recall the equation, we cannot resolve the question and we are deemed to have a 'not so smart' brain. On the other hand, if someone can recall the equation and thereby answer the question he is considered to have a smart brain. In this regard the difference is only the difference of their memory, or maybe of their training.

Memory is a function of the interest of mind. The person who could recall the Pythagorean equation must have had a need for or interest in it, while the person who could not do so must not have had this incentive. For another example, somebody can remember a melody after listening to it whereas somebody else cannot. The person who can remember the melody well is not necessarily 'smart,' but he may well be good at music due to his concern or interest. Likewise, the fact that somebody cannot remember a melody well may not be because he is not smart, but he may not be good at music due to lack of his concern or interest. We cannot say that a person who can remember a mathematical equation can also remember a melody. If the brain can think by itself and has an ability to remember or memorize, a person who has a smart brain should remember a mathematical equation as well as a melody better than a person who has a less smart brain, but this is not correct because the capability to memorize depends not on the smartness of brain but on the interest of the mind. One's power of memory has nothing to do with the smartness of the brain. One's power of calculation, analysis, extrapolation, synthesis, creativity or any other mental activity is also a function of interest and focus, as it is with memory.

Having said this, we must acknowledge that many western neuroscientists believe that the mind or consciousness comes from the brain, that the brain is the organ which generates them. In fact, most neuroscientists believe that the mind or consciousness is a by-product, or epiphenomenon of the brain; mind vanishes when the brain dies and that is all there is to it.[17] In the medical or neuroscience research literature they have attempted to prove that the brain thinks by researching the changes or phenomena which occur in the brain during the process of thinking.

A Nobel laureate, Francis Crick, OM, FRS, contends that "your joys and your sorrows, your memories and your ambitions, your sense of personal identity and free will, are in fact no more than the behavior of a vast assembly of nerve cells." On the other hand, many cognitive neuroscientists believe that consciousness emerges from the collective activity of those nerve cells throughout the entire brain and is a function of millions or billions of neurons firing together.[18] However, Christof Koch, Ph.D. and Crick believe that the secret may lie in the discrete firing of a much smaller group of neurons. They contend "Evolution has created amazing speci-

---

[17] B. Alan Wallace, *Buddhism with an Attitude,* Snow Lion Publications, New York (2003), p 51

[18] Andrea Rock, *The Mind at Night,* Basic Books, New York (2004), pp. 175-176

ficity at the level of molecules and individual cells, and Crick and I [Koch] think this will also be the case for consciousness. We're looking for very specific neuronal properties that give rise to consciousness, rather than assuming it's the collective activity of the entire brain." Francis Crick defines the neuronal requirements for generating consciousness as neuronal correlates of consciousness (NCC). He contends that whenever information is represented in the NCC you are conscious of it. His goal is to discover the minimal set of neuronal events and mechanisms jointly sufficient for a specific conscious percept.[19] If an NCC which gives rise to consciousness were identified it may definitely prove the belief that the brain thinks. However, who knows when, or if, the NCC will be discovered.

If the brain is not able to think, calculate, analyze, extrapolate or synthesize, what is the brain? What is the identity of the brain that, we believe, is an organ of the human body which is considered to be the locus of judgement and all kinds of human capabilities?

The scientific hypothesis that the brain is the source of thought or consciousness started to be criticized in Western science during the 19th century. William James, M.D. and Professor of Philosophy pointed out more than a century ago that the evidence for mind/brain correlations may indeed imply that the brain produces mental events, that it has the lesser role of simply releasing or permitting them, or that it merely transmits them as light passes through a prism resulting in a spectrum of colors. In this regard B. Alan Wallace, Ph.D., criticizes that with their bias toward materialism, most cognitive scientists simply assume that the first hypothesis is correct despite the lack of compelling scientific evidence.[20]

The Western scientists who assert that the brain thinks by itself and the mind comes from the brain present experimental and material evidences that the brain is activated during thinking. But Deepak Chopra, M.D., counterclaims that their assertion is

---

19 Christof Koch, *The Quest for Consciousness*, Roberts and Company Publishers, Colorado (2004), p 16

20 B. Alan Wallace, p 95

a Western perspective based on our bias for solid, tangible things. The Western scientists insist that the brain must be the source of mind because the brain is a visible object, which is like saying that a radio must be the source of music because it is a visible object from which music emerges. However, Deepak Chopra responded that "It may seem significant that the brain is active during thought, but a radio is active during a broadcast."[21]

We must also consider the plasticity theory of the brain which posits that the structure of the brain can be changed by the mind. According to Norman Doidge, M.D., a Canadian-born psychiatrist, psychoanalyst, and researcher, one reason we can change our brains simply by imagining is that, from a neuroscientific point of view, imagining an act and doing it are not as different as they sound. Dr. Doidge asserts that when people close their eyes and visualize a simple object, such as the letter 'a,' the primary visual cortex lights up just as it would if the subjects were actually looking at the letter 'a,' and that brain scans show that many of the same parts of the brain are activated in both action and imagination.[22]

Alvaro Pascual-Leone, M.D., Ph.D. is Professor of Neurology and Director of the Berenson-Allen Center for Noninvasive Brain Stimulation at Beth Israel Deaconess Medical Center and Harvard Medical School. He also serves as Program Director of the Harvard-Thorndike Clinical Research Center and has written over 350 technical articles on the brain and its functioning. His experiments have shown that we can change our brain anatomy simply by using our imaginations.[23]

Having considered the body's initiation of the digestive process in response to the thought stimulation in the case of remembering the taste of a juicy plum, and the nocturnal emission in a

---

21 Deepak Chopra, *Life After Death*, Three Rivers Press, New York (2006), pp 218-219

22 Norman Doidge, *The Brain That Changes Itself*, Penguin Books, London (2007), pp 203-204

23 Norman Doidge, p 196

Probing the Mind: How does Consciousness Work?

'wet dream,' we turned from thought experiments to the findings of renowned scientists as they considered the functioning of the brain. We first considered William James' hypothesis that the brain merely transmits mental events as light hits a prism, thereby transmitting a spectrum of colors. We also considered Doidge's plasticity theory of the brain, the theory that the hypothesis that the brain is an organ which is passively operated by a thought or mind is more persuasive than any of the other hypotheses. Finally, we noted that Alvaro Pascual-Leone has shown that we can literally change the anatomy and functioning of our brain by simply using our mind. If we agree to this, what is the thought or mind which operates the brain? How does thinking occur? What **is** the mind?

2

Five Sense Consciousnesses

In order to comprehend thought or mind we have to comprehend consciousness first; and in order to comprehend consciousness, we have to comprehend sense awareness. Consciousness encompasses sense awareness, thought and mind. Consciousness is defined as 'the state or quality of awareness, or, of being aware of an external object or something within oneself.'[24,25] Consciousness is also defined as 'all mental activities that someone is sensing or aware of something.'[26] Being aware of an external object is called sense, being aware of something conceptual within oneself is called thought or cognition, and the internal state arising from a sense or thought or cognition is called mind or feeling or emotion.

There are five sense consciousnesses which are common to nearly all members of the animal kingdom. Humans share these capabilities since humans also have an animal body. The five sense consciousnesses we will discuss relate to the five physical organs: the eyes, ears, nose, tongue and body (skin). These are funda-

---

24 "consciousness". Merriam-Webster. Retrieved June 4, 2012.

25 Robert van Gulick (2004). "Consciousness". *Stanford Encyclopedia of Philosophy*.

26 http://ko.wikipedia.org

mental sense organs which are used to recognize or perceive external objects. The eyes perceive light (color), the ears detect noise (sound), the olfactory sense of the nose detects scents (odors), the tongue distinguishes flavors (taste), and the skin perceives or 'feels' tactile objects. These can be considered to be eye consciousness, ear consciousness, nose consciousness, tongue consciousness, and body (touch) consciousness. To look at an object through the eyes and to recognize whether it is a book or it is a desk relates to an eye sensation. To hear a sound through the ears and to recognize whether it is a piano or a trumpet requires an ear sensation. Sensation is a fundamental prerequisite for life and a criterion for distinguishing life and death. Accordingly, the physical organs relating to the sensations have been important subject matters for study in the fields of medicine and science for a long time.

We have discussed the five sense consciousnesses which we consider to be 'normal' attributes of the animal and human bodies, but this assumes that the sense organs are operating in the expected manner. This is not always the case, however, and we find instances wherein the eyes are not operating normally and sight consciousness cannot be generated. In this case the person is considered to be blind. Likewise, if the ears are not functional, sound consciousness cannot be generated and a person is considered to be deaf. Smell consciousness, taste consciousness and skin (contact) consciousnesses may also fail and the person will be handicapped by the lack of one or more of the sense consciousnesses in the same manner.

We have discussed how the senses may fail us in some instances, so what is required for them to support us and our manifestation in this world? We see that the basis for any sense consciousness is that the relevant sense organ must contact or perceive the respective objects. If there is no contact between the organs and the objects, the sense consciousnesses do not arise. Although you have eyes, sight consciousness does not arise when you close your eyes or when there is nothing to see, such as in a dark room. The object of sight consciousness is light. As light is perceived with an attribute of color, light is interpreted as color. As light reflects a particular object, light also reveals form. Noise is the object of

Probing the Mind: How does Consciousness Work?

sound consciousness. A noise must be detected with the ears in order to generate a sound consciousness. The object of nose (smell) consciousness is a scent, the object of tongue (taste) consciousness is a flavor, and the object of skin consciousness is a tactile object. All things of the external world are classified into the five objects—light, noise, scent, flavor and tactile objects—with respect to sense consciousnesses, and the five objects are perceived by the respective organs of the physical body.

As we have noted, sense consciousness arises only when an organ of a physical body contacts an object of the external world. We are considering only the five senses which are common to the human body, but these organs do not generate the respective sense consciousnesses by themselves. In order to generate the five consciousnesses, the organs must be connected to the brain via the nervous system. Although the brain is not able to think or judge by itself, it is absolutely necessary for interpreting a sense input and generating a sense consciousness.

(sense organ)	eye	ear	nose	tongue	body (skin)
	|	|	|	|	|
(object)	light (color)	noise	scent	flavor	tactile objects
	|	|	|	|	|
(consciousness)	sight	sound	smell	taste	touch

A living animal recognizes objects through the respective five organs, as does a human being. Humans perceive light or color through the eyes, but not all kinds of light can be seen by human eyes. The region of light we can see is just that we call visible rays, those whose wavelength is from about 390 to about 700 or 780 nanometers. We cannot see ultraviolet rays or infrared rays, those which are beyond the wavelengths of the visible spectrum. This does not allow us to say that ultraviolet rays or infrared rays do not exist, however, simply because we cannot see them. Even though human eyes are only able to perceive visible rays, we have utilized the infrared spectrum to create equipment for wireless communication, to warm or cook food, to create motion detectors and home security systems, etc. We also use ultraviolet rays to disinfect water to make it safe to drink, to characterize properties of distant objects in astronomical studies, for 'black lights' to excite fluorescent materials, for lasers, etc. We should also note that there are animals which are able to 'see' far beyond the human visual spectrum, with many insects and birds being capable of seeing into the ultraviolet spectrum. Bees are a particularly interesting case of animals which have this extended color vision since they are also peculiarly sensitive to traces of polarization in the light, as von Frisch in Munich found out not long ago; this aids their orientation with respect to the sun in a puzzlingly elaborate way. To a human being, even completely polarized light is indistinguishable from ordinary, non-polarized light.[27]

Sound is very similar to light in that the frequency of sound that we can hear with normal ears is in the range from about 20 hertz to 20,000 hertz, with some humans having the ability to 'hear' sound with frequencies from as low as 12 Hz to as high as 30,000 Hz. As we saw with light, however, there are animals who can hear sounds far outside our normal range of hearing. For instance, elephants and whales hear and communicate using subsonic frequencies; i.e., frequencies which are below the range of human hearing. On the other end of the spectrum, bats, porpoises, shrews and many insects are sensitive to extremely high frequency vibrations ('ultrasound') far beyond the upper limit of human hearing. Many of these animals produce the ultrasound themselves and emit it not only to communicate with each other, but also using it as a sort of 'radar' to detect prey and avoid obstacles.[28] Dogs, elephants, bears, sharks, many insects, etc. have a much better sense of smell than does a human, and the senses of taste and touch are also greatly expanded by other members of the animal kingdom.

---

27 Erwin Schrodinger, *What is Life? with Mind and Matter and Autobiographical Sketches*, Cambridge University press, Cambridge (2008), p 158

28 Erwin Schrodinger, *What is Life? with Mind and Matter and Autobiographical Sketches*, Cambridge University press, Cambridge (2008), p 158

Probing the Mind: How does Consciousness Work?

The five sense consciousnesses are each two step processes—a simple sensation and a recognition (or discrimination). The simple sensation step generates a neurophysiological consciousness and the recognition step generates a recognizing consciousness. The sensation step is carried out by the respective organs in association with the brain and nervous system, while the recognition step is carried out by the respective organs, brain and nervous system in conjunction with experience or learning. For example, when an object appears far away, if the eyes can see it, it is the first step consciousness of sight – the simple sensation step. At this step, the eyes do not recognize or discriminate whether it is a bird or an airplane. The first step consciousness is merely a neurophysiological consciousness.

Once the simple sensation step resulting from the eyes and an object is processed through the brain and nervous systems, however, the recognition step is made possible by previous experience or learning. The sensation at the first step should be distinguished from the recognition or discrimination of the second step. When a person sees an airplane without first having an experience or learning concerning airplanes, the information on airplanes will be stored in his consciousness for the first time. The next time he sees an airplane he will recognize that the object is an airplane from the information which is stored in his consciousness. This is an example of how the information which is stored in one's consciousness is formed through experience or learning. Accordingly, the second step consciousness of recognition arises based upon one's experience or learning. An experience or learning about airplanes must precede the visual sensation if one is to perceive that it is an airplane.

When the simple sensation step resulting from the eyes 'seeing' an object is transmitted through the nervous system to the brain, the brain functions like the CPU of a computer. If the first step consciousness of the sensation is not generated normally, the eyes or nervous system should be treated by a medical doctor so that the sight might be recovered. When the recognition step does not work, however, medical treatment is not necessary. Accordingly, we can conclude that the simple sensation step is carried out in the physical system including eyes, brain and nervous system, while the recognition step is carried out in the consciousness system which is a nonphysical and nonmaterial system.

Sound (ear) consciousness is similar to sight (eye) consciousness. If someone hears sound coming from a piano the simple sensation step is to hear something playing, and the recognition step is to recognize that the sound is from piano. When a person hears the sound of a piano for the first time in his life he does not have any experience or learning about the piano and he cannot tell that the sound is from a piano. This 'hearing' will result in information about the piano being stored in his consciousness, however, so that the next time he hears the sound he will recognize it based on the information which was just stored. In order to recognize the sound of a piano, an experience or learning about a piano must precede the hearing. The remaining sense consciousnesses are generated in the same manner. A simple sensation at the first step is generated by the nose, tongue or body (skin) and transmitted to the brain by the nervous system, and a recognition or discrimination is derived from the information based on experience or learning which has been stored in the consciousness.

As we have shown, experience or learning is something that has occurred in the past, and to recognize or discriminate something is only possible if we have information produced from a prior experience or learning. If this is the case, where is the information which was produced from the experience or learning stored? Where is the information on the airplane or piano stored? Where is the information sensed and recognized by the five organs stored? Many people will think that the information could not be stored in their heart or body; western science will say that the information is stored in the brain; and many psychologists will say that the information is stored in the subconscious or unconscious. Which, if any of these, is really correct?

3

Storage of Consciousness— Store Consciousness

A person who has eaten an apple can recall what an apple is. He knows about the apple as a fruit as well as about the taste of an apple. On the other hand a person who has not eaten a durian, or possibly even heard about it, cannot know what a durian is. Likewise, some people can remember the Pythagorean Theorem which they learned in school, others cannot. If someone uses the Pythagorean equation frequently he may recall it without any difficulty, even if a few decades have passed, whereas if someone does not use it or has not been interested in it at all since he learned it the equation will have been lost to his memory.

We can say that the information about the apple has been produced by experience, but where is this information stored? Where is the information on the Pythagorean Theorem which has been produced by learning stored? If we were discussing a computer we could say that the information is stored in a memory device and is recalled and utilized when necessary. What about humans? Where is the information which has been produced by experience or learning stored? Will the information be stored in the brain?

Steven Pinker, professor of psychology at Harvard University, said "The mind is what the brain does; specifically, the brain processes information, and thinking is a kind of computation. The mind is organized into modules or mental organs, each with a specialized design that makes it an expert in one arena of interaction with the world. The modules' basic logic is specified by our genetic program."[29] According to his assertion, our physical organs owe their complex design to the information in the human genome; and so, I believe, do our mental organs.[30] Francis Crick and Christof Koch contend that all mental interaction is in fact no more than the behavior of a vast assembly of nerve cells. They contend that there will exist very specific neuronal cells that give rise to consciousness, rather than assuming it's the collective activity of the entire brain.[31]

According to Pinker, Crick and Koch, the belief that the information produced by experience or learning is stored in the brain extends to the neuronal cells. Of course any scientific evidence to support this has not been discovered yet, so the belief that all mental interaction is generated from the neuronal cells is also a hypothesis or an opinion.

Information regarding the five sense consciousnesses which is obtained through the five sense organs is another form of information regarding consciousness, just as is the information which is produced by experience or learning. In other words, the information generated by the five senses, or by experience or learning, is neither analog data nor digital data, but is rather stored somewhere in the form of consciousness and not in analog or digital form. Western scientists may say that the information is stored in the brain or nerve cells, whereas psychoanalysts like Sigmund Freud and Carl Jung may say that the information is stored in the unconscious or subconscious.

---

29 Steven Pinker, *How The Mind Works*, W.W. Norton & Company, New York (1997), p 21

30 Steven Pinker, *How The Mind Works*, W.W. Norton & Company, New York (1997), p 31

31 Andrea Rock, *The Mind at Night*, Basic Books, New York (2004), pp. 175-176

Probing the Mind: How does Consciousness Work?

Freud envisioned the psychic structure as being in three layers: the top or cortex level he called *consciousness*; next was knowledge of which we are not conscious at all times but which can always be called on—this he named the *preconscious*; and the third layer, the largest and most mysterious, he called the *unconscious*. The *unconscious* is the realm which we do not know and cannot find in our waking conscious lives, and yet which exerts a vast influence on our behaviour throughout life. The unconscious mind is constantly active in our inner psychic world and drives us to find solutions to instinctual drives (which are often in conflict with the demands of the external world). The unconscious mind, Freud would say, is all of humanity, all that we have inherited from centuries of humanity. He called this our phylogenetic heritage as opposed to our ontogenetic heritage which is made up of all that one person has experienced from the time of birth.[32]

Within Mahayana Buddhism there is a concept of Alaya, a storehouse of consciousness. Alaya is the all encompassing field of consciousness which encapsulates and contains all types of consciousnesses including the five sense consciousnesses, experience, learning, mental activities, and all information regarding these. Alaya is called Store Consciousness since it is like a huge storehouse including all consciousnesses which a person has perceived, recognized, thought or felt. It is likened to a huge memory device of a supercomputer, but no such memory device could be even remotely comparable with the volume of memory in the Alaya of a person.

Information regarding consciousness is itself a form of consciousness, so it is neither analog data nor digital data and cannot be converted to physical or material data. The Pythagorean equation expressed by $a^2 + b^2 = c^2$ can be expressed as either analog data or digital data, but as we have seen, the equivalent concept stored in consciousness is neither analog nor digital. Being stored in consciousness it is stored in and encapsulated within Alaya.

---

32 Francisco J. Varela, *Sleeping, Dreaming, and Dying*, Wisdom Publications, Boston (1997)

Although Buddhism establishes Alaya as a store of consciousness information, since the consciousness information is nonphysical and nonmaterial we cannot locate the Alaya physically in the body. We can certainly see that the all-encompassing field of consciousness cannot be contained in either the brain or the heart, or in any other physical part of the body, but we cannot deny the existence of the store consciousness. If we were to deny the existence of Alaya we would have to deny whatever information we might have received concerning an apple as a result of our experience, or the information about the Pythagorean Theorem which we learned as a function of our studies. This principle may also be applicable to mind; we cannot deny the existence of mind simply because we cannot prove the characteristics of mind scientifically. Descartes may tell us *cogito ergo sum*, "I think, therefore I am," but this only posits the existence of mind and does not provide any information which would definitively prove it.

In the physical world, light, sound, scent, flavor and tactile objects perceived by the respective five organs all have physical properties. The five sense consciousnesses generated from responding to the interactions with the five sense organs are all nonmaterial, however, just as the information obtained through experience or learning is nonmaterial. Likewise, the information stored in Alaya is also nonmaterial.

Although the information stored in Alaya is nonphysical or nonmaterial, there is a type of power associated with it. Information which is subject to frequent recall, that which is beneficial to maintain and enhance important relationships or which improves our ability to perform our role in life more effectively, will command a greater and more readily accessible role in Alaya. The information on one's own name or birthday, for instance, or our parents' name or birthday as well as similarly useful information is stored in Alaya with strong power so that it cannot be forgotten. Such information can be recalled for use anyplace or anytime when necessary. On the other hand the information on friends' birthdays or clients' phone numbers has a relatively weak power and may not be available for quick and easy recall. If we use the Pythagorean Theorem frequently, the information on the equation will be associated with a strong power and stored in Alaya for ready recall and it will not be difficult to summon the information on the equation for use when necessary. However, if we have not used the equation since we learned it in school the information concerning the equation will have a weak power in Alaya and it will not be easy to remember the equation for use if we need it.

Storing consciousness information in Alaya is the same as storing articles in a warehouse or a storage area. We do not leave something valuable such as a diamond ring, a luxury Swiss watch, a designer handbag etc. laying just 'any old place.' We keep the valuable items in predefined special places with special attention given them. But we can also associate special importance to items such as umbrellas, slippers, towels etc., since if we are unable to locate the right item when it is needed we will not be able to perform a task as desired. Although the item may not be of high monetary value, it will have high utility value so we must be able to locate it when needed.

The five sense consciousnesses associated with the five sense organs are all stored in Alaya. When we walk along the street we see many things: buildings, signboards, passing crowds, passing cars, shops, window displays etc. We do not recognize all of the things which we see, and in fact not only are there things which we do not recognize, but there are many things which we do not even become consciously aware of even though they are in our line of sight. The range of things which we recognize is partially determined by our areas of concern or interest. Although we do not recognize everything, the things that have come into our sight are stored in Alaya. This is very similar to a photograph. When we take a picture, the thing we had focused on is certainly included, but the surroundings which we had not focused on are also in the picture. The surroundings in a picture will correspond to the unconscious as defined by Freud. Consequently, the conscious, preconscious and unconscious which Freud structured as three layers are all stored in Alaya.

The consciousness associated with sound is quite similar to that associated with sight. When we walk along the street many noises impinge upon our ears: music from the shops, noises from street vendors, sounds of people bargaining, sounds associated with traffic, the honking of horns, etc. But as with sight, we do not recognize all the noises that come into our ears. The things which we recognize are limited—we recognize sounds which concern us or in which we have an interest. Although we do not recognize all the sounds, the noises that have come into our ears are stored in Alaya. The smell, taste or skin consciousness works in the same manner.

It will be meaningless to only store the information regarding the five sense consciousnesses or the information gained through experience or learning in Alaya—we must be able to recall the information for subsequent use. This is like a computer memory. If a lot of data is saved in the memory device without being retrievable for any purpose, the data is not valuable. The consciousness information should likewise be recalled and used whenever it is necessary. We can recall the information about our name or birthday or height from the store consciousness anytime we find it necessary to use it. Likewise, the Pythagorean equation is useful and valuable when it is recalled from the Alaya and utilized.

This leads us to ask how can we recall or retrieve the necessary information from the store consciousness? How can we perceive the consciousness information of Alaya? Which organ in the physical body can perceive the consciousness information? How can we memorize our birthday or the Pythagorean equation? Will the brain do? In order to answer these questions we must further consider the five sense consciousnesses. It will be necessary to look back at how we perceive the five sense objects using the respective five organs, and we must ask "Does the brain perceive the consciousness information?" Unfortunately, there is no scientific evidence that the brain can read the consciousness information. It is probable that the Mind will be able to read the consciousness information stored in Alaya, but this leads us to ask "What is the Mind?"

4

A Sense Organ for Reading Consciousness Information—Mind

We can postulate that the mind will read the consciousness information stored in Alaya, and if the mind were a physical organ in our body we would not have any question or any doubt as to the reality of consciousness. The mind is not physical or material, however, just as the consciousness information is not physical or material. If the consciousness information stored in Alaya could be digitized (which we have seen it cannot) and the mind could read the digitized data, human beings would be mere machines like computers. This will never be the case, however, since it will be forever impossible to define the mind and the consciousness information correctly due to the nonmateriality or nonphysicality of their nature.

The Korean dictionary definition of mind is a state of consciousness or intelligence which appears as a complex of thought, recognition, memorization, emotion, willingness, imagination and the like for others or external things.[33] The mind is also defined as the set of cognitive faculties that enables consciousness, perception,

---

33   http://ko.wikipedia.org

thinking, judgement, and memory—a characteristic of humans, but which also may apply to other life forms.[34]

However, when we define the mind in the same manner as a dictionary we acknowledge that thought, recognition, memorization, emotion, willingness, imagination, perception, judgement and the like have not been clearly defined yet. Therefore, the more we try to define the mind the further we shall immerse ourselves into a mystery. To define the mind correctly will be more difficult than to discover the cosmogenesis or to find a planet where there is life. Up to now in the 21st century humans have been to the moon and the computer is a common device, but the definition of mind has not been established.

Even though the mind and consciousness are not material, there is an ongoing attempt to depict the materialization of the mind, consciousness, or consciousness information. Psychologist and scientist Steven Pinker defines a language of thought as *mentalese* to inscribe the statements in a knowledge system.[35] Further, Pinker said "The combinatorics of mentalese, and of other representations composed of parts, explain the inexhaustible repertoire of human thought and action. A few elements and a few rules that combine them can generate an unfathomably vast number of different representations, because the number of possible representations grows exponentially with their size."[36] Though it will take time to discover and define *mentalese*, we can see the stated desire to convert the nonmaterial information of mind into materialized information.

Norman Doidge, M.D., is also aligned somewhat with Steven Pinker in that he said "we can see our 'immaterial' thoughts too have a physical signature, and we cannot be so sure that thought

---

34 http://en.wikipedia.org

35 Steven Pinker, *How The Mind Works*, W.W. Norton & Company, New York (1997), p 70

36 Steven Pinker, *How The Mind Works*, W.W. Norton & Company, New York (1997), p 88

Probing the Mind: How does Consciousness Work?

won't someday be explained in physical terms."[37] If thought or mind could be explained in physical terms, as Doidge desires, we may some day easily devise a robot with high intelligence which could read thoughts or the mind, and could be operated and controlled upon the command of thought or mind.

The reason we could not have defined these concepts correctly up to now is because we could not figure out the constitution of mind. We have confusingly misused the terms relating to consciousness such as mind, thought, emotion, feeling, desire etc. For instance, when we say "My mind is well aware of that," 'mind' is the subject of the action. On the other hand, when we say "I have a sad mind when I see that" (as we do in Korea), 'mind' is the object or phenomenon of the master, which abides inside. In other words, the term 'mind' can be a subject or an object or phenomena as the case may be. Although there is a big difference between subject and object, we have misused the term interchangeably from case to case. Nevertheless, the misuse has gained general acceptance because the term is nonmaterial, conceptual or abstract.

The eye is an organ which perceives light or color, the ear is an organ which perceives sound, the nose is an organ which perceives scent, the tongue is an organ which perceives flavor, and the skin is an organ which perceives tactile objects. If the mind is considered to be an organ in a like fashion, the mind in the subjective sense must be an organ which perceives consciousness information. The mind as subject is therefore named as an 'organ of mind' or 'mind organ' and the consciousness information as the object to the mind organ as 'mind information' in this book.

---

37 Norman Doidge, *The Brain That Changes Itself*, Penguin Books, London (2007), p 214

(SENSE ORGAN)	Eye	Ear	Nose	Tongue	Body	Mind
|	|	|	|	|	|	|
(OBJECT)	Light (Color)	Noise	Scent	Flavor	Tactile Object	Mind Information
|	|	|	|	|	|	|
(CONSCIOUSNESS)	Sight	Sound	Smell	Taste	Touch	Sixth Consciousness

In Buddhism the sense organ is defined as the 'root of sense.' The eye is a root of sight, the ear is a root of sound, the nose is a root of smell, the tongue is a root of taste, the body is a root of touch feeling, and the mind is a root of sixth consciousness. Also, the mind information is defined as 'dharma' and the sixth consciousness as 'dharma consciousness.' What is the dharma as an object of the mind organ? There is no explanation about the sixth object, dharma, either in the Thirty Stanzas[38] or in the *Ch'eng Wei-shih-Lun*.[39]

In Buddhism the dharma generally has two meanings. One is Dharma, spelled with a capital D, which is the Buddhist term for what we would call 'Buddhism.' The Dharma is the teachings of the Buddha, the laws that characterize existence, the truth. The other is dharma (uncapitalized) which means an experiential datum. It might be translated as 'object' or 'thing.' It might be defined as all sentient beings as well as all non-sentient beings. It might encompass all material things as well as psychic factors including mind, consciousness and mental activities.[40] The explanation of the dharma as the sixth object is not wrong, but neither is it crystal-clear. Will any other object except the five objects which can be perceived by the five sense organs exist? All the external objects can

---

38 *The Thirty Verses on Consciousness-Only* written by Vasubandhu

39 *Demonstration of Consciousness-Only* written by Hsuan Tsang, Tripitaka-Master of the T'ang Dynasty

40 Francis H. Cook, *Three Texts on Conscious-Only*, Numata Center for Buddhist Translation Research, California (1999), p.5

be perceived by the five organs. However, the mind organ cannot perceive any of the five objects. Likewise, any of the five organs cannot perceive consciousness information. Consequently, the sixth object, dharma, of the mind organ should be consciousness information (or mind information). If so, what is the sixth consciousness like which is generated when the mind organ contacts mind information?

The sixth consciousness which is generated when the mind organ contacts mind information will be the sixth sense in a general term. The sixth consciousness will be called telepathy or extrasensory perception (ESP). Walking along a crowded street, when you looked back because you had a hunch that somebody was following you, and you found that a friend of yours was actually following you, the hunch would be telepathy, a sixth sense, an ESP or the sixth consciousness. No matter what the name is, nobody can deny its existence.

Frederic W. H. Myers, one of the founders of the Society for Psychical Research, was the first person to introduce the term 'telepathy' at the Society's meeting in December 1882. Telepathy, he said, was intended "to cover all cases of impression received at a distance without the normal operation of the recognized sense organs." It should be noted that Myers' definition did not specify that the impressions in question had to emanate from another mind or consciousness. The word telepathy, however, was commonly assumed to imply a supernatural or paranormal connection with some other mind—either that of a living person or that of a disembodied spirit. Telepathy is necessarily related to other 19th century forms of communication from a distance through new and often invisible channels including telegraphy, photography, telephone and gramophone. If disembodied words could be transmitted in an instant across vast distances, why couldn't thoughts and other 'psychic impressions' be transmitted in an analogous manner? Indeed, Sigmund Freud referred explicitly to this analogy when, a few decades later, he speculated that thought-transference might be regarded as 'a psychical counterpart to wireless telegraphy.' Richard Francis Burton, that master of intrusiveness, was the originator of the term that we now call ESP. Richard Burton did not believe in an afterlife but he clearly did believe in a 'sixth sense.' And even now, over 120 years after the founding of the Society for Psychical Research, the question of whether telepathic communication really exists is still in dispute. On the one hand are the inveterate skeptics—people such as Charles Hansel and James Randi. They have repeatedly challenged the validity of studies purporting to have found evidence for ESP, and they have documented many instances in which the results could be attributed to other factors including cheating, fraud, collusion, and insufficient experimental controls. On the other extreme are the credulous enthusiasts: they take it for granted that ESP exists; they believe the apparently supportive research findings; and they vigorously resist any skeptics' attempts to 'explain it all away.' Occupying the middle ground between these two positions are people whose own skeptical need to be convinced is balanced by a genuine open-mindedness. Their position is represented by a current generation of scientists who seek to investigate ESP and other anomalous experiences without bias or prejudice, using the most valid and defensible methods available. Surveying the studies conducted by these scientists, respected scholars such as Daryl Bem, Charles Honorton, Ray Hyman, and Robert Rosenthal have carefully reviewed the results, and the general consensus of these reviewers is that it is difficult to explain away all of the evidence for extrasensory perception. Although the existence of ESP has not been definitively proved, neither has it been definitively discredited.[41]

In the Consciousness-Only Theory of Buddhism, all consciousness is stored in Alaya as consciousness information or mind information. The consciousness information or mind information has a meaning of 'seeds of mind' and is called 'cittas' in the Pali language. The Theory also explains that mental activities or mental associates are produced in the sixth consciousness which is generated when the mind organ contacts the mind information. The

---

41 William Ickes, *Everyday Mind Reading*, Prometheus Books, New York (2003), pp 299-303

mental activities or mental associates are called 'caittas' in the Pali language. The mental activities are like loving mind, happy mind, sad mind, angry mind etc. Buddhism understood the constitution of mind about 2,000 years ago and explained the 'mind' as a structure of the mind organ (the sixth organ: subjective of mind), *citta* (seeds of mind: mind information), and *caitta* (mental activities or mental associates).

Let's consider the process as it would be when we meet a foe. The first step is to perceive the simple sensation with the eyes, and the second step (the recognition step) is recognizing that it is a foe. Due to the recognition, the mind organ retrieves the information regarding that foe which had been produced in the past and has been stored in Alaya. Thereafter an angry mind arises as a mental activity.

Mind Organ

| ⇒⇒⇒⇒⇒⇒⇒⇒⇒⇒⇒⇒**Mental Activity (caitta)**

Mind Information (citta)

We can understand the mental activity better than the mind organ or the mind information because we experience many mental activities such as a loving mind, a happy mind, a sad mind, an angry mind, etc. The mental activities are internal phenomena which are generated from the sixth consciousness. Although the mental activities cannot be proved physically or materially, we cannot deny their existence. We cannot deny the existence of the mind information because we recall a lot of information which has been obtained through experience or learning. We may think of the mind information as the subconscious or unconscious, but we almost never think about the mind organ. We do not know about the existence of the mind organ.

5

Fifty One Mental Activities (Caittas)

Although each of us experiences feelings, moods and emotions, we cannot objectify or materialize them. We have a belief that the mental activities are generated from our mind, but we do not know where the mind is or how these mental activities arise. It must be said, however, that we are surely confident that something arises inside the mind because we experience physical sensations in response to these thoughts. As a result of such mental activities we sometimes find ourselves in an excited or agitated state, we grimace in pain, we find that we are breathing heavily, or we suffer indigestion.

Mental activities are mental phenomena which arise when the mind organ perceives and acts upon mind information. The mental activity is analogous to the smoke which is produced when fuel is burned in a fire. If we consider the fire which is operating on the fuel to be similar to the mind organ, then the fuel will be the equivalent of the mind information which is being operated on by the mind. If the fuel is dry firewood it will produce white smoke, if the fuel is a heavy oil it will produce black smoke, and if the fuel is a good charcoal it will burn without producing hardly any smoke. The mental activity will likewise be a function of the mind information; if it is pleasant information one will feel happiness, but if it is unpleasant information one will experience an unpleasant or agitated mental state. In this regard, it is very important what information is stored in Alaya.

Mental activities include all kinds of feelings, moods, emotions etc. Buddhism explains that there are fifty one mental activities (caittas) which can be classified as being in six categories: good caittas, vexing passions, secondary vexing passions, indeterminate mental associates, universal caittas and discriminating caittas. These can be seen in Table 1 on the next page.

There are eleven caittas in the good caittas, and these produce pleasant mind states which are experienced as enjoyable and fulfilling experiences.

There are six vexing passions (*klesas*), which are attitudes which lead to frustration and ineffective coping with the situations we encounter. *Klesas* in Sanskrit mean 'seeds of *dukkha*,' and *dukkha* in Sanskrit is frequently translated as pain or suffering, so *klesas* mean 'seeds of pain' or 'seeds of suffering.' This might better be presented as being 'out of joint' such as rolling on a wheel which has its axle off-center so that the ride is very bouncy and uncomfortable. It is being 'out of sync' with the true Reality by living from the false ego. This is the First Noble Truth in Buddhism: the Buddha said 'Life is dukkha.'

We have seen that there are six vexing passions which throw us out of kilter in our living, but there are twenty secondary vexing passions (upaklesas) which are more definitive ways in which the vexing passions are expressed in our life.

There are also four mental activities in the indeterminate mental associates which are neither pleasant nor painful within themselves, but which provide a basis for us to respond in either a positive or a negative way. The five universal caittas can likewise be considered as stimuli for either positive or negative reaction, and finally there are five discriminating caittas which can be stepping stones to spiritual growth and harmony.

Probing the Mind: How does Consciousness Work?

Table 1: The mental activities (caittas) as described in the Consciousness-Only school of Buddhism

good caittas (11)	belief, sense of shame, sense of integrity, non-covetousness, non-anger, non-delusion, zeal, composure of mind, vigilance, equanimity, harmlessness
vexing passions (klesas) (6)	covetousness, anger, delusion, conceit, doubt, erroneous views
secondary vexing passions (upaklesas) (20)	fury, enmity, concealment (or hypocrisy), vexation, envy, parsimony, deception, duplicity (or fraudulence), harmfulness, pride, shamelessness, non-integrity, agitation (or restlessness), torpid-mindedness, unbelief, indolence, idleness, forgetfulness, distraction, non-discernment
indeterminate mental associates (4)	remorse, drowsiness, reflection, investigation
universal caittas (5)	mental contact, attention (caution), sensation, attention (imagination), volition
discriminating caittas (5)	desire, resolve, memory, meditation, discernment

The nature of mind information is classified as *good*, *no-good* and *non-defined*. The mental activities associated with these types of activity are pleasure, pain, and indifference respectively. When the mind organ works with *good* mind information, one will experience pleasant feelings; when the mind organ responds to *no-good* mind information, one will feel pain; and when the mind organ interacts with a *non-defined* type of mind information, one will feel indifference or will invoke the pain-pleasure threshold based upon internal biases or interpretations.

Neither the mind organ nor the mind information can affect the brain directly, but the mental activity does affect the brain. The brain responds to this activity by sending an order to the appropriate organs of the body resulting in various physical changes in the body in relation to pulse rate, blood pressure, breathing rate, facial color, tremor, and so on. The resultant physical phenomena depend on the mental activities which initiate them, and these may result in a response such as fear, or 'fight or flight' with the corresponding release of hormones like endorphines or adrenaline. Stress may also release glucocorticoids, which can help relieve pain and inflammation, but which can also kill cells in the hippocampus.[42]

As excessive drinking damages the liver and smoking harms the lungs, negative thoughts undermine the brain and finally the physical body. Every time you are angry, or have an unkind thought, a sad thought, or a cranky thought, your brain releases chemicals that make your body feel bad. Every time you have a good thought, a happy thought, a hopeful thought, or a kind thought, your brain releases chemicals that make your body feel good. Think about the last time you were mad. How did your body feel? When most people are angry their muscles become tense, their heart beats faster, their hands start to sweat, and they may even begin to feel a little dizzy.[43] Mental activities such as anger are not a physical force but just a phenomenon in the mind, but mental activities nevertheless have the power to cause physical changes in the body.

The brain systems that are most intimately involved with our behavior are explained as being in five parts – deep limbic system, basal ganglia, prefrontal cortex, cingulate system, and temporal lobes. Scientific studies such as sophisticated quantitative EEG (brain wave) studies and nuclear medicine brain studies called

---

[42] Norman Doidge, *The Brain That Changes Itself*, Penguin Books, London (2007), p 248

[43] Daniel G. Amen, *Change Your Brain Change Your Life*, Three Rivers Press, New York (1998), pp 57-58

Probing the Mind: How does Consciousness Work?

SPECT (single-photon emission computed tomography) show visual evidence of brain patterns depending on psychological or psychiatric problems.[44] The deep limbic system, at the center the brain, is the bonding and mood control center. An angry thought, an unkind thought, a sad thought, or a cranky thought activates your deep limbic system; whereas a good thought, a happy thought, a hopeful thought, or a kind thought cools your deep limbic system. A deep limbic dysfunction results in symptoms of nausea, social withdrawal, crying spells, depression and the like.[45] The basal ganglia, large structures deep within the brain, control the body's idling speed. When this part of the brain works too hard anxiety, panic, fearfulness, and conflict avoidance are often the result. Meditation, respiration practice or self hypnosis is recommended to overcome the symptoms coming from the basal ganglia. The prefrontal cortex, at the front top of the brain, is your supervisor, the part of the brain that helps you stay focused, make plans, control impulses, and make good or bad decisions. When this part of the brain is underactive people have problems supervising themselves and also have significant problems with attention span, focus, organization, and follow-through. Learning how to activate the prefrontal cortex in a positive way leads to better internal supervision. The cingulated system (limbic cortex), a part of the brain that runs longitudinally through the middle part of the frontal lobes, allows you to shift attention from thought to thought and between behaviors. When this part of the brain is overactive, people have problems getting stuck in certain loops of thoughts or behaviors. Understanding its function will help you deal with repetitive worries. Lastly, the temporal lobes, underneath the temples and behind the eyes, are involved with memory, understanding language, facial recognition, and temper control. When there are problems, especially in the left temporal lobe, people are more

---

44 Daniel G. Amen, *Change Your Brain Change Your Life*, Three Rivers Press, New York (1998), p 3

45 Daniel G. Amen, *Change Your Brain Change Your Life*, Three Rivers Press, New York (1998), p 49

prone to temper flare-ups, rapid mood shifts, and memory and learning problems. Optimizing this part of the brain may help you experience inner peace for the first time in your life.[46]

Scientists say that all psychological or psychiatric problems are caused by abnormalities of the brain systems—deep limbic system, basal ganglia, prefrontal cortex, cingulate system, and temporal lobes. We may, however, advance a hypothesis that the abnormality of the brain system is caused by psychological or psychiatric problems. We may also consider that the psychological or psychiatric problems are caused by the mental activities. This is the equivalent of we cannot answer the question of which came first, the chicken or the egg; we do not know which came first, the psychological or psychiatric problems or the abnormality of the brain systems. In Buddhism, as only consciousness truly exists, the mental activities may affect the brain and finally the body. It is also in accordance with the Buddhist tradition that consciousness, including mental activities, exists without the physical body, and that consciousness may exist even after the dying of the body. If that is the case we can say that the psychological or psychiatric problems came first rather than the abnormality of the brain systems. All mental activities will affect the brain, and, once the brain is affected by a mental activity the brain will deliver an order to the respective physical organ to protect the organ and finally the body from the mental activity. We may conclude that the brain functions as a control tower which delivers a necessary order to the body in response to the mental activities.

The mental activity (caitta) which is produced when the mind organ contacts mind information (citta) produces another mind information which is stored in Alaya. We can recall and experience the same feeling, mood, emotion and the like for a particular event as when it was first produced because the mental activities we had experienced have been stored as mind information in our Alaya.

---

[46] Daniel G. Amen, *Change Your Brain Change Your Life*, Three Rivers Press, New York (1998), p 9

6

The Difference between Thinking and Memorizing

When you meet one of your friends on the street, you remember the friend's name because the friend's name has been stored in your Alaya and is recalled as soon as you meet. The remembrance of the friend's name is verification that your mind has located the right mind information in Alaya, not that your brain has located the information in the brain.

Mind Organ
↑↓
Mind Information (Citta)

We should note, however, that it is sometimes difficult to remember a friend's name when you see him or her on the street without any advanced notice. This may leave you trying to remember the name even after you shook hands and said good-bye if you were unable to recall it during the social interaction. If you fail in your search for the right information from the Alaya you will try to retrieve other information related to or associated with this person in order to recall the name. You may recall the house where he had lived, his brothers or sisters, his favorite friends or the like. Even then you may or may not locate the right information from the Alaya.

It is analogous to remembering the Pythagorean equation when you face a mathematical question relating to the Pythagorean Theorem. If you are quite familiar with the Theorem you will retrieve the right equation, $a^2 + b^2 = c^2$, immediately without difficulty. If not, you will try to search for similar equations, $a + b = c$, $a^2 x b^2 = c^2$, $(a + b)^2 = c^2$ or the like to determine the right one. As long as you do not give up on the question, you will repeat the same process.

Mind Organ

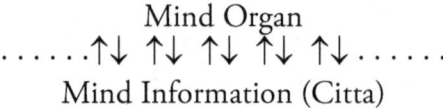

Mind Information (Citta)

Memorizing is a process to enable retrieving right information which one wishes to recall. This enables the mind organ to retrieve the right information from the Alaya, not that the brain retrieves it from the brain. Your birthday or the name of your close friend can be retrieved without any effort. In this case, an active act of thinking is not required in order to recall it, but in the case where you cannot recall your friend's name or the Pythagorean equation immediately a concerted act of thinking is required to bring about the recall. An immediate recall of right information means that the mind organ contacts the right information immediately without any thinking, whereas thinking means that the mind organ contacts various pieces of mind information continuously until the mind organ finds the right information or the solution that one is seeking.

Although one finally finds the necessary information from the Alaya through thinking, the thinking process does not stop there. Returning to the mathematical example above, once one recalls the Pythagorean equation he will try to solve the question by using the equation to calculate something. The thinking process keeps on going. Even if one recalls his friend's name immediately or through thinking, a lot of information relating to his friend will be continuously contacted by the mind organ. For example, he will think of things in the past with the friend—how he is doing, where he is living, what his occupation is, etc.

We say that our mind, in general terms, is always busy. It is said that on an average day the average person runs about sixty thousand thoughts through his mind.[47] This means that the mind organ contacts sixty thousand pieces of information in the Alaya in one day. The thinking mind of a human being is analogous to monkeys swinging from branch to branch using their arms. The thinking process is performed either (1) with a particular purpose in order to find a right piece of information or a solution that one wishes to seek, or (2) in a random or free-associating manner without any particular purpose. This means that the mind organ is continuously trying to contact pieces of mind information to locate right information in the first case, or the mind organ is contacting pieces of mind information randomly or freely as they appear to the mind organ in the second case. The former is referred as thinking, thought or cognition, and the latter as imagination, delusion or daydreaming.

In Buddhism, the consciousness generated through the thinking process has been separated from the six consciousnesses and has been defined as Manas consciousness, the seventh consciousness. The seventh consciousness, however, is quite different from the six consciousnesses in that the six consciousnesses are generated when the six organs contact the corresponding objects, but in the seventh consciousness there is neither organ nor object. As the sixth consciousness is generated when the mind organ contacts mind information, we can say that the Manas consciousness is a continuous repetition of the sixth consciousness.

The thinking process which is performed by searching mind information in the Alaya is not performed spontaneously or automatically. Although it seems to us that thinking is proceeding by itself, it is not, and there must be a reason. When we are talking

---

47 S. Sharma, *The Monk Who Sold His Ferrari*, Harper, San Francisco (1997), p42

about something we sometimes ask ourselves "why are we talking about this now?" For example, while talking about elephants with friends we might ask ourselves "why are we talking about elephants?" before we realize that our talking about elephants was related to a tour of Thailand by a friend, and that the Thailand tour was from the summer vacation which he received as a special bonus from his company. This string of related realizations is a specific example of how the thinking process is started from a starting information A, A triggers B, B triggers C, C triggers D and so on. If this is the case, what is the starting point of thinking?

The starting point of consciousness or thinking is the five sense consciousnesses. When the five sense organs contact their respective objects the five sense consciousnesses are brought into our awareness, an invoking of the five sense consciousnesses. If our eyes perceive a visible object X, we think of A from X, B from A, C from B and so on. During that thinking, if a sound Y comes into our ears we think of L from Y, M from L, N from M and so on. Again, if a scent Z comes into our nose we think of P from Z, Q from P, R from Q and so on. Our thinking continues going on and on in this manner. The mind information in Alaya is continuously contacted by the mind organ which constitutes a continuous thinking process. The thinking is developed or evolved by contacting new pieces of information one by one, and since this process is continuously building upon itself as it goes 'round and round,' it may be useful to envision this repetitive nature as a 'spirally thinking cycle,' ever onward through recurring iterations.

As we have noted, thinking is started mostly from the five sense consciousnesses, but mind information can also be the starting point of consciousness since a piece of mind information can contact the mind organ suddenly without any initiating sensation. For instance, if the mind organ contacts mind information regarding an apple it will contact further pieces of information one by one. This is an example of how consciousness, including thinking, is not necessarily generated independently but may be generated as a result of earlier processes. Previous information results in a subsequent consciousness; i.e., the previous information becomes a

Probing the Mind: How does Consciousness Work?

cause of the next consciousness. This is analogous to causationism, a theory in the Buddhist tradition that every event is the result of a preceding cause. The self-nature which results from dependence on others consists of discriminations produced by causes and conditions. This characteristic of consciousness is called 'Nature of Dependence on Others' in the Consciousness-Only Theory[48] of the Yogacara school of Mahayana Buddhism.

In Buddhism, nothing exists independently—all things exist dependent on each other; this exists due to that, and that exists due to this. We cannot exist without air, and although we have air, we cannot exist without water. We cannot exist independently. Accordingly, the self-nature in us does not exist. All things do not have their own self-nature. All things exist temporarily only due to the interdependence with other things. All things are temporary manifestations due to causality.

We are searching mind information in Alaya all the time in order to find a particular information or a solution to a question, or without any purpose. As we noted, an average person runs about sixty thousand thoughts through his mind a day; we are thinking of something while eating, driving, walking, talking, or even sitting in a lecture room. We say that our mind or our brain is busy all the time. Such a characteristic of consciousness is called the 'Nature of Mere-Imagination' in the Consciousness-Only Theory. All things are imagined; i.e., all things are perceived by the imagination. What is conceived by the imagination has no nature of its own.[49] If we comprehend both characteristics of consciousness, Nature of Dependence on Others and Nature of Mere-Imagination, we shall approach the mechanism of consciousness more easily.

---

48 *The Thirty Stanzas* by Vasubandhu, 21st Stanza

49 *The Thirty Stanzas* by Vasubandhu, 20th Stanza

7

The Epitome of Thinking and Its Contamination

Thought or thinking is very important to all sentient beings, but this is especially true for human beings since thought has been at the root of our development and evolution. All developments and achievements in science and technology, as well as civilization and culture, have evolved from human thought. Rene Descartes, a 17th century French philosopher, regarded thought as being the fundamental essence of existence for human beings and stated this by declaring *Cogito ergo sum*, "I think, therefore I am."

According to the Consciousness-Only school of Buddhism, the seventh consciousness (Manas consciousness) is the continuation of the sixth consciousness. If the five types of sense objects are perceived by their respective organs, the sixth consciousness is generated as a result of extending this awareness to contact mind information so as to identify the sensed object, and the seventh consciousness is generated as the mind continues to identify other characteristics associated with the object. For example, when we see an apple it is perceived by the eyes to generate a visual consciousness. The mind organ then contacts the mind information regarding the object and discriminates it as an apple, which constitutes the sixth consciousness. The sixth consciousness does not stop there, however, as the mind organ continues to seek other information relating to 'apple.' It will contact information regarding the taste, variety or type, even it's conversion to cider and other qualities or uses. The seventh consciousness includes all intellection, cogitation, mental operations, imagination and the like. Buddhism defines the thinking process as the seventh consciousness, Manas, separately from the sixth; i.e., sixth consciousness is opening up to and contacting mind information, whereas seventh consciousness is the act of manipulating or using the information. All of these mental activities are stored in the eighth, Alaya consciousness.

In the Consciousness-Only Theory, the seventh consciousness surpasses the other consciousnesses. It means that thinking, cogitation or intellection in the seventh consciousness surpasses sensation, perception or discrimination in the six consciousnesses, as well as the mind information stored in the eighth, Alaya. It should be understood, however, that the cogitation or intellection in the seventh is processed with and within the information stored in Alaya.

We should also note that thinking is not restricted to human beings. A lesser developed creature such as an ant or an earthworm, as well as more developed animals like chickens or dogs think. Dogs distinguish their master from others, and understand what they are saying and act on it; chickens protect their chicks from an outside threat; ants know how to store their food for winter and earthworms can move to the suitable place to live. All sentient beings have the mind organ and mind information, thereby generating both the sixth consciousness and the seventh. The only difference between human beings and other living things is the amount of mind information which is stored in their Alaya. The amount of mind information is greatly expanded by use of the spoken language and written letters. Human beings can store a tremendous amount of mind information due to the use of language and letters, and the more information which is stored the more the intellect has to process. We store information (which we call knowledge) in Alaya through experience or learning during our lifetime, and we understand how important education is. On the other hand as the

Probing the Mind: How does Consciousness Work?

lesser creatures do not have a spoken language or letters, even if many of them do make sounds and have other modes of communication, they have the ability to store only a very limited amount of information in their Alaya. Most of the information relates to their instincts. We therefore say that they act on instinct. Due to the tremendous amount of mind information, human beings have an opportunity to develop a remarkable theory or to devise a fantastic invention during the processing of mind information. We call it research in ordinary language.

The Consciousness-Only Theory says that the Manas consciousness, which surpasses other consciousnesses, is contaminated in the thinking cycle since the process of thinking continuously revises and reorganizes the mind information. The Theory says that the Manas consciousness is always accompanied by four *klesas* or vexing passions. The Theory explains six vexing passions (*klesas*): covetousness, anger, delusion, conceit, doubt and erroneous views. However, four *klesas* are pertinent to the seventh consciousness: self-delusion, self-belief, self-conceit and self-love.[50] The proclamation that the Manas consciousness is always accompanied by the four *klesas* or vexing passions is one of remarkable characteristics of the Theory.

Self-delusion means lack of understanding. It means ignorance of the true nature of the Atman (the 'inner self' or 'higher self') or individual divine essence, and delusion as to the principle that there is no Atman (egolessness). Self-belief means adhering to the view that Atman exists, erroneously imagining certain dharmas (transitory conditions which cause creation) to be the self when they are not so. Self-conceit means pride; basing itself on the belief in an Atman, it causes the mind to feel superior and lofty. Self-love means a greedy desire for the self; because of its belief in the Atman it develops deep attachments to it.[51] The four vexing passions are from the wrong view that we believe in 'individual ego' and attach

---

50 *The Thirty Stanzas* by Vasubandhu, 6th Stanza

51 Wei Tat, *Ch'eng Wei-Shih Lun: The Doctrine of Mere-Consciousness*, Hong Kong: The Ch'eng Wei-Shih Lun Translation Committee 1973, p 289

to it. In a word, the four vexing passions may be called 'self-view.' The following quotation explains the meaning of the four klesas, especially self-view.

A university professor once visited a Japanese master, asking many questions about Zen. The master served tea, filling his guest's cup, and then continuing to pour. The professor watched the overflow exclaiming that the cup was full without room for any more. "Just like this cup," the master replied, "you are so full of your own views and opinions that there is no room for any new understanding. To experience the truth you must first empty your cup."[52]

The vexing passions come from self-view and the self-view comes from attachment to individual ego. As social animals, human beings live in interrelation with others, but, they live always in pain due to the self-view. They come into conflict with others due to the self-view and go through a difficult time. The following quotation also provides understanding about the self-view or individual ego.

If a man is crossing a river and an empty boat collides with his own skiff, even though he be a bad-tempered man he will not become very angry. But if he sees a man in the boat, he will shout at him to steer clear. If the shout is not heard, he will shout again, and yet again, and begin cursing, and all because there is somebody in the boat. Yet if the boat were empty, he would not be shouting, and not angry. If you can empty your own boat crossing the river of the world, no one will oppose you, no one will seek to harm you.[53]

A pure information is contaminated by the self-view, self-delusion, self-belief, self-conceit and self-love, in the thinking process of the seventh consciousness. When the thinking process is carried out we hardly obtain a right view because the self-view interjects itself in and disturbs it. The thinking process is self-centered and the pure information is contaminated with self-view. This is analogous to someone who draws water to one's own mill.

---

52 Joseph Goldstein, *The Experience of Insight*, Shambhala Publications, Boston (1976), p158

53 Joseph Goldstein, *The Experience of Insight*, Shambhala Publications, Boston (1976), p166

Probing the Mind: How does Consciousness Work?

After almost 2,000 years a social psychologist has confirmed the insight of Buddhism that our thinking is accompanied by the vexing passions, resulting in being contaminated. Daniel Gilbert, Professor of Psychology, Harvard University, says:

People have a tremendous talent for changing their views of events so that they can feel better about them. We're not immediately delighted when our wife runs away with another guy, but in fairly short order most of us start to realize that "she was never really right for me" or that "we didn't have that much in common." Our friends snicker and say that we are rationalizing—as if these conclusions were simply wrong because they are comforting. ..... What matters is that human beings are exceptionally good at discovering them when it is convenient for them to do so.[54]

---

54 Edited by John Brockman, *Thinking*, Harper, New York (2013), pp59-60

8

The Delusion of Thinking—Why Do We Not See the True Nature?

A little Korean-American boy who just learned an English word 'apple' and visited a Korean relative was quarrelling with a little Korean boy who just learned a Korean word '*sagwa*' which means apple. The American boy argued that the fruit is an apple, but the Korean boy argued the fruit is a *sagwa*. For the same fruit, Americans call it an apple, Koreans call it *sagwa*, and Japaneses call it *ringo*. Although the object is the same, we say it differently because the mind information in Alaya is different for each of us. Americans who do not know Korean do not have information about *sagwa* in Alaya. If the apple is red, American, Korean, Japanese and others see it as being red. Nobody sees it as yellow or black. Everybody also perceives the apple as being rounded; nobody perceives it as a cubic shape. The color or shape of an apple does not change from person to person, so the color or shape of an apple can be considered a reality, but the name is variable from language to language so it is not a reality. We do not see the reality, the true nature or true self; each sees only in accordance with the mind information of his own self-view resulting in disputes, quarrels, arguments and so on.

Walking down the street I may pass a woman with bright red lipstick, a faint whiff of wine on her breath from lunch at a restaurant, and with no hat on her head. In my worldview none of these facts triggers any particular emotion or judgement so this is a neutral encounter that barely registers with me. You might therefore assume that nothing happened in my brain, yet, as meme theory points out, a great deal happened tacitly. The sight of this woman entered my brain as raw data along the optic nerve but I couldn't actually 'see' her until that data passed through my worldview. Imagine a series of filters marked 'memory,' 'beliefs,' 'associations,' and 'judgements.' Each filter alters the raw data in some way, invisibly and instantaneously. Should a person with a different worldview encounter the same woman, he would 'see' her through his filters. If he happened to be a traditional Muslim, or a Victorian or a medieval monk, all the innocuous features that entered my brain—the lipstick, the smell of alcohol, the absence of a hat—might cause a violent reaction in his brain and generate considerable stress. Two people with different worldviews can see the same facts and give totally divergent interpretations of them.[55]

Taking the examples of the apple and the woman into account, we may outline the mechanism of consciousness from generation to storage as five steps as follow:

Sensation (Perception) ⇨ **Discrimination** ⇨ **Thinking** ⇨ **Mental Activities** ⇨ **Storage.**

When an object appears far away, we can see it with our eyesight but we cannot know whether it is an apple or a woman. This is the first step of sensation or perception. The first step is performed by the corresponding organ (eye), the nervous system and brain. If the object is approaching us we can discern whether it is an apple or a woman. This is the second step of discrimination. The second step is performed by the mind organ and mind information. You

---

55 Deepak Chopra, *Life After Death*, Three Rivers Press, New York (2006), pp 229-230

Probing the Mind: How does Consciousness Work?

may say *apple, ringo* or *sagwa* according to the mind information stored in Alaya. You may even discriminate the woman as a drunk woman due to the mind information on lipstick, wine and the like. The following quotation describes the process for searching necessary mind information from the Alaya.

Let's say someone walks up to you and greets you by name. The person is smiling; there's an expectant look on her face. How do you come up with a response? Your mind does several things at once. It consults its stored picture files for familiar faces. It looks for a name to attach to the right face. If neither can be found immediately, the mind doesn't feel stymied yet-it has backup resources. It rummages through faces that could fit this person but are younger or fuzzily recorded. It tosses up sample names that might jog your memory. It runs through recent events that this apparent stranger may have played a part in. If all this doesn't work, the mind starts thinking of what to say to cover up your memory lapse. We're all familiar with such situations, and we are so accustomed to matching names and faces that we don't marvel at how astonishing the whole process is. Not only can the mind Google itself for information with incredible swiftness, it performs multiple operations with backup plans if they fail. This implies an amazingly complex but invisible structure.[56]

The third step of thinking follows the second step of discrimination. In this step in our earlier example an American boy thinks that he is right, he is seeing an apple., A Korean boy also thinks that he is right, that is a *sagwa*. We may likewise get different views when seeing the same woman. In this step the thinking is accompanied by self-delusion, self-belief, self-conceit or self-love. We could not see the true nature of the woman and the information on her is contaminated by the self-view.

Our minds are constantly churned up by our thoughts and our emotions, by what we see, hear, smell, taste, and touch. Because of this, they do not accurately reflect what is happening outside. In other words, when something happens outside, we immediately interpret it

---

56   Deepak Chopra, *Life After Death*, Three Rivers Press, New York (2006), pp 89-90

in accordance with our biases and prejudices. We do not see things as they really are, but rather as we interpret them. This happens so automatically that we are not conscious of what is going on. If you talk to a number of people who have experienced the same event, each one will describe it differently.[57]

The mind information which is stored in Alaya is very important because the quality of our thinking is dependent on the validity of the mind information. We cannot control the sensation which is perceived by the five organs (in order to avoid the sensation we cannot close our eyes or ears and hope to continue to function effectively), but our thinking depends on the information which is stored.

The quantity of mind information in the human being's Alaya gradually increased due to the contribution of the invention of paper and the development of printing techniques since visual information increased with these developments. The quantity of mind information took another leap forward after the radio was invented early in the 20th century and radio stations were founded in 1920s; auditory information had been increased. The mind information in the human Alaya continued to increase explosively with the invention of the TV, also in the 1920s, since both visual and auditory information had been increased. We are now living in a flood of information since the internet was developed late in the 20th century. Dr. Michael Merzenich, PhD, a neuroscientist, said that the internet is just one of those things that contemporary humans can spend millions of 'practice' events at, that the average human a thousand years ago had absolutely no exposure to. Our brains are massively remodeled by this exposure—but so too, by reading, by television, by video games, by modern electronics, by contemporary music, by contemporary 'tools,' etc.[58]

---

57 Tenzin Palmo, *Reflections on a Mountain Lake*, Snow Lion Publications, New York (2002), pp 87-88

58 Norman Doidge, *The Brain That Changes Itself*, Penguin Books, London (2007), p 306

Probing the Mind: How does Consciousness Work?

In our modern, highly secular world, we are not only overwhelmed with information but we are cast into an ocean of conflicting religious, philosophical, and scientific claims about the nature of the universe and human existence. No human society in recorded history has ever been presented with such a diversity of views, many of them presented as if with great authority.[59] This is because everybody produces his own views depending on the mind information stored in Alaya. Worse still, the mind information becomes impure or polluted by being accompanied by self-delusion, self-belief, self-conceit or self-love in the third step of thinking.

We can see how our thinking is going on in the third step if we closely observe it. We can try not to employ self-delusion, self-belief, self-conceit or self-love. We might observe the thinking closely, and if we do this we may have a right view which is not contaminated by the vexing passions and we can therefore store uncontaminated information in Alaya. This sounds simple, but when the five types of sense objects are contacted by the corresponding organs it is very difficult to see the true nature of the objects. That is because their true nature is covered with the contaminated information due to the four vexing passions. Therefore, the Buddha taught in the Diamond Sutra that "In a place where there is something that can be distinguished by objects, in that place there is deception. If you can see the objectless nature of objects, then you can see the Tathagata."[60] This means that since the concepts, ideas, images, or mental phenomena of the objects could deceive you, you should not be deceived by them. We may be deceived by the drunk appearance of the person, but we cannot see the true nature of him or her. If you are not deceived, you can see the reality or true nature of the objects and further the Tathagata, the Buddha nature.

Mental activities (the fourth step) also occur in the second step of discrimination as well as in the third step of thinking. These

---

59 B. Alan Wallace, *Buddhism with an Attitude,* Snow Lion Publications, New York (2003), p 67

60 *The Diamond Sutra (The Vajrachedika Prajnaparamita Sutra)*, Chapter 5

mental activities are also dependent on the mind information, and if it is good, a good mental activity will make you feel good and happy. The mental activities will affect the physical body directly. It is also very important to observe the mental activities which arise in the mind. How to observe the mental activities will be discussed in the later chapters.

In the fifth step, all consciousnesses which were generated in the preceding four steps will be stored in Alaya. The sensation, discrimination or recognition, thinking, and mental activities will be stored as mind information. The mind information has a different force due to the degree of importance, attention, concern or interest of the matter with which it is associated.

9

A Dog Has a Better Mind Organ than a Human

We generally understand mind reading as telepathy, which is the transfer of information between individuals by means other than the five senses. The five senses are perceived by the five sense organs of the physical body, so what would be the means other than the five senses? Buddhism clearly defines the means as mind organ and the objects for the mind organ as dharmas which we explain as mind information. According to Buddhism, mind reading or telepathy means that the mind organ perceives and recognizes mind information. Telepathy is not a physical term and cannot be demonstrated in a scientific manner. As the mind organ or dharmas or mind information is non-material or non-physical, they also cannot be substantiated physically or scientifically. However, a lot of instances occur around us.

Many pet owners will attest to the ability of a dog or cat to know what the owner is thinking. A few minutes before going on a walk, a dog gets excited and restless; on the day when a cat is going to be taken to the vet, it disappears and is nowhere to be found. These casual observations led the ingenious British researcher Rupert Sheldrake, a trained biologist now turned speculative thinker, to conduct controlled studies to find out if dogs and cats can actually read their owners' minds. One study was very simple: Sheldrake phoned sixty-five veterinarians in the London area and asked them if it was common for cat owners to cancel appointments because their cats had disappeared that day. Sixty-four vets responded that it was very common, and the sixty-fifth had given up making appointments for cats because too many couldn't be located when they were supposed to come in.

Sheldrake decided to perform an experiment using dogs. The fact that a dog gets excited when the time comes to go for a walk means little if the walk is routinely scheduled for the same time every day, or if the dog gets visual cues from its owner that he is preparing to go out. Therefore, Sheldrake placed dogs in outbuildings completely isolated from their owners; he then asked the owner, at randomly selected times, to think about walking their dogs five minutes before going to get them. In the meantime, the dog was being videotaped in its isolated location. Sheldrake found that when their owners started thinking about taking them for a walk, more than half the dogs ran to the door wagging their tails, circling restlessly, and keeping up this behavior until their owners appeared. No dog showed anticipatory behavior, however, when their owners were not thinking about taking them for a walk.

This suggests something intriguing, that the bond between a pet and its owner creates a subtle connection at the level of thought. Polls show that about 60% of Americans believe they have had a telepathic experience, so this result is not completely startling. The next leap is quiet startling, however. After writing up his results with telepathic pets, Sheldrake received an e-mail from a woman in New York City who said that her African gray parrot not only read her thoughts but responded to them with speech. The woman and her husband might be sitting in another room, out of sight from the bird, whose name is N'kisi, and if they were feeling hungry, N'kisi would suddenly say, "You want some yummy." If the owner and her husband were thinking about going out, N'kisi might say, "You gotta go out, see ya later."[61]

From the cats' study and the dogs' experiment above, we can say that cats and dogs can read their master's mind. It seems to

---

61 Deepak Chopra, *Life After Death*, Three Rivers Press, New York (2006), pp 89-90

us that animals have a more developed mind organ than human beings in certain areas. If the experiments had been about human beings instead of cats or dogs we would not have obtained similar results. That's not to say that human beings are inferior to cats or dogs; there's no need to put ourselves down about the experimental results, but we should rather note that a human consciousness is much more complicated than that of cats or dogs. Cats and dogs devote themselves to their caretaker. He provides them with food when they are hungry and takes care of them when they get sick. They haven't got the time to concern themselves with other things except their master. To them their master is an absolute being as important as themselves. What they do not tune in with within the awareness of the master's mind could be a major threat and a significant danger to them. The sixth organ for reading the master's mind couldn't help being developed. Likewise, bees have the ability to see even into the ultraviolet spectrum, so bees are superior to human beings when it comes to sight consciousness; bats perceive ultrasonic waves with much higher frequency than human beings; and dogs have a more developed smell consciousness than do humans.

Although animals have some aspects of their sense organs or mind organs more developed than human beings, no animal can compete with a human being when it comes to the amount of mind information which we call knowledge. The tremendous amount of mind information stored in the human Alaya is due to the use of language and letters, and humans reorganize and rearrange the thinking cycle very fast based on the tremendous amount of mind information. Animals, including even the very primitive, also see evolution of their thinking cycle, but their thinking cycle is too slow for major disruption due to the limited amount of mind information which mostly relates to their instincts.

We have explained that the mind organ perceives the mind information which is stored in Alaya. More precisely, Buddhism says that the sixth organ, the organ of mind, perceives the sixth object, dharmas, and that the Alaya, the eighth consciousness, stores all consciousnesses including mind information or dharmas.

Like in the experiment with the dogs, if dogs understand their master's thinking then the object that the mind organ contacts is not limited to the mind information stored in their own Alaya. This may be even more powerfully presented in the story of the parrot which can read its owner's minds. The object is extended to the mind information stored in others' Alaya. If the object is limited to the mind information stored in its own Alaya, the sixth object will be identical to the Alaya, eighth consciousness. But the sixth object is not only the mind information stored in its own Alaya, but also includes and accesses the mind information stored in others' Alaya. Accordingly, I infer that Buddhism defines the sixth object, dharmas, as being separate from the Alaya, the eighth, and that the dharmas as a sixth object encompass all mind information of all sentient beings. The sixth object is without boundaries in consciousness.

We have seen that dogs can read their owners' mind, but will it be possible for humans to read a dogs' mind or another's mind? According to *Ch'eng Wei-Shih Lun*, one's mind is said to understand the mind of the other person, but it cannot understand another mind directly. What it does understand directly is only what it itself develops. The point is that when consciousness is born it manifests a semblance of another thing, and from this semblance it is able to comprehend that thing. In this way, one's own mind perceives a representation of another person's mind as an object as it develops concepts of related items or actions, etc.[62] For example, suppose that someone is thinking about taking me to the hospital. What I read in his mind is neither to see a sentence "He will take me to the hospital." nor to hear the sentence. This is because we cannot understand another mind immediately and directly. Instead, what we perceive in his mind is to see some material things such as hospital, white gown doctors and the like, which are visually developed or manifested. We may occasionally hear some sound, too.

---

62 Wei Tat, *Ch'eng Wei-Shih Lun: The Doctrine of Mere-Consciousness*, Hong Kong: The Ch'eng Wei-Shih Lun Translation Committee 1973, p523

Probing the Mind: How does Consciousness Work?

Finally, we understand from the material things that he will take us to the hospital.

It is not easy for humans to see what is going to happen from the mind information. Human consciousness is more complicated. Unlike dogs or cats, we do not have a master to whom we dedicate our life. Each individual is busily crafting his own evolving cycle. When we believe ourselves to be a god, we are furthering the evolving cycle. On the other hand, believing ourselves to be lost we are shaping the evolving cycle to seek for something from the outside. We are crafting the evolving cycle to correspond with the vexing passions. We are forming the evolving cycle in accordance with eight mundane concerns consisting of four pairs of priorities: the pursuit of material acquisitions and the avoidance of their loss; the pursuit of stimulus-driven pleasure and the avoidance of discomfort; the pursuit of praise and the avoidance of blame; and the pursuit of good reputation and the avoidance of bad reputation.[63] The eight mundane concerns are to satisfy the five sense organs. We have never tried to develop the sixth organ. We have never tried to see the true nature or reality of objects through the sixth organ. Instead, we have been developing the evolving cycle faster and faster in the pursuit of mundane concerns.

We pay a lot of attention to our bodies. We clean them, adorn them, feed them, and exercise them. But how much attention do we give to our real home? How often do we clean out our mind? How much do we exercise it? How much do we adorn it? How much nourishment do we give it?[64]

It takes a lot of time for a baby to learn a spoken language. It takes several years for babies to learn it from their parents or brothers or sisters even if it is their native tongue. They have to repeat listening and pronouncing spoken words in order to train their ears. They also have to repeat reading and writing letters to learn

---

[63] B. Alan Wallace, *Buddhism with an Attitude,* Snow Lion Publications, New York (2003), p 19

[64] Tenzin Palmo, *Reflections on a Mountain Lake,* Snow Lion Publications, New York (2002), p 132

written letters and sentences for several years through kindergarten, elementary school, middle school, high school and so on. That is for training their eyes as associates in the language arts. It likewise takes a lot of time and practice for a sommelier to distinguish the taste of wine. We have addressed the difficulty associated with a child learning his native tongue, and it is much more difficult for grown-ups to learn a foreign language.

What can we learn from the above? We have to train our five sense organs for a considerable amount of time in order to generate the right corresponding consciousness. We might ask, then, why should it be different for the sixth organ, mind organ? Note that we have not tried to train the sixth organ for the entire length of our lifetime. Due to our overwhelming focus of attention on the perceptions developed through our sense organs we have tried only to satisfy them so far in our lifetime which raises an interesting question: how could we develop our sixth organ without practicing using it to read the sixth objects, mind information?

10

An Inanimate Being Has a Mind Organ

In Buddhism, all beings have their own Buddha nature. This includes both sentient beings and nonsentient beings, animate beings and inanimate beings. In the Diamond Sutra beings are classified into nine categories, but these are first defined as animate beings or inanimate beings. There are four species of animate beings: those born from eggs, born from a womb, born from moisture, and born spontaneously. In inanimate beings, there are five species: species with form, species with no form, species having perception, species having no perception, and species neither having perception nor not having perception.[65]

All birds and fowls are born from eggs; turtles, snakes, crocodiles and the like are also born from eggs. All mammals, including humans, are born from the womb. Some worms are born from moisture, whereas the cicada is born spontaneously from cicada larva. In another instance a pupal state is spontaneously changed to another form to give another birth; e.g., a caterpillar to a moth or a butterfly. Species with form would include stone, metal, a desk, a

---

65 *The Diamond Sutra*, Chapter 3

chair, etc., and species with no form include ghost, phantom, soul, etc. If the species with form or with no form has perception, it will be categorized as a species having perception, whereas if a species with or without form has no perception it will be categorized as a species having no perception. The ninth category of species not having perception and not having no perception is difficult to comprehend and to explain in ordinary language, and is comprehended more as a mystical realization to those who have *touched* such a state of consciousness.

We know that the first four species of animate beings have consciousness. They think by themselves not because they have a brain, but because they have a mind organ and mind information. Their thinking cycle is ordered and pursued based on the mind information which is available to them in Alaya. The only difference among them is the amount of mind information and the speed of the thinking cycle. The thinking cycle of humans is the quickest and the most complex among the species born from the womb, or of any of the other categories of beings. The thinking cycle of the species born from the womb or the species born from eggs is faster than that of species born from moisture or the species born spontaneously, and this may be considered a measure of the brightness of consciousness or the level of consciousness of the relevant species. Humans have the highest brightness and then dogs, chimpanzees, cats, species from the womb, species from eggs, species from moisture, and species born spontaneously. The level of brightness gradually decreases as we go down this list.

Plants and vegetables have a low level of consciousness, but science has revealed that they do possess a level of consciousness even if it is much lower than that of the four species of animate beings. In religion "Do not kill an animate being" means "Do not kill the four species." Most plants or vegetables grow heliotropically, that is, they seek the sun. A scientific experiment revealed that in addition to their response to light, those which were grown in the presence of classical music grew faster than those who were not stimulated by music as they were grown. Plants were also found to react with frenetic energy discharges when a person who had previously mutilated one of the plants in their group walked into the room. We find that like animate beings, we can say plants have similar five sense organs as well as the mind organ.

Bernard Grad, a biologist and professor at Mcgill University did experimental work and observed how barleys grow in pots when watered from three different bottles. One water bottle was grasped and blessed by a naturalist who loves the plants, another by an insane person, and the third one was not grasped by anyone. Each of these three bottles was used to water different pots, with the result that the barley in the naturalist's water grew the biggest, the barley in the nobody's water was second, and the barley in the insane person's water was the smallest.[66]

Another experiment showed different results on cooked rice. Cooked rice was put into two glass bowls. One bowl was attached with labels 'LOVE' and 'THANK YOU,' the other with labels 'HATE' and 'DAD-BLAMED.' A month later, the rice of the former bowl had been changed into well fermented yeast, but the rice of the latter into badly spoiled mold.[67]

Quantum physicists explain such phenomena as characteristics of particles. The particles are explained as having an infinite number of possibilities. The particles seem to communicate with all cosmic information. The theory of quantum physics posits that subatomic units called quanta are the building blocks of reality. Matter, energy, time and space are all composed of some variant of quanta, and material quanta appear to be both particles of matter and waves of energy. Physicists have repeatedly proven the truth of these principles, both experimentally and mathematically. In trying to determine whether a given subatomic unit is a particle of matter or a wave of energy, physicists devise experiments to look for one or the other, the most famous of which being the Double-Slit Experiment. The more they have conducted these experiments, the more they have found that particles of matter are actually waves of

---

66 Sangwoon Kim, *Watching*, Seoul, Jungshinsegyesa (2014), pp 26-27

67 Sangwoon Kim, *Watching*, Seoul, Jungshinsegyesa (2014), p 28

energy until they are observed, at which point they become particles of matter; although if physicists are looking for a wave of energy, then the wave remains a wave. Not only do physicists' own minds influence the results of their experiments, but their minds may actually be creating matter or energy at the instant that they make their observations.[68]

The roots of physics, as of all western science, can be traced to the Greek philosophy of the sixth century B.C., in a culture where science, philosophy and religion were not separated. The sages of the Milesian school in Ionia were not concerned with such distinctions; their aim was to discover the essential nature, or real constitution of things they called 'physis.' The term 'physics' is derived from this Greek word and originally meant the endeavor of seeing the essential nature of all things. This, of course, is also the central aim of all mystics, and the philosophy of the Milesian school did indeed have a strong mystical flavor. The Milesians were called 'hylozoists', or 'those who think matter is alive,' by the later Greeks, because they saw no distinction between animate and inanimate, spirit and matter. In fact, they did not even have a word for matter since they saw all forms of existence as manifestations of the 'physis,' endowed with life and spirituality. Thus Thales declared all things to be full of gods (the nature of gods) and Anaximander saw the universe as a kind of organism which was supported by 'pneuma', the cosmic breath, in the same way as the human body is supported by air.[69]

According to the Consciousness-Only Theory, as all animate beings and inanimate beings have consciousness, barley, water, cooked rice and the like have consciousness. What 'inanimate beings with no physical body have consciousness' means is that they have their own mind organ and that the mind organ reads mind information, thereby their mental interaction affects the growth or change of their body.

---

68 Roberta Grimes, *Fun of Dying*, Greater Reality Publications (2010), pp 28-29

69 Fritjof Capra, *The Tao of Physics*, Shambhala, Boston (2010), p 20

Probing the Mind: How does Consciousness Work?

Species with no form such as ghosts, demons, soul or the like also possesses consciousness. They also have their own mind organ which can read mind information, and they also utilize a thinking cycle. If they do not have any consciousness, or if they do not think, why are we scared of them? If they were a stone or a piece of dry wood alongside the roadside we would not be scared of them. We are scared of them because we believe they possess consciousness, or have the capability to think about something.

Their thinking cycle operates very slowly compared to humans, or even to any animate beings. The five sense organs of humans are always open to the five objects, and humans receive a lot of information from outside through these five organs. Information received by the organs stimulates the mind information in Alaya resulting in excitation of the thinking cycle. Ghosts, demons, souls or the like do not have the five sense organs; they have only the sixth organ. Their thinking cycle cannot help but being slow because other information is not received by the five organs to initiate retrieval of mind information by the mind organ.

We should note that Buddhism defined eight consciousnesses about 2,500 years ago, and in particular, the sixth organ and the sixth object are defined like the five sense organs and the corresponding five objects. Remarkably, Buddhism declared the fact that mental activities are produced when the sixth organ, mind organ, contacts the sixth object, dharma, mind information. Western philosophy has tried to discern the secrets of the existence of matter and spirit for more than 2,000 years, but they did not establish scientific theories for the physical world until the 17th century. At the stage of the Newtonian universe, classical physics started to explain the order and constitution of the material world. In view of consciousness, however, classical physics found that it could only cover principles on the five objects which are all matter, and found that Newtonian physics could not touch the realm of consciousness or mind.

The mechanistic world view of classical physics is useful for the description of the kind of physical phenomena we encounter in our everyday life and thus appropriate for dealing with our daily environ-

ment, and it has also proven extremely successful as a basis for technology. It is inadequate, however, for the description of physical phenomena in the submicroscopic realm. Opposed to the mechanistic conception of the world is the view of the mystics which may be epitomized by the word 'organic,' as it regards all phenomena in the universe as integral parts of an inseparable harmonious whole. This world view emerges in the mystical traditions from meditative states of consciousness. In their description of the world, the mystics use the concepts which are derived from these non-ordinary experiences and are, in general, inappropriate for a description of macroscopic phenomena.[70]

Both of the cited experiments on barley and cooked rice are factual occurrences. Although quantum physics explains the phenomena in its own way, it has not uncovered the mechanism behind them. Phenomena beyond scientific reasoning are called mysteries. Mystical knowledge cannot be demonstrated conclusively and has to be experienced in a direct intuitive (or unitive) way. Mystery, mystical knowledge, mysticism and the like are separate from but complementary to the frontiers of science. From the standpoint of the Consciousness-Only Theory, a mystery is a result of phenomena by mental activities which are generated when the mind organ contacts mind information, and mystical knowledge is mind information obtained through intuition or insight. Our thinking is initiated in response to outside information obtained through the five organs and developed sequentially, whereas our intuition or insight is encountered as an immediate awareness when the thinking is stopped. Intuition or insight is a capacity in which one's mind organ can contact mind information without being triggered by an outside information or without thinking.

Early in the 20th century an extraordinary intellectual feat by Albert Einstein initiated a change in the whole of theoretical physics with two revolutionary developments: relativity theory and his formulation of quantum physics based on Max Planck's work on Black-Body radiation. It may be said that modern physics started to overtly discover and recognize the realm of consciousness or mind

---

[70] Fritjof Capra, *The Tao of Physics*, Shambhala, Boston (2010), pp 303-304

Probing the Mind: How does Consciousness Work?

with the work of Einstein. In the Consciousness-Only Theory, the mind can be defined in ordinary terms as a triangular relationship between the mind organ, mind information and mental activities. Can modern physics, oriented towards quantum mechanics, discover the constitution of mind information or mental activities in the same way as it did in matter and energy?

A similarity between the ways of the physicist and mystic is the fact that their observations take place in realms which are inaccessible to the ordinary senses. In modern physics, these are the realms of the atomic and subatomic world; in mysticism they are non-ordinary states of consciousness in which the sense world is transcended. Mystics often talk about experiencing higher dimensions in which impressions of different centres of consciousness are integrated into a harmonious whole. A similar situation exists in modern physics where a four-dimensional 'space-time' formalism has been developed which unifies concepts and observations belonging to different categories in the ordinary three-dimensional world. In both fields, the multi-dimensional experiences transcend the sensory world and are therefore almost impossible to express in ordinary language.[71]

Many things about mind information or mental activities could be explained in the same way that quantum physics clarified the physical structure or constitution of matter or energy, but quantum physics will not help us understand the meaning of mind information or mental activities. The meaning of the mind information or mental activities will be read and understood by the mind organ, but the mind organ does not have any power, unlike mind information or mental activities. The mind organ only has the ability to read mind information and change it into consciousness so that we might become aware of it. Quantum physics has not solved the secrets of the mind organ yet. In order to understand the meaning of the mind information or mental activities, or to discover the identity of the mind organ, we shall have to wait for the birth of the third generation physics.

---

71 Fritjof Capra, *The Tao of Physics*, Shambhala, Boston (2010), pp 305-306

11

See Your Mind (I): See Your Mind Interactions (Mental Activities)

In Korea, and probably in other oriental countries, we often hear 'see your mind' (probably similar to 'see with your heart' in western cultures). That is not 'see your mind with your eyes' but 'see your mind with your mind,' or 'with your *mind's eye*.' How can we make sense of this dichotomy of subject and object?

In Buddhism 'see your mind' means 'see your mental activity or mental interaction with your mind organ.' Buddhism defines fifty one mental activities (*caittas*), and yet we have trouble even seeing the five objects correctly. We hardly ever see the true nature or true self of the five objects because we are plausibly deceived by the form of the objects. Even worse we do not see the mental activities, and worse yet, we find that we follow the mental activities; in other words, the mental activities lead us. Our true self is captivated by the mental activities rather than being in charge.

Anyone who is willing to commit suicide in anguish and hopelessness is captivated by the agony and despair which will lead to suicide. If he sees and recognizes the agony and despair, or recognizes the mind (mental activity) to be willing to commit suicide, however, suicide will not follow. Likewise, if someone curses bitterly before you, anger or fury will arise inside you but you will hardly be aware of the anger or fury because you will react immediately to the situation before you are cognitively aware of the emotions. The mental activities will lead you as if on autopilot and a counter reaction such as abusive language or physical attack will follow. When we see our mental activities, however, we can see them in the third person and know that they do not last and they will finally disappear. One of the important teachings in Buddhism is that *all things change* and are impermanent. Nothing is certain in this world. Mental activities are the same.

If we can see a generating mental activity and be aware of it, we can change it in a way that we like. This is analogous to changing the TV channel. When a TV channel is not interesting we can change the channel to an interesting channel. Similarly, we have a tremendous amount of interesting information in our Alaya, and if we summon the interesting information from Alaya a new mental activity appears. Conversely, if we do not see the proceeding mental activity we are captivated by it and do not have room to call other interesting information from Alaya, and if we do not see the mental activities such as anger, fury, agitation, suffering and the like when they arise, it is not easy to escape from them.

When we experience an insulting event in front of many people it can trigger many things: our thinking cycle busily jumps around accessing a lot of information stored in Alaya and we feel like crawling into a hole somewhere, we think about revenge someday later, we think ourselves incompetent or worthless, or we even think so far as to give up on life. Our thinking cycle triggered by the event keeps going and never stops. On the other hand if we see the generating mental activities we know they are changing, coming and going. When a shameful activity arises, we need to see it. When it does not disappear and keeps going on we need to keep seeing it and then the shameful activity will be gradually weakened and finally disappear. The result is that the shameful activity will become trivial. This can sometimes take a significant amount of time, but it is the path of healing.

To say that we see our mental activities means that we are aware of them. 'Seeing mental activities' is 'Being aware of mental

Probing the Mind: How does Consciousness Work?

activities.' 'Thinking' is the opposite of 'Being aware of.' *Thought* is the opposite of *awareness*. Thinking is that the mind organ contacts mind information continuously, while 'being aware of' is achieved by stopping the thinking cycle and simply *knowing* or *having a realization about* the mental activities including thinking.

If we see the generating mental activities, our thinking stops. If we see the shameful activity, the thinking about revenge, inferiority complex, suicide or the like does not follow. Nevertheless, if a next activity arises after the previous one we need to try to also see the next. If we try to see the mental activity as it arises, the thinking cycle will begin to slow down and finally stop. Whether we excite the thinking cycle busily with mind information or we become aware of the mental activities by stopping the thinking cycle depends on one's own practice.

Thinking and *being aware of* are complementary functions. *Thinking* is stopped during *being aware of*, and as long as *thinking* keeps going on, the *being aware of* mental activities is difficult to maintain. It is not easy to simultaneously be aware of the mental activity and to think something by contacting mind information because the subject for doing both is the same mind organ. This is analogous to watching two channels on one TV set. It is also impossible to simultaneously watch two channels with two TV sets. The five sense organs are the same. Strictly speaking we cannot simultaneously see and focus on two or more objects with the eyes or simultaneously perceive two or more different sounds with the ears. On the other hand it is possible for more than two sense organs to perceive their corresponding objects at the same time. We can perceive a visual object with the eyes and hear a sound with the ears simultaneously. Each of the five sense organs, as well as the sixth organ, perceives the corresponding objects sequentially in accordance with time. Therefore, *thinking* and *being aware of* by the mind organ are not occurring at the exact same time.

Although we are aware of mental activities in the spirally-thinking (ST) cycle, the awareness does not last very long. William James reported on research that showed that it is possible to focus the attention continuously on an unchanging object for only two to three seconds, and this continues to be the position of cognitive scientists today. Without further investigation of basic assumptions one could get the impression that two to three seconds is the hard-wired upper limit of the brain's capacity for attention.[72] Even if we concentrate on the mental activities, if a beam of light flies into our eyes or a noise comes into our ears, the concentration is scattered and the thinking cycle begins to change due to the light or sound. The five external objects and the sixth object divert awareness from continuing. If awareness is stopped for a moment, thinking forces its way into the mental process like the rising tide. Due to this propensity for interruption, awareness is apt to be a momentary phenomenon. In this view awareness is therefore referred to as momentary consciousness or instant consciousness, which means extremely short duration consciousness.

According to Buddhism, if you see into the true nature of your true self you will attain Buddhahood. To see into the true nature of the true self means to see your mental activities, to be cognizant of your mental activities. There is a Korean or Chinese word '見性' whose meaning is 'seeing into one's true nature.' The meaning of the word expands to 'attaining Buddhahood or achieving enlightenment.' The word has two Chinese letters. The first letter means 'see,' the second 'nature' literally. The second actually is a combination of two letters again, mind (心) and arise or generate (生). Thus, to see into one's true nature is to see the generating mind, the mental activities; i.e., to be aware of it.

Though enlightenment is explained in various ways, the most persuasive explanation of it is 'being aware of what is going on here and now.' This does not come easy to us, however. For example, we may become cognitively unaware upon receiving surprising news that a parent died from a heart attack or that a child was a victim of a traffic accident. As soon as we hear the news we will rush to the hospital. After regaining a quiet mind, however, we will be unable to remember how we took a taxi, how we paid the fare,

---

72 B. Alan Wallace, *Buddhism with an Attitude,* Snow Lion Publications, New York (2003), p 80

etc. Likewise, many actions or experiences occur without our being aware of them. Although they are not surprising events, we do actions without awareness. If we take off our glasses just anywhere instead of in a habitual place when we go to bed, we may find that we will need to search for them here and there or everywhere the next morning. We may call it forgetfulness or amnesia, but the fact is that forgetfulness is caused from no-awareness. If we had been aware of the place when we took off the glasses we could easily locate them. One way to avoid forgetfulness is to talk to oneself in a whisper, or loudly, as "I put the glasses on the dining room table" or "I put the glasses on the desk." If we do so, we can attain awareness by sound conscious actions. Alzheimers' syndrome is much more serious than amnesia and is reported to be caused by damage to a special part of brain. In view of consciousness, we are not sure whether the syndrome is caused from the brain damage or whether it results from no-awareness. We may presume that no-awareness might also cause damage to the brain. If so, if we keep the habit of awareness of consciousness we shall prevent the brain from being damaged.

In Buddhism, among all the sentient and non-sentient beings only humans can get enlightenment and finally reach nirvana. We have discussed that all beings, whether animate or inanimate, have their own mind organ and mind information so as to generate mental activities, but it seems to us that animals cannot get awareness, and as enlightenment is attained through awareness it seems that enlightenment is a monopoly of humans. This is the second difference between humans and animals. The first difference is the amount of mind information in Alaya. Humans have an extremely large amount of mind information in their Alaya compared to animals due to the use of spoken languages and written letters. Humans have a very fast-paced consciousness based on the huge amount of mind information compared to animals. After all, humans have achieved civilization and cultural developments through the mind information by use of the spoken languages and written letters, and further thoughtful use of the mind information.

12

See Your Mind (II): How?

If we stop thinking and become aware of the arising mental activities we can see them in the third person. To use a simile, if muddy water is agitated we cannot see the bottom; we have to calm down the muddy water in order to see the clear bottom. We have to likewise calm down the thinking or mental activities in order to see the true self, the true nature, and there are fortunately many practices which have been developed for seeing the arising mental activities.

Meditation is an important way to see the arising mental activities to attain awareness. It is for stopping the thinking cycle from running away (the *monkey mind*). We do find, however, that often when we sit for meditation we experience more and more thoughts. The problem here is that we are *trying* to stop thinking; i.e., we are *thinking* about *not thinking*. The harder we try to stop thinking the more thoughts or mental activities seem to arise. Regardless of the seemingly continuous stream of mental activities we need to just be aware of them and release them, not become involved with them, or seek to banish them, but simply let them go from our consciousness. Meditation is not that we do not think about anything, but rather that we see the thinking and mental activities but do not get *hooked* by them. Nisargadatta Maharaj says:[73]

> A QUIET MIND...
> You begin by letting thoughts flow and
> watching them. The very observation slows
> down the mind till it stops altogether.
> Once the mind is quiet, keep it quiet.
> Don't get bored with peace, be in it,
> go deeper into it....Watch your thoughts
> and watch yourself watching the thoughts.
> The state of freedom from all thoughts
> will happen suddenly and by the bliss of it
> you shall recognize it.

There is another useful and simple practice to stop the frenetic thinking cycle and maintain awareness—that is to focus on our breathing. Breath is life itself. We all breathe from the time of birth until the time of death, and ceasing to breathe means to cease to live, so respiration is an object of attention that is familiar to and readily available to everyone. It is a universally accessible, universally acceptable object of meditation. Breath reflects the mental state. If the mind (mental activity) is peaceful and calm, breathing becomes deep and regular, whereas if a negative mental activity such as anger, jealousy or fear arises, breathing becomes harsh and shorter. Therefore, breath is an important object or means for mental training as well as for physical health. Being aware of breathing is to be aware that 'we are breathing in' when we breathe in, and 'we are breathing out' when we breathe out. Awareness of respiration is awareness of consciousness of the present moment. If we observe our breathing we can stop thinking. We can stop the endlessly cycling thinking process in Manas, the seventh consciousness. Observation of breathing does not allow any distractions to break the chain of awareness. We can maintain the state of aware-

---

73 Nisargadatta Maharaj, *I Am That*, p.224.

ness in the Manas. Thus, it is said that the breath acts as a bridge between the conscious and unconscious mind because it functions both consciously and unconsciously.[74]

It should be said, however, that most of us are unaware that we are breathing even though we are always doing so. The reason is that we are always thinking about something. So, what are we thinking about all the time? We are indulged in thinking without knowing what we are thinking about. We are just thinking unconsciously. By observing the breath, we can observe our present mind.[75]

If we observe our breath, the thinking process will be stopped. Once the thinking cycle is stopped, a mental activity will not be generated. Such practice is called 'awareness of respiration' (*anapana-sati*), which corresponds to 'mindfulness (正念),' one of the Eightfold Paths.[76] The first letter means 'right' and the second '念' means 'mindfulness' which is a combination of two letters, 'present (今)' and 'mind (心).' Thus, the right mindfulness is to see the present mind. As with meditation, it is also not easy to maintain the respiration practice. The thinking cycle that had been stopped will begin again in spite of oneself when one of the five sense objects is contacted by the respective organ, or when mind information is contacted by the mind organ.

In order to address the meditation on the breath adequately, we should provide a very brief introduction to the history of Buddhism. After the Buddha's death, Buddhism developed into

---

74 William Hart, *Vipassana Meditation*, Harper One, New York (1987), p 75

75 U Jotika (translated by Eunjo Park), *Geography of Mind*, Yonbangjuk, Seoul (2008), p 57

76 In order to understand the Eightfold Paths, first we have to understand the Four Noble Truths that the Buddha preached to his former fellow hermits after his awakening: *dukkha* (suffering), *trishna* (cause of suffering; clinging), ending of suffering, and prescription to end suffering. The Eightfold Paths are the prescription to end suffering: right view, right intention, right speech, right action, right livelihood, right effort, right mindfulness, and right concentration.

two main schools: Hinayana and Mahayana. Hinayana, or Small Vehicle, is an orthodox school which sticks to the letter of the Buddha's teaching, whereas Mahayana, or Great Vehicle, shows a more flexible attitude, believing that the spirit of the doctrine is more important that its original formulation. The Hinayana school established itself in Ceylon, Burma and Thailand, whereas the Mahayana spread to Nepal, Tibet, China, Korea and Japan and became, eventually, the more important of the two schools.[77]

In Hinayana, vipassana (*mindfulness meditation*) is the most powerful practice for keeping aware of the mind and body. Vipassana teaches us to be always aware of four objects: body, sensation, mind and dharmas. Walking on the street we move our legs and arms, but we are not conscious of moving them. We move our legs and arms without thinking about it since such movement has become a kind of unconscious action. Likewise, most of our body movements are performed as habitual actions without conscious awareness of them. It is like a zombie. In philosophy, a zombie is an imaginary being who behaves and acts just like a normal person but has absolutely no conscious life, no sensations, and no feelings.[78] According to the vipassana practice we have to be aware of every moment of our body. We also have to be aware of sensation which is generated by the five external objects through the five organs. Thirdly, we have to be aware of mental activities including thinking, and finally, we have to be aware of mind information, dharmas. Without being aware of our body, sensation, mind and dharmas, we will be misled by the sensation, mental activities or thinking.

An alternate approach in Mahayana Buddhism is a Zen practice for attaining enlightenment. The name *Zen* was derived from a Chinese word (禪), *Ch'an* in Chinese, *Zen* in Japanese, and *Seon* in Korean. The Chinese word is a combination of two letters, (視) and (單). The first means 'see' and the second 'only.' The literal

---

77 Fritjof Capra, *The Tao of Physics*, Shambhala, Boston (2010), pp 93-94

78 Christof Koch, *The Quest for Consciousness*, Roberts and Company Publishers, Colorado (2004), p 3

meaning of Zen is to see only, thus to see the mind, mental activities. The Zen practice uses a unique means for attaining enlightenment which is called '*koan*' (公案). The literal meaning of *koan* is official correspondence, official statement, public question or the like. In short, *koan* may be interpreted as an unsolvable question.

In Zen Buddhism, there are 1,700 *koans*. One of them is: You can make the sound of two hands clapping. Now what is the sound of one hand clapping? It sounds paradoxical. *Koans* cannot be solved by intellect, rationality, logic or scientific methods. *Koans* cannot be solved in the material world. Here is another: *An old lady set fire to the temple and left.* An old lady was in attendance on her master monk at a temple with her grown-up daughter. One day she tried to test his practice, how deep his practice is, and let her daughter enter his room and seduce him. But, he was never moved and sat like a rock. Her daughter came out of his room and told her mother that he was a great monk and never moved. Then, she set fire to the temple and left, saying that I had subserved a bad guy instead of a great master. Why? Why did the old lady set fire to the temple? Why was the monk a bad guy? As with the other, this *koan* cannot be solved in the intellectual or logical domain.

In Zen Buddhism a student or a practitioner receives a *koan* from his master. The irrational wording and paradoxical content of the *koans* makes it impossible for us to solve them by thinking. They are designed precisely to stop the thought process and thus to make the student ready for the non-verbal experience of reality. The solving of a *koan* demands a supreme effort of concentration and involvement from the student.[79] It is like that a cat stares at a mouse straight to catch it. The cat hasn't got the time to look elsewhere. By concentrating on an unsolvable question the thinking process is stopped. If an external object triggers the thinking cycle, the student should be aware of it and try to concentrate on the *koan* again until he finds the solution. The master will determine whether the student has found a right solution or not. Once the solution is found, the *koan* ceases to be paradoxical and becomes

---

79   Fritjof Capra, *The Tao of Physics*, Shambhala, Boston (2010), pp 48-49

a profoundly meaningful statement made from the state of consciousness which it has helped to awaken.[80]

There is another word for *koan*, *whadu* (話頭), in oriental countries. The first letter means 'speech' and the second 'head.' The real meaning of the word is 'what is that before the speech is made?' For a speech, a mind or a thinking comes first. The *koan* or *whadu* is to seek the mind before the speech is made.

It is impossible to find the solution to a *koan* without understanding the mind. We cannot solve the old lady *koan* without understanding her mind. When the student has got the solution it means that he understood her mind. In other words, it means that his mind organ contacted her mind information regarding the story, and thus finally got enlightenment.

In fact, since *koans* cannot be solved in the material world, it is not proper to say a solution to a *koan*. However, for the purpose of just understanding the Zen practice, we would provide a hint on the old lady *koan*. One of the most important teachings in Buddhism is not to have a self-view. In the *koan*, the old lady thought that the monk had still his self-view; i.e. "I am a monk, so I should not be seduced." Although this is one hint, we should understand the state of mind and be able to communicate from mind to mind in order to get the right solution and finally enlightenment.

---

80 Fritjof Capra, *The Tao of Physics*, Shambhala, Boston (2010), p 49

13

See Your Mind (III): See Your True Nature

If we try to see our mind precisely, mental activity including thinking, we can see it. We can also stop our thinking cycle through the respiration practice, vipassana, *koan* or other meditation practice, and see the mental activity. However, we still have questions about the next and final state of mind or consciousness. Can we ultimately get enlightenment? If so, what will the state of mind be? What capability will we have after enlightenment? What will be the true nature of the enlightened mind?

It is sometimes said that it is impossible to describe enlightenment or the enlightened mind in rational thought. It is also said that it is impossible to describe them correctly in ordinary languages. In fact, the realm of the enlightenment, the enlightened mind, or the true mind of enlightened mind is not the realm of the Conditioned World, the physical or material world, but is of the realm of the Unconditioned World. It is similar to saying that the mechanistic world view of classical physics is inadequate for the description of physical phenomena in the submicroscopic realm of quantum mechanics.[81]

---

81 Fritjof Capra, *The Tao of Physics*, Shambhala, Boston (2010), pp 303-304

Many sages tried to convey a description of the enlightenment or the enlightened mind in different words. They named it True Nature, Buddhahood, Tathagata, Rigpa, Transcendent Consciousness, Cosmic Consciousness, Self-Consciousness, Pure Consciousness, Ultimate Reality, Being, etc. Here are some examples:

When one seeks one's mind in its true state, it is found to be quite intelligible, although invisible. In its true state, mind is naked, immaculate, not made of anything, being of the voidness, clear, vacuous, without duality, transparent, timeless, uncompounded, unimpeded, colorless, not realizable as a separate thing but as the unity of all things, yet not composed of them, of one taste, transcendent over differentiation.[82]

Then there is the very nature of mind, its innermost essence, which is absolutely and always untouched by change or death. At present it is hidden within our own mind, our sem, enveloped and obscured by the mental scurry of our thoughts and emotions. Just as clouds can be shifted by a strong gust of wind to reveal the shining sun and wide-open sky, so, under certain special circumstances, some inspiration may uncover for us glimpses of this nature of mind. These glimpses have many depths and degrees, but each of them will bring some light of understanding, meaning, and freedom. This is because the nature of mind is the very root itself of understanding. In Tibetan we call it Rigpa, a primordial, pure, pristine awareness that is at once intelligent, cognizant, radiant, and always awake. It could be said to be the knowledge of knowledge itself.[83]

The Upanishads bring out Being as the ultimate reality which is imperishable and eternal. The hymns of the Vedas and Bhagavad-Gita sing the glory of the imperishable Self, Being, the ultimate reality, the Brahman which is the supreme ultimate absolute. They say: *"Water cannot wet It nor can fire burn It. Wind cannot dry It and weapons*

---

82 Joseph Goldstein, *The Experience of Insight*, Shambhala Publications, Boston (1976), p156

83 Sogyal Rinpoche, *The Tibetan Book of Living and Dying*, Harper One, New York (2002), pp 47-48

Probing the Mind: How does Consciousness Work?

cannot slay It. It is in front, It is behind, It is above and below, It is to the right and left. It is all-pervading, omnipresent, divine Being."[84]

This state of pure consciousness, or state of absolute pure Being, is called Self-consciousness. When this Self-consciousness is not lost, even when the mind comes out of the transcendent and engages itself once more in the field of activity, then the Self-consciousness gains the status of cosmic consciousness. The Self-consciousness is then eternally established in the nature of the mind. Even when the mind is awake, dreaming, or in deep sleep, the Self-consciousness is naturally maintained and is said to be cosmic consciousness. Cosmic consciousness means that consciousness which includes the experience of the relative field along with the state of transcendental pure Being.[85]

Astonishing! The ongoing awareness and clarity called **the mind** exists, but does not exist even as a single thing. It arises, for it manifests as **samsara** and **nirvana**, and as a myriad of joys and sorrows. It is asserted, for it is asserted according to the twelve vehicles. It is a label, for it is named in unimaginable ways. Some people call it **the mind-itself**. Some non-Buddhists call it **the self**. The **sravakas** call it **personal identitylessness**. The **Cittamatrins** call it **the mind**. Some people call it **the middle way**. Some call it **the perfection of wisdom**. Some give it the name **tathagatagarbha**. Some give it the name **Mahamudra**. Some give it the name **ordinary consciousness**. Some call it **the sole bindu**. Some call it **the absolute nature of reality**. Some label it **the universal ground**.[86]

No words can describe it. No example can point to it. Samsara does not make it worse. Nirvana does not make it better. It has never been born. It has never ceased. It has never been liberated. It has never

---

84 Maharishi Mahesh Yogi, *Science of Being and Art of Living*, PLUME, New York (2001), pp 15-16

85 Maharishi Mahesh Yogi, *Science of Being and Art of Living*, PLUME, New York (2001), p 245

86 *Padmasambhava:* B. Alan Wallace, *Buddhism with an Attitude*, Snow Lion Publications, New York (2003), pp139-140

been deluded. It has never existed. It has never been nonexistent. It has no limits at all. It does not fall into any kind of category.[87]

In a fashion, Buddha-nature exists, but to say that it exists is more like a metaphor. You can only really refer to it in an oblique fashion; you cannot pin it down so easily, because Buddha-nature in itself is nothing; it is not a substance. Buddha-nature is not a psychic substance of any kind. It is intrinsically empty, but at the same time, Buddha-nature is the source of enlightenment. Without Buddha-nature, we would not be able to attain enlightenment. If there were only ignorance, conflicting emotions and conceptual proliferation, it would be impossible to find a way out. So in that sense, Buddha-nature exists, but it does not exist as a substantial entity. According to Mahayana Buddhism, Buddha-nature is not part of causes and conditions, but is self-presenting. We develop a whole new perspective in relation to how we see ourselves when we no longer operate from within the conventional context of ego identity. We have a more expansive view in relation to our abilities and how we are able to see things. We are less opinionated; one is able to embrace things more.[88]

According to Fritjof Capra's study, the spiritual world of the enlightened mind can be easily compared to quantum physics. The conception of physical things and phenomena as transient manifestations of an underlying fundamental entity is not only a basic element of quantum field theory, but also a basic element of the Eastern world view. Like Einstein, the Eastern mystics consider this underlying entity as the only reality: all its phenomenal manifestations are seen as transitory and illusory. This reality of the Eastern mystic cannot be totally identified with the quantum field of the physicist, however, because it is seen as the essence of all phenomena in this world and, consequently, is beyond all concepts and idea. The quantum field, on the other hand, is a well-defined concept which only accounts for some of the physical phenomena.

---

[87] Dudjom Rinpoche: Sogyal Rinpoche, *The Tibetan Book of Living and Dying*, Harper One, New York (2002), p 50

[88] Traleg Kyabgon, *The Essence of Buddhism*, Shambhala Publications, INC., Boston (2001), pp 94-95

Probing the Mind: How does Consciousness Work?

Nevertheless, the intuition behind the physicist's interpretation of the subatomic world, in terms of the quantum field, is closely paralleled by the Eastern mystic who interprets his or her experience of the world in terms of an ultimate underlying reality. Subsequent to the emergence of the field concept, physicists have attempted to unify the various fields into a single fundamental field which would incorporate all physical phenomena. Einstein, in particular, spent the last years of his life searching for such a unified field. The *Brahman* of the Hindus, like the *Dhamakaya* of the Buddhists and the *Tao* of the Taoists, can be seen, perhaps, as the ultimate unified field from which spring not only the phenomena studied in physics, but all other phenomena as well.[89]

Looking back to the Consciousness-Only Theory, the Cosmos encompassing the material world and the non-material world consists of eighteen realms: six realms of objects, six realms of organs, and six realms of consciousnesses. Besides the six consciousnesses, two more consciousnesses are defined in the Theory: the seventh consciousness of thinking and the eighth consciousness of storage. The various consciousnesses manifest themselves in what seem to be two divisions: the perception and the object of perception. The perception is the perceiving division, and the object is the perceived division. The manifestation of the perceiving division is termed 'discrimination' because it apprehends the perceived division.[90] A question which we might ask is "Where is the enlightened mind in the eighteen realms?"

The five objects are in the perceived division. The five organs are in the perceiving division. The five sense consciousnesses are not reality. The sixth object, dharma, is mind information but not reality. The seventh consciousness is an extended concept of the sixth consciousness. The eighth consciousness may be included in the sixth object. The finally remaining thing is the sixth organ, the mind organ. I dare to conclude that the sixth organ will be the

---

89 Fritjof Capra, *The Tao of Physics*, Shambhala, Boston (2010), p 211

90 Wei Tat, *Ch'eng Wei-Shih Lun: The Doctrine of Mere-Consciousness*, Hong Kong: The Ch'eng Wei-Shih Lun Translation Committee 1973, p LXXXI

subject of enlightenment and the true nature or true self. When the mind organ gets enlightenment, it will be the Mind Organ. The Mind Organ is like the Great Mirror. The Great Mirror reflects objects as they are. To get enlightenment means to clean the dirty mirror so that it might reflect objects as they are. The Great Mirror is free from errors in its perception of all objects. As the mind organ is dirty with vexing passions, it cannot see the reality. The Great Mirror Wisdom is developed through the Great Mirror.

14

Ways of Thinking in Oriental and Western Cultures

The western culture is frequently said to be a 'culture of knowledge' which is based on an active focus on language which emphasizes analysis and logic, whereas the eastern culture is said to be a 'culture of wisdom' which is based on the passive acceptance of language and emphasizes comprehensive awareness and intuition. Because of this difference, many eastern philosophies or religions are considered to be less systematic or analytic than those of the western world.[91]

Westerners have a strong interest in categorization which helps them to know what rules to apply to the objects in question, and this is supported by formal logic which also plays a role in problem solving. East Asians, on the other hand, consider objects in their broader context. The world seems more complex to Asians than to Westerners, and understanding events always requires consideration of a host of factors that operate in relation to one another in no simple, deterministic way. Formal logic plays little

---

91 Myungjin Kim, *East and West*, Yedam, Seoul (2008), p 96

role in problem solving for the oriental. In fact, the person who is too concerned with logic may be considered immature.[92]

Easterners are almost surely closer to the truth than Westerners in their belief that the world is a highly complicated place and Westerners are undoubtedly often far too simple-minded in their explicit models of the world. Easterners' failure to be surprised as often as they should may be a small price to pay for their greater attunement to a range of possible causal factors. On the other hand, it seems fairly clear that simple models are the most useful ones, at least in science, because they're easier to disprove and consequently to improve upon. Most of Aristotle's physical propositions have turned out to be demonstrably false. But Aristotle had testable propositions about the world while the Chinese did not: It was Westerners who established what the correct physical principles are. The Chinese may have understood the principle of action at a distance, but they had no means of proving it. When it was proved true, it was by Western scientists who did not initially believe in it and who were actually trying to establish that all motion was of the billiard ball type, with objects moving only because they come into contact with some other object. Westerners' success in science and their tendency to make certain mistakes in causal analysis derive from the same source. Freedom to pursue individual goals prompts people to model the situation so as to achieve those goals, which in turn encourages modeling events by working backward from effects to possible causes. When there is systematic testing of the model, as in science, the model can be corrected. But Westerners' models tend to be limited too sharply to the goal object and its properties, slighting the possible role of context. When it is everyday life – all too often a buzzing confusion – that is being modeled, recognition of error is more difficult. A mistaken model will be difficult to correct. So despite their history of scientific-mindedness, Westerners are particularly susceptible to the Fundamental Attribution Error and to overestimating the predictability of human behavior. As we shall see next, Westerners' preferred simplicity and Easterners' assumed complexity encompass more than their approaches to causality.

---

92 Richard E. Nisbett, *The Geography of Thought*, Free Press, New York (2003), p xvi

Probing the Mind: How does Consciousness Work?

Their preferences extend to the ways that knowledge is organized more generally.[93]

The western arts also present a striking contrast to the eastern. The mainstream of western arts is dynamic and active, while the eastern is static and silent. The figure paintings of western art provoke emotional excitement, while the landscape paintings of eastern art are calming. A symphony orchestra may evoke aesthetic emotions, while the traditional music of the east may compose the emotions. In the dancing, naturally rhythmical sense, western music such as ballet or tango pursues dynamic beauty, while the traditional Korean dancing pursues the beauty of configuration and the static beauty in the dynamic. In poetry, the eastern tradition seeks a contemplative or meditative view rather than a sentimental or dramatic view such as that of the west. In a similar vein, the western world has not developed art such as calligraphy which expresses energy of life free from all thoughts.

In the research on consciousness, westerners dissected the brain and applied electric shock to it and observed the physical phenomena. When they obtained experiment data and presented an analysis of the data, at last it was accepted as an uncontroversial theory. In order for a hypothesis about the unseeable world to be accepted as uncontroversial theory, experimental data has to be presented. Experience gained through intuition or insight remains an outsider to westerners.

From where do the differences between the eastern and western world originate? All of them have the same five sense consciousnesses and the sixth consciousness by the mind organ contacting mind information, so why do they take such different approaches to seeing objects or to seeking solutions? Norman Doidge postulated that the differences are from the brain's structure.

It was often observed that Westerners approach the world 'analytically,' dividing what they observe into individual parts. Easterners tend to approach the world more 'holistically,' perceiving by looking at 'the

---

93 Richard E. Nisbett, *The Geography of Thought*, Free Press, New York (2003), pp 134-135

whole,' and emphasizing the interrelatedness of all things. It was also observed that the differing cognitive styles of the analytic West and the holistic East parallel differences between the brain's two hemispheres. The left hemisphere tends to perform more sequential and analytical processing, while the right hemisphere is often engaged in simultaneous and holistic processing. Were these different ways of seeing the world based on different interpretations of what was seen, or were Easterners and Westerners actually seeing different thing?[94]

From the viewpoint of the Consciousness Theory, the westerners were eager to enlist their thinking cycle. They stored a lot of knowledge (mind information) through learning or experience, discriminated dichotomically on the basis of logical analysis and obtained what they wanted. As a result, they reached notable achievements in science, technology and human civilization.

The easterners, on the other hand, tried to stop their thinking cycle as much as they could instead of relying on it. They tried to contact and know the true nature or true self of objects, matter and mind through their mind organ, and they could reach important conclusions through intuition and insight without proving them through the scientific process. They considered mind more important than matter. They understood that matter is manifested by mind. They understood that spoken words come after mind. *Koans* were made from this concept. *Koans* are for seeing the mind before words were spoken. Thus, *koans* could not be solved or understood by scientific methods or logical analysis.

Westerners preferred self-assertion to amalgamation, analysis to comprehensive insights, rational knowledge to intuitive wisdom, science to religion, competition to cooperation, development to preservation. They researched using their thinking cycle until they reached what they wanted. On the other hand, easterners stopped the thinking cycle and tried to encounter true wisdom. They consider mind as the origin of wisdom, while the westerners consider matter as key to knowledge. A lot of scientific principles and useful

---

94 Norman Doidge, *The Brain That Changes Itself*, Penguin Books, London (2007), p 301

technology have been developed in western science, while the principles of cosmogony and introspection for human beings have been revealed in the eastern traditions.

The eastern approach is more interested in the unseeable world. Thus, easterners began to know about the existence of *ghi* (氣), a kind of energy flowing in the universe and the meridian system in the body. The principles of cosmogony were introduced in the oriental philosophy of Changing (I Ching, or Book of Changes) or the principles of human nature in the four pillars of destiny.

The basic ordering principle of the patterns in the philosophy of Changing is the interplay of the polar opposites *yin* (–) and *yang* (+). The *yang* is represented by a solid line (—), the *yin* by a broken line (--), and the whole system of hexagrams is built up naturally from these two lines. By combining them in pairs, four configurations are obtained,

and by adding a third line to each of these, eight 'trigrams' are generated:

In Korea, we believe that the eight trigrams were created by the Emperor Taeho-Bokhee at the ancient dynasty of Korea, Baedal Dynasty, around 3,500 BC. The trigrams were considered to represent all possible cosmic and human situations.[95] It is said that the German philosopher Leibniz created the binary system of numbers from the eight trigrams he had learned in the 17th century, and this binary system is the basic principle behind computers.

---

95   Fritjof Capra, *The Tao of Physics*, Shambhala, Boston (2010), p 279

In the four pillars of destiny, the order of heaven repeats ten stems and the order of earth also repeats twelve branches.

10 Stems:	Gap	Eul	Byung	Jung	Mu	Ki	Kyung	Shin	Im	Kye	**Gap**	**Eul**	**Byung**
	|	|	|	|	|	|	|	|	|	|	|	|	|
12 Branches:	Ja	Chuk	In	Myo	Jin	Sa	Oh	Mi	Sin	Yu	Sul	Hae:	**Ja**

The four pillars mean birthyear, birthmonth, birthday and birthtime. Each pillar has one stem and one branch in the order. For example, if this year is Gap-Ja year, the next Gap-Ja year comes 60 years later because the pillar is a combination of 10 items and 12 branches in the order. The order of 10 stems and 12 branches constitutes the order of the cosmos as well as human destiny. According to the four pillar philosophy, 2016 is Byung-Sin year. 1956 was the last Byung-Sin year, the next Byung-Sin year will be 2076. We have noted that the Emperor Taeho-Bokhee set up the ten stems and twelve branches around 3,500 BC. If the ten stems and twelve branches had not been correctly set up at the beginning, the philosophy could not have applied until now. Such theory cannot be created by a scientific method such as experiments. Such a theory could not have been created without the wisdom of enlightened sages.

15

The Amalgamation of Oriental and Western Philosophies

Until the mid-20th century, the ways of thinking were quite different between the west and the east. The west considered individualism to be more important than a holistic approach, and the east just the opposite. The western culture pursued more knowledge based on individualism and rationalism using information stored in Alaya, and predicated their thinking cycle on knowledge. The western approach was to seek the truth on matter and nature through experimental means and breaking the problem down into ever smaller parts. They considered the human being to be a part of matter or nature. After all, science and technology were making great progress resulting in developments in all kinds of industry. The development of industries resulted in the amassing of huge capital, and the resulting wealth led to a feeling of great triumph. The resultant prosperity enticed people from all over the earth to move towards the capital and wealth, and more and more easterners crossed over to the western countries to learn the western knowledge of science and technology.

The pre-industrial eastern approach was to explore the mystery of the human being. They tried to see their mind and human nature through intuition or insight, but not through scientific analysis or experiments. To them the cosmos is a part of a human being, just as a human being is part of the cosmos; i.e., all is one.

Even though this eastern way of thinking that tried to see the true nature of objects holistically had served them well for centuries, the scientific and technological advances of the western world in the 20th century, and the resultant prosperity and accumulation of wealth, were too much to resist and eastern thinking became gradually westernized. They concentrated more and more on science and technology and began to reorient their thinking process along the lines of the west. As a result of this reorientation, the eastern cultures began to produce accomplished scientists and technological experts and made great scientific achievements matching up with those of the westerners. Easterners were fascinated by the power of capital and the material sciences and dedicated themselves to pursuing them more and more.

The eastern approach now is to store a lot of information on science and technology just as the westerners do, and to strive to create new technical ideas. The eastern inferiority to the western in science and technology has diminished, or disappeared, and capital and wealth are moving from the west to the east. On the other hand, the oriental philosophy, education, medicine, sports, entertainments and the like are becoming mainstream in the western world.

Since mid to late 20th century we have been inundated with information due to the availability of the computer and the internet, and the boundary of knowledge between east and west has been collapsing. The necessities of life as well as culture, philosophy, education, arts, sports etc. began to be integrated, and the integration accelerated by the early 21st century. Prior to the sufficient development of science and technology we could feed ourselves, or a new theory or a new item could be made successfully if we focused on only one thing; specialization or diversification was enough for a living. We reached the breaking point however toward the end of the 20th century and the boundaries between specialties began collapsing. Engineering needs humanities and humanities require natural science or applied science. Engineering is introduced into business administration or politics and it also needs arts or economics. The medical world began to amalgamate. Traditional medicine or alternative medicine began to attract attention in the west, and the eastern medical methods such as acupuncture, moxa cautery or acupressure therapy entered into the west. There has also been the emergence of hybrid media and hybrid cars, and cars are no longer simply feats of mechanical engineering any more. They are products of information technology and the arts. Knowledge in one field is not enough for exploring an academic theory or developing a technological item any more. Fritjof Capra pointed out that the analytical methods prevailing in modern science are obstacles to academic developments, that a whole and comprehensive analysis is required. In fact, we find that new theories presented in the fields of physics, psychology, ecology, economics and so on are developed by the integrated synthesis approach.

By the 21st century the creative and inventive mind was being emphasized. Change and innovation were stressed, and everybody searched desperately for something new and many dreams of the imagination became realized. The world in the movie has become a reality, and the cyber world is not a cyber world any more.

Both western and eastern scientists and engineers have conducted research toward manufacturing a human being. They have already manufactured some artificial organs like an artificial heart and artificial kidney as well as body tissue. They are anxious to make the brain and create robots having artificial intelligence, a robot who thinks and judges like a human. They have already made synthetic versions of the five sense organs. They have made an artificial visual sensor perceiving light, an auditory sensor perceiving sound, a smell sensor perceiving scents, a taste sensor perceiving flavor, and a tactile organ perceiving sense of touch. The only problem is whether we can make the sixth organ. The five material objects are all over the outside world, but the sixth object, mind information, is in the Alaya. The five material or physical organs can be made, but the sixth organ, being an immaterial or non-physical organ, will be difficult to make. Although the results are yet insignificant, some information on consciousness can be changed to an electric signal so that a computer might read it, and if we could make the mind organ we could make a human being or humanoid.

A human Alaya may store a lot of information during life. All consciousness information produced by the six organs, and the thoughts and mental activities produced by the thinking process in the seventh consciousness are stored in Alaya. If one's life repeats the cycle of *samsara*, the Alaya shall store all the information of the previous lives. We have said that no supercomputer could be comparable to a human Alaya in the amount of information, but thanks to the development of technology we can now make a computer which has more information than a human Alaya. Further, the computer may retrieve and utilize necessary information from the memory faster than the human who must initiate the thinking cycle. We will be able to make a humanoid which can save all the poems of this world in its memory, and we may be able to program to let the humanoid search for the saddest poem from the memory or recite the most beautiful, but it will not be able to write a line of poetry by itself. This will be a limitation of the humanoid and the computer.

The eastern approach to thinking has taught about wisdom rather than knowledge. It was considered that wisdom could be obtained when the Alaya became empty of knowledge and the thinking process stopped. In a classical summary of four lines, Zen is described as

> "A special transmission outside the scriptures,
> Not founded upon words and letters,
> Pointing directly to the human mind,
> Seeing into one's nature and attaining Buddhahood."[96]

However, more and more individuals from the east abandoned this approach and went to the western way, storing more and more knowledge in their Alaya. Instead of stopping their thinking cycle

---

96   Fritjof Capra, *The Tao of Physics*, Shambhala, Boston (2010), p 122

and seeing into the true nature, they are competing in technical ideas for wealth and power.

Westerners believed that the human mind existed in the brain, and the brain was considered to be the most marvelous structure in the cosmos. They believed that all the secrets are in the brain, and they tried to uncover them by dissecting it, or applying electric shock therapy, or taking photographs, etc., but the secrets could not be discovered from the brain. In the end they criticized that they had enslaved neuroscience to the electric signal. They also realized that material affluence and physical power could not fulfill their ultimate happiness and ultimate desire, and more and more people began to seek their true mind and true nature. They began to have an interest in oriental philosophy and religion, and a new way of life like meditation or healing began to enter into their life. Many meditation centers, Zen centers, healing centers, oriental clinics, yoga centers and the like began to emerge in the society. This has enabled many to stop their thinking cycle which was based on processing a tremendous amount of knowledge, and to see reality as they touch their inner world.

16

Four Wisdoms through Consciousnesses

We can stop both the continuous thinking cycle and dichotomous discrimination by being consciously aware of the thinking cycle, including mental activities. We can also attain wisdom and grasp the truth through stopping the mind and opening to wholeness. At last, both philosophy and science are coming to know that we can find enlightenment through the truth. Wisdom is a habit or disposition to perform our actions with the highest degree of integrity under any given circumstance. It is a disposition to find the truth coupled with an optimum judgement as to what actions should be taken. The Oxford English Dictionary defines wisdom as the "Capacity of judging rightly in matters relating to life and conduct; soundness of judgement in the choice of means and ends."[97]

There are many truths, and Buddhism teaches many of them. Among them, the most valuable truths are the Three Marks of Existence (the Three Dharma Seals) and the Four Noble Truths.

---

97   www.wikipedia.org

The Three Marks of Existence are:

1. "All conditioned things are impermanent"
2. "All conditioned things are unsatisfactory and suffering," and
3. "All conditioned or unconditioned things are not self."

The Four Noble Truths are:

1. the Truth of *Dukkha* (Suffering),
2. the Truth of the Origin of *Dukkha,*
3. the Truth of the Cessation of *Dukkha,* and
4. the Truth of the Path of Liberation from *Dukkha* (the Eightfold Path: right view, right intention, right speech, right action, right livelihood, right effort, right mindfulness, and right concentration).

The ultimate truth in Buddhism which we must grasp is 'Emptiness' (*Sunyata*), which means simply that one cannot identify anything as one's own self.

Buddhism describes the transformation of the Eight Consciousnesses into the Four Wisdoms. The Consciousness-Only philosophy explains that four transcendental wisdoms are attained by transformation of the mental attributes of consciousness. Consciousness consists of the first five consciousnesses and the post three. The first five are physical sense consciousnesses whereas the post three are not related to the physical senses; i.e., the mind (dharma) consciousness, the thinking (discriminating) consciousness, and the store consciousness. The four wisdoms are attained from the respective consciousness.

The Four Wisdoms are:

1. the Perfect Achievement Wisdom,
2. the Profound Contemplation Wisdom,
3. the Universal Equality Wisdom, and
4. the Great Mirror Wisdom.

Probing the Mind: How does Consciousness Work?

The Perfect Achievement Wisdom is attained by virtue of the transformation of the five sense consciousnesses, the Profound Contemplation Wisdom by the transformation of the sixth, the Universal Equality Wisdom by the transformation of the seventh, and the Great Mirror Wisdom by the transformation of the eighth.

The welfare and happiness of all sentient beings are promoted through the Perfect Achievement Wisdom. The mind associated with this Wisdom manifests itself through the desire to promote the welfare and happiness of all sentient beings in a diversity of consciously-realized actions of the body, the voice, and the mind. The five sense consciousnesses arise on the basis of our material world consisting of the five objects, and this world cannot be ignored even though it contains no *true* self in and of itself, and even though it is not the ultimate reality. In spite of what we perceive as our operating environment, the Perfect Achievement Wisdom must be attained through living in the material world which obeys the laws of nature; i.e., water always flows to a lower level, the law of gravity applies to all objects, an onion will not produce a rose, and as one sows so shall he reap, etc. Someone with a troubled emotional nature, or pursuing a get-rich-quick scheme, is acting from a lack of the Perfect Achievement Wisdom. Bribery scandals or seeking goods or gifts for free (without compensation) is another act of one who does not find the Wisdom. Accordingly, the Perfect Achievement Wisdom is important in this material world and we can attain it through the right awareness of the five sense consciousnesses. We can bring the sentient beings into a state of being profitable and edified with the Wisdom.

The mind associated with the Profound Contemplation (Observing) Wisdom discerns the peculiar and common characteristics of all dharmas in insightful ways: it manifests itself without any hindrance; it can manifest itself in infinite activities, in all of which it possesses self-mastery; it cuts away all doubts; and it enables all sentient beings to obtain blessings and joy. The Profound Contemplation Wisdom is attained by the transformation of the sixth consciousness. With this Wisdom the sixth organ (mind) perceives the sixth objects (mind information) with profound clarity and without hindrance. The sixth objects means the mind information of one's own Alaya as well as all others' Alaya. This Wisdom is not observed in common sentient beings; this is beyond the physical world. The laws of nature do not apply to the world of the sixth consciousness any more. This is the spiritual world where the mind organ experiences wonderful observations. If the Profound Contemplation Wisdom is attained the mind organ can see unseeable objects, hear soundless sounds, smell scentless scents, taste food without flavor, and be free from space and time. This is why it is also called the Profound Observing Wisdom, for it is in this stage that the six transcendent powers which transcend the senses are obtained. One has the ability to see anything at any distance, the ability to hear any sound at any distance, the ability to go anywhere at will and to transform himself or objects at will, the ability to know others' thoughts, the ability to know the former lives of himself and others, and the ability to destroy all evil passions. In this world a stone Buddha can drop tears and a sterile woman can be pregnant. We call it the metaphysical world, but the world is operated by the sixth organ.

The Universal Equality Wisdom is attained by the transformation of the seventh consciousness. The mind associated with this Wisdom sees the identity of all dharmas, and the complete equality between its own self and other sentient beings. This Wisdom is always united with great benevolence, great compassion, etc., and is the special supporting basis for the Profound Contemplation Wisdom. Note that this Wisdom deals with Equality, which is the opposite of discrimination. In the lower levels we habitually discriminate all dharmas in the thinking process; we discriminate dichotomously all dharmas such as good and evil, right and wrong, virtue and vice, black and white, oneself and others, etc., and are always in conflict between them. The Universal Equality Wisdom cannot be obtained as long as the dichotomous discrimination and the conflict continue in the thinking process. By stopping discrimination in our normal thinking cycle we can attain the Wisdom and at last realize that all sentient beings including myself are equal. In the world of this Wisdom, there is no discrimination between good and evil, right and wrong, virtue and vice, black and white, oneself and others, etc. It is ALL right.

The Great Mirror Wisdom is attained by the transformation of the eighth consciousness. The mind associated with this Wisdom is entirely dissociated from all mental discriminations. When the mind organ gets enlightenment, it will be the Mind Organ. The Mind Organ is like the Great Mirror. The Great Mirror reflects objects as they are. To get enlightenment means to clean the dirty mirror so that it might reflect objects as they are. The Great Mirror is free from errors in its perception of all objects. Like a big mirror reflects all objects as they are, this Wisdom reflects the absolute reality of all things as they are. We do not presently see the absolute reality of all things because the mind information in Alaya is contaminated with ego and personal views. When all contaminated information dissipates, however, all delusion and agony will disappear and the Wisdom will be attained, and at last we see the reality through the Wisdom.

In the stage of the Perfect Achievement Wisdom, a mountain is a mountain and a river is a river. In the Profound Contemplation Wisdom, a mountain is not a mountain and a river is not a river. Getting up to the Universal Equality Wisdom, a mountain is a river and a river is a mountain. The Great Mirror Wisdom sees again that a mountain is a mountain and a river is a river. However, in the first stage, the mountain and river are contaminated with personal views and personal thoughts. In the last stage, the mountain and river are reflected as they are, without being discriminated and contaminated. They are *known*, rather than being *perceived*.

The Eight Consciousnesses have the Nature of Ultimate Reality. Ultimate Reality is the complete and perfect 'real nature' of all dharmas which is revealed by the Emptiness (Voidness: *sunyata*) of Atman (self) and dharmas. The Eight Consciousnesses are explained to have the three Natures: the Nature of Mere-Imagination, the Nature of Dependence on Others, and the Nature of Ultimate Reality. All things are imagined due to the Nature of Mere-Imagination and the previous information becomes a cause of the next consciousness due to the Nature of Dependence on Others.

The Four Wisdoms seem to be attained from the transformation of the Eight Consciousnesses due to the Nature of Ultimate Reality.

According to the Consciousness-Only Theory, there are five stages of progress or development towards enlightenment. The stages of progress toward enlightenment are: \

1. the stage of moral provisioning (the path of preparation),
2. the stage of intensified effort (the path of application),
3. the stage of unimpeded penetrating understanding (the path of seeing),
4. the stage of exercising cultivation (the path of meditation), and
5. the stage of final attainment or ultimate realization (the path of no more learning).

The five stages are the steps to reach the holy path of attainment. The first two, the path of preparation and the path of application, are normally referred to as worldly paths, whereas the last three are known as supramundane paths. On the last three paths, there is a greater development of wisdom. From the Buddhist perspective, without wisdom we operate on the level of a worldly person. No matter how kindhearted we are, or how well behaved we may be, if we are devoid of wisdom we are still operating within the context of this world and not the world of spirituality. Wisdom does not necessarily mean being clever. Wisdom in Buddhism has more to do with having a real understanding of ourselves and the phenomenal world. On the *Shravaka* level it means understanding impermanence, and on the level of the *Bodhisattva* it means understanding emptiness. A really spiritual person must possess the qualities of compassion and love as well as wisdom. Even if compassion and love are present in the mind-stream of a particular individual, if that person is lacking in wisdom he or she is still not a fully developed person.[98]

---

98 Traleg Kyabgon, *The Essence of Buddhism*, Shambhala Publications, INC., Boston (2001), pp. 97-98

17

What Is Emptiness?

Buddhism explains that there is no true self (inherent existence) in us or in any sentient being, or in any of the dharmas. This is the so called 'No-Self Doctrine.' The Doctrine is the same as the Emptiness (*Sunyata*) Doctrine in which all sentient beings including 'I' and all dharmas lack inherent existence or a permanent enduring essence. In early Buddhism it was called 'No-Self Doctrine,' and later in Mahayana Buddhism it was called the 'Emptiness Doctrine.' This Doctrine is the most important in Buddhism and also the most difficult to understand. Clearly I am here, and all sentient beings exist and all dharmas exist too. Despite this, if a true self of 'I' or all sentient beings do not exist, who am I and what are all sentient beings? The Doctrine appears to us like a sophism.

Various aspects of Mahayana Buddhist philosophy are often used as the basis of insight meditation. There are two major schools in Mahayana Buddhism: one is *Madhyamaka*, the School of the Middle Way, and the other is called *Yogacara* or *Chittamatra*, the School of the Mere-Consciousness.[99]

---

99 Traleg Kyabgon, *The Essence of Buddhism*, Shambhala Publications, INC., Boston (2001), p71

In *Madhyamaka* philosophy 'Emptiness' does not mean that things do not exist, that our everyday experience of the world is somehow completely erroneous, that it is all a dream. Many people in the West think this is exactly what the Mahayana tradition is saying, but just because things lack inherent existence or a permanent enduring essence does not mean they don't exist. Mountains, chairs, tables, houses, people, cars, and televisions all exist, but they do not have inherent existence. Realizing that there is no permanent essence inherent in empirical objects diminishes our tendency to cling to things. Understanding emptiness allows us to see the world as it is and not believe the world as it appears to our deluded mind.[100]

Madhyamaka introduced the causality doctrine to prove that all sentient beings do not have inherent existence. The founder of *Madhyamaka*, Nagarjuna said "There is no being that can exist on its own without depending on anything else; no self-sufficient being. Everything is interdependent. Everything that exists on both the physical and mental plane involves the idea of interdependence, or *pratitya-samutpada*." All sentient beings come into being because of what is called interdependent origination, or *pratitya-samutpada*—that is, due to causes and conditions. This implies that all things do not have inherent existence, because if they had any kind of essence or independent existence there would be no need for the whole idea of causality.[101]

Both the Buddha and Nagarjuna have said that the idea of interdependent origination is identical with the concept of Emptiness. Nagarjuna said that Emptiness is interdependent origination and interdependent origination is emptiness. So when we say that things are interdependently produced, or that things come into being through the interdependence of causes and conditions, it is the same as saying things are empty by nature. Through the

---

100 Traleg Kyabgon, *The Essence of Buddhism*, Shambhala Publications, INC., Boston (2001), p 72

101 Traleg Kyabgon, *The Essence of Buddhism*, Shambhala Publications, INC., Boston (2001), pp 73-74

understanding of Emptiness based upon interdependent origination, we are able to form the right view, which voids these two extremes of externalism and nihilism. In *Madhyamaka* philosophy, ultimate reality is not seen as something that exists outside of or above the empirical reality with which we are confronted every day. Rather, Emptiness is the nature of the very world that we live in, so the nature of the empirical world is ultimate reality.[102]

Emptiness is the reality underlying all phenomena. Emptiness is beyond all forms and defies all description and specification. It is often said to be Formlessness or Voidness, but Emptiness is not to be taken for mere nothingness. It is, on the contrary, the essence of all forms and the source of all life. It has an infinite creative potential. It is a living Void which gives birth to all forms in the phenomenal world.[103]

It is said that the concept of Emptiness was originated from the digit zero (0). The digit zero means nothing.

$$0 = 000 = 00000 = 0000000$$

One zero, three zeros, five zeros and so on are all zero, and mean nothing.

$$10 \neq 1000 \neq 100000 \neq 10000000$$

However, 10 is not equal to 1000 or 10000. In the numbers, the zero does not mean 'nothing.' In the numbers, one zero mean 'ten times,' which is powerful and potential. Because of the digit '1,' the zero is not 'nothing' but 'emptiness.' The digit '1' is a form as individuality. Because of the form, the zero has an important meaning of emptiness. The relationship of form and emptiness cannot be conceived as a state of mutually exclusive opposites, but

---

[102] Traleg Kyabgon, *The Essence of Buddhism*, Shambhala Publications, INC., Boston (2001), p 75

[103] Fritjof Capra, *The Tao of Physics*, Shambhala, Boston (2010), pp 211-212

only as two aspects of the same reality, which co-exist and are in continual co-operation.[104]

The Emptiness is compared to the quantum field of subatomic physics. Like the quantum field it gives birth to an infinite variety of forms which it sustains and, eventually, reabsorbs. The phenomenal manifestations of the mystical Void, like the subatomic particles, are not static and permanent, but dynamic and transitory, coming into being and vanishing in one ceaseless dance of movement and energy. Like the subatomic world of the physicist, the phenomenal world of the Eastern mystic is a world of *samsara* – of continuous birth and death. Being transient manifestations of the Void, the things in this world do not have any fundamental identity. This is emphasized in Buddhist philosophy which holds that the idea of a constant 'self' undergoing successive experiences is an illusion. Buddhists have frequently compared this illusion of a material substance and an individual self to the phenomenon of a water wave, in which the up-and-down movement of the water particles makes us believe that a 'piece' of water moves over the surface. Physicists have used the same analogy in the context of field theory to point out the illusion of a material substance created by a moving particle.[105]

On the other hand, the Consciousness-Only Theory of Yogacara is that only consciousness exists. Yoga in this context means 'meditation,' while chara means 'practice' so Yogacara has been translated as 'the school of meditation,' emphasizing the primacy of meditation in understanding ultimate reality. This school is also called *Chittamatra* – a term that has given rise to much confusion in the West where it has usually been translated as 'mind only.' This has led many interpreters of Mahayana Buddhism to think that this particular school denies the existence of the external world, positing that everything exists only in the mind. As a result they consider Mahayana to be the same as the Western theory

---

104 Fritjof Capra, *The Tao of Physics*, Shambhala, Boston (2010), p 215

105 Fritjof Capra, *The Tao of Physics*, Shambhala, Boston (2010), pp 212-213

Probing the Mind: How does Consciousness Work?

known as idealism. British idealists such as Bishop Berkeley assert that only ideas in the mind are real and that apart from ideas, nothing exists. This is not what the Chittamatrins mean when they say that everything is 'mind only,' however. What they mean is that our perception of external reality is mind-dependent. In other words, we can only have access to the external world through our mind.[106]

The Yogacharins say that when we look at things on all different levels—on the sensory level, the conceptual level, or the moral level—we can see that what we experience is colored by our presuppositions, prejudices, and predilections. This means that there is no such thing as objective reality in the ultimate sense. On a sensory level, for example, we perceive a tree or car with our visual sense, but there is no tree or car existing of its own accord independently of the mind. Insects would not perceive a tree or a car in the way we would, because they lack our concepts relating to trees and cars.[107]

The Consciousness-Only Theory explains that each of the eight consciousnesses is the basis or infrastructure for a twofold manifestation, the perceived division and the perceiving division. Atman (self) and dharmas (mind information) are merely conventional designations of this double manifestation of consciousness. There definitely is no 'real' Atman or dharmas aside from what is thus evolved from consciousness. There are no 'real' things apart from these two aspects, the perceived division and the perceiving division. Everything phenomenal and noumenal, everything seemingly 'real' and 'false' alike, is inseparable from consciousness. In consequence 'all is mere consciousness,' or 'nothing exists but consciousness.'[108]

The external spheres of matter (color, sound, etc.) are clearly immediately apprehended and corroborated by the five conscious-

---

106 Traleg Kyabgon, *The Essence of Buddhism*, Shambhala Publications, INC., Boston (2001), p 79

107 Traleg Kyabgon, *The Essence of Buddhism*, Shambhala Publications, INC., Boston (2001), p 80

108 Wei Tat, *Ch'eng Wei-Shih Lun: The Doctrine of Mere-Consciousness*, Hong Kong: The Ch'eng Wei-Shih Lun Translation Committee 1973, pp 503-505

nesses (eyes, ears, etc.). How can we deny the existence of that which is perceived through immediate apprehension? *Ch'eng Wei-Shih Lun* replies to this question: When the external spheres are apprehended through immediate perception they are not regarded as external. It is only later that *Manovijnana (the sixth consciousness)*, through its discrimination, erroneously creates the notion of externality. Thus, the objective spheres immediately apprehended are the 'perceived division' of the consciousnesses themselves. Since they are manifestations of consciousness, we say they exist. But inasmuch as they are regarded by *Manovijnana* as constituting external and real matter, etc., and are thus erroneously imagined to be existent, we say they are non-existent. Furthermore, objective spheres of color and so forth are not colors though they seem to be so, and are not external though they seem to be so. They are like in a dream, which cannot be regarded as real and external.[109]

If the things seen during one's waking state are all like objects in a dream and are inseparable from consciousness, why, when we are awake, do we not know that the sphere of objects perceived by us is Mere-Consciousness? *Ch'eng Wei-Shih Lun* replies to this question: As long as we have not awakened from the dream we are incapable of realizing that the objects of the dream are unreal. It is only after we have awakened that, in retrospect, we come to realize this. We should know that the same is true of our knowledge regarding the sphere of material objects in our waking life. Until we have truly awakened we cannot ourselves know, but, when we reach the state of true Awakening (Enlightenment), we shall be able, in retrospect, to realize it. Before this genuine Awakening is achieved, we perpetually remain as in a dream. This is why the Buddha spoke of the long night of transmigratory existence, characterized by ceaseless rounds of birth and death.[110]

---

[109] Wei Tat, *Ch'eng Wei-Shih Lun: The Doctrine of Mere-Consciousness*, Hong Kong: The Ch'eng Wei-Shih Lun Translation Committee 1973, p 521

[110] Wei Tat, *Ch'eng Wei-Shih Lun: The Doctrine of Mere-Consciousness*, Hong Kong: The Ch'eng Wei-Shih Lun Translation Committee 1973, p 521

Probing the Mind: How does Consciousness Work?

All information for external objects is contaminated by our personal view, presuppositions, prejudices, and predilections. We cannot see the reality of things due to the contaminated information. If Alaya were stored with uncontaminated information we could see the reality of external objects and dharmas. If Alaya were even free from uncontaminated information and empty, we could also see Emptiness. If the mind organ were not covered with contaminated information, the mind organ would appear as the Great Mirror, which would reflect the suchness of things as they are, Emptiness. After all, both *Madhyamaka* and Yogacara arrive at the same destination. *Madhyamaka* sees the reality of things through the interdependency of causes and conditions, and Yogacara sees it through the eight consciousnesses. Both reach the Emptiness.

The Emptiness Doctrine is the Buddhists' conclusion and final destination. Buddhism concludes "Form is emptiness, and emptiness is indeed form. Emptiness is not different from form, form is not different from emptiness. What is form that is emptiness, what is emptiness that is form."[111]

Buddhism does not claim to advocate idealism or nihilism. The Buddha did not deny the existence of the apparent world of shapes and forms, colors, tastes, smells, pains and pleasures, thoughts and emotions, of beings, oneself and other. He stated merely that this is not the ultimate reality. We perceive only the large-scale patterns into which more subtle phenomena organize themselves with our ordinary vision. Seeing only the patterns and not the underlying components, we are aware primarily of their differences and therefore we draw distinctions, assign labels, form preferences and prejudices, and commence liking and disliking, the process that develops into craving and aversion.[112]

The Buddhists' final goal is to get enlightenment on the Emptiness Doctrine. If so, we see that form is emptiness and emp-

---

111 *Prajna-paramita-hridaya Sutra*, in Fritjof Capra, *The Tao of Physics*, Shambhala, Boston (2010), p 215

112 William Hart, *Vipassana Meditation*, Harper One, New York (1987), pp 119-120

tiness is form. The mind organ will be open and become the Mind Organ which can read all kinds of mind information. The Mind Organ will see oneness in the unified field and will not cling to the six objects any more, so the *dukkhas* will cease. Above all, the Mind Organ will see the reality of the six objects without any delusion like the Great Mirror. The world of *samsara*—of continuous birth and death—will also cease and the Nirvana will be unrolled for eternal life.

PART II

The Mind and the Dream World

18

The Mystery of Dreams— Dream Consciousness

We spend about one third of our life sleeping, but we do not know very much about it. Neuroscience started off with the idea that sleep is like switching off the lights of the house and that human beings left alone with nothing to do will fall asleep. This provides a perspective that sleeping is a passive act, but advances in research very quickly made it clear that sleep is an active phenomenon, a state of consciousness with its own laws. It was Sigmund Freud who first articulated that sleep is an active process. Around 1900 the first researchers tried to define sleep physiologically, and around 1920 a French scientist named Henri Pieron expressed the dominant modern view of sleep as having three characteristics: first, it is a periodic biological necessity; second, it has its own internally produced rhythm; and third, it is characterized by an absence of motor and sensory functioning.[113]

The fact that sleep is characterized by an absence of motor and sensory functioning is true in a general sense, but it should be noted that sleep does not bring complete loss of motor and sensory

---

113 Francisco J. Varela, *Sleeping, Dreaming, and Dying*, Wisdom Publications, Boston (1997), p 24

functioning. The complete loss of motor and sensory functioning means death, not sleep. While sleeping we twist and turn our body, and our body responds to hot or cold. Strictly speaking, the motor and sensory functioning is alive while sleeping as well.

Sensory functioning is a result of the five physical organs working in conjunction with the brain and nervous system, and this continues while sleeping even though our consciousness is not aware of it. Accordingly, if a sensory awareness happens during sleep, the brain responds to it and gives a command to a particular part of the body resulting in a corresponding action or phenomenon. Because we are unaware of it at the conscious level, we call it a state of unconscious. If an external stimulus is strong enough to awaken us from sleeping, however, we will once again experience waking state consciousness.

Sleep has been one of our major concerns when considering the physical body, medicine or physiology, but not when considering consciousness or the psyche. If we cannot get a normal night's sleep we consider whether medical treatment is required. However, in view of consciousness, our primary concern is the dream state rather than sleep, and we do not have to see a doctor because we do not have a good dream, or a clear consciousness after dreaming.

We dream during sleep, and what we dream is a recollection or recognition of something. What we recognize is a result of the five consciousnesses which arise through the five sense organs. Although the consciousnesses do not arise through the physical organs during a dream, we recognize them as though they do: we see something, hear something, smell something, etc. In psychoanalysis we consider the dream to be manifested from the subconscious or unconscious. Freud said that a dream is a shortcut for reaching the unconscious and proved that dreaming is an activity of consciousness. A half century of dream research has demonstrated that dreaming is a rich form of consciousness that we should prize no less than we do our experience of the world in waking hours.[114]

---

[114] Andrea Rock, *The Mind at Night*, Basic Books, New York (2004), pp 199-200

Probing the Mind: How does Consciousness Work?

Dreaming is pretty much an unknown science even now, however. It is still a mysterious realm for us to understand, just as is consciousness of the waking state.

A dream is a different form and reflection of our real life. Human beings dream a lot during their life. Insights into the unconscious as presented in dreams are glimpses into a world of Absolute knowledge, and the unconsciousness which is transpersonal is connected to the Cosmic Mind and functions to communicate with the sea of information in the multidimensional world. Clairvoyance, which is obtained by extrasensory persons through meditation, can be achieved through understanding the realm of dreams. Even though everybody experiences extrasensory perceptions about past events of the previous lives, present events of the present life, and future events of the future lives in a dream, we neglect the important messages of dreams because we do not consider their viability. This is the reason why we live solely in the form of a human being, but not in the form of a higher dimensional being. A dream is a manifestation of our unconsciousness which begins from the world of the Absolute knowledge. Therefore, the world of dreams is a fantastic and magical realm.[115]

In a dream we experience becoming a king or being bitten by a poisonous snake. Though we become a king in a dream, it is just a dream, and though we are bitten by a snake in a dream, poison does not spread throughout our body. We therefore think that a dream is just a dream, that a dream is vain, transient, and far away from reality.

While we are in the midst of a dream we are experiencing an alternate reality, but we believe that all of the events which we experience are solid and real without ever realizing that we are dreaming.[116] When we awaken we come out of the dream state and return to the waking state. During dreaming, we respond to events like we do in the waking state. Believing the events in the dream to be

---

[115] Young-shik Choi, *Possession, The Homeless of Soul*, Inwha, Seoul (2004), pp 40-41

[116] Sogyal Rinpoche, *The Tibetan Book of Living and Dying*, Harper One, New York (2002), p. 348

solid, actual events, we sometimes scream, are tormented, or break out in a cold sweat. When we awaken we dismiss the dream events as being just a dream which is worthless to mention or consider. Since we often do not fully remember or truly understand what occurred in the dream, we dismiss it as unimportant despite the fact that we suffered or enjoyed our dream as though it were composed of actual events.

First, let us consider the case of the Russian chemist, Dmitri Mendeleev, who had been working for years in an effort to discover a way of classifying the elements according to their atomic weights. One night in 1869 the chemist fell into bed exhausted after devoting many long hours in an attempt to solve the problem. Later that night he "saw in a dream a table where all the elements fell into place as required." Upon awakening he immediately wrote down the table just as he remembered it on a piece of paper. Amazingly, Mendeleev reported, "Only in one place did a correction later seem necessary." Thus the Periodic Table of the Elements, a fundamental discovery of modern physics, was first brought forth in a dream.[117]

Paul McCartney woke up one morning in May of 1965 with a haunting tune running through his mind. In the dream he'd just awakened from, he'd been listening to the same melody being played by a classical string ensemble. He was so taken with the sound that he immediately got up and began playing the notes he'd heard on the keys of the upright piano next to his bed in his mother's home in London, where the Beatles were filming Help! ....(He) finally plunged in and composed the lyrics to 'Yesterday,' which was then recorded with a string arrangement just as he'd originally heard it in his dream. Nearly forty years later, 'Yesterday' still ranked as the most frequently played single of all time on American radio. Reflecting on the song later in life, McCartney said it was 'the most complete thing' he'd ever written. "For

---

117 Stephen LaBerge, *Lucid Dreaming*, Sounds True, Colorado (2009), pp 36-37

Probing the Mind: How does Consciousness Work?

something that just happened in a dream, even I have to acknowledge that it was a phenomenal stroke of luck," he concluded.[118]

Elias Howe picked up the idea from the spears with eye-shaped holes that he had seen in his dream, and finally invented the sewing machine. Many significant inventions or academic achievements have been born from dreams. There are also many stories about dreams in which the dreamer received a hint from the dream concerning a real event, directly or indirectly. Someone won the lottery after a good dream. Someone passed an examination after a good dream. A dream is not a mere dream; a dream gives something to our real life and has something to do with it. Though a dream is explained as a form of consciousness from the unconscious or subconscious, many things are left as a mystery: how it is made, why it is made, how it gives revelation, and so on.

---

118 Andrea Rock, *The Mind at Night*, Basic Books, New York (2004), pp 135-136

19

A History of Dream Research

The earliest record of dreams comes from Mesopotamia, where clay tablets recounting the adventures of the legendary hero Gilgamesh included accounts of dreams and how to interpret their symbolic and metaphorical imagery. The tablets were found in the library of a king who ruled in the seventh century B.C., but oral versions of the dream-rich stories are believed to have circulated hundreds of years earlier. It is believed that texts had been written on how to decipher the meaning of dreams by about 1000 B.C. in both India and China. These early conceptions of dreams revolved around the notion that they were messages from the gods that could foretell the future, and dreams are still believed to have that power in many cultures.[119]

The roots of modern scientific thought about dreams can also be found in ancient times. Aristotle proclaimed that far from being a product of divine origin, "dreaming is thinking while asleep." The Upanishads, philosophical treatises written in India between 900 and 500 B.C., proposed that it is the dreamer himself who creates horses, chariots, and other objects appearing in the dream

---

119 Andrea Rock, *The Mind at Night*, Basic Books, New York (2004), pp ix-x

world, and that dream objects were expressions of the dreamer's inner desires.[120]

The notion which dominated both scientific and popular thought about dreams throughout most of the first half of the 20th century was at the heart of Sigmund Freud's dream theory. Freud described dream interpretation as "the royal road to understanding the unconscious activities of the mind." In his view, the unconscious consisted of both innate information that had never entered consciousness as well as experiences or thoughts that had been shunted off to the unconscious and remain repressed because they were memories, wishes, or fears that were unacceptable. The repressed desire to sleep with one's mother and kill one's father became perhaps the iconic example of Freudian theory.[121]

Published in 1900, Freud's *The Interpretation of Dreams* argued that dreams spring from subconscious wishes (primarily sexual and aggressive desires, which Freud called libidinal drive) that the censoring ego normally suppressed in waking hours. To protect sleep from being disrupted, the mind then imagined these wishes being fulfilled by creating dreams—symbolic, disjointed tales that were filled with visual metaphors designed to disguise the desires and fears actually being expressed. These wishes sometimes arose from 'day residue,' meaning consciously remembered wishes that were aroused during the preceding day but were unfulfilled, or desires bubbling up from the unconscious once sleep relaxed the controlling grip of the mind's censor.[122]

Freud's insistence that most dream content reflected repressed sexual wishes was one of the major factors leading to the split that occurred between Freud and his one-time protégé, Carl Jung, whose dream theories also influenced popular thought on the subject throughout much of the past century. In addition to meaning that could be extracted based on each individual's personal expe-

---

120 Andrea Rock, *The Mind at Night*, Basic Books, New York (2004), p x

121 Andrea Rock, *The Mind at Night*, Basic Books, New York (2004), p x

122 Andrea Rock, *The Mind at Night*, Basic Books, New York (2004), p x

rience, Jung proposed that there was another level of meaning in dreams. In fact, he believed the most important dreams we have are the products of what he called the 'collective unconscious,' which reflects the inherited experiential record of the human species. As human anatomy bears telltale signs of its evolutionary past, such as vestiges of a tailbone in the human fetus, so Jung theorized that the mind "can no more be a product without history than is the body in which it exists." He argued that the collective unconscious was expressed through archetypes that appear not only in dreams but throughout history in the content of myths, fairy tales, and religious ceremony. Archetypal dreams are linked with strong emotions and occur more often around times of crisis or transitions in our lives, Jung contended.[123]

The dream, which had been researched within the perspective of psychoanalysis, entered upon a new phase in the perspective of neurophysiology in the 1950s when rapid eye movement (REM - sleeper's eyes dart back and forth beneath closed lids) during sleep was proved by Eugene Aserinsky and Nathaniel Kleitman. Some define it narrowly as the creation of hallucinatory narratives complete with characters and a discernable plotline that occurs primarily during that period of rest known as REM sleep, while at the other end of the spectrum are researchers who classify any mental activity that occurs during any stage of sleep as dreaming.[124]

The period of the 1950s and 1960s was a golden age of dream research by Eugene Aserinsky, Nathaniel Kleitman, William Dement and others at Chicago University. What Allan Hobson and Robert McCarley eventually found using an EEG (electroencephalogram) and REM studies, published in 1977 as the activation-synthesis model of dreaming, was a controversial neurophysiological explanation of dreaming that effectively kicked the legs out from under Freudian theory and most other existing psychological

---

123 Andrea Rock, *The Mind at Night*, Basic Books, New York (2004), pp xi-xii

124 Andrea Rock, *The Mind at Night*, Basic Books, New York (2004), p viii

approaches to interpreting dream content.[125] The Freud or Jung theory used in psychology or psychoanalysis was subject to criticism from the neurophysiological theory of Hobson and McCarley who argued that the sense of judgement we need to recognize that we're dreaming and the ability to remember exactly what we dreamed are limited because the two neuromodulators needed for those functions are in short supply until we awaken. We therefore forget most of our dreams simply because we lack the neurochemicals needed to imprint them on memory, not because we have a Freudian censor in our mind furiously working to repress their taboo content. Hobson was eviscerating Freudian dream theory. As for Freud's former disciple Carl Jung, Hobson dismissed his notion of the collective unconscious and archetypal symbols as a form of religion—something for which he had no patience—but he agreed with Jung that dreaming was a creative process in the brain and any meaning that resulted was absolutely transparent.[126]

In the 1980s, dream theory opens a new chapter by virtue of Steven LaBerge's research on lucid dreaming. Just as the discovery of REM had required a rethinking of previous notions of sleep as a state in which the brain essentially shut down, LaBerge's research into an unusual phenomenon known as lucid dreaming eventually shifted scientific thought about the nature of the dreaming mind.[127]

In the late 1990s there is progress in the neurophysiological research on dreams with the imaging studies of the dreaming brain which revealed that structures in the limbic system—the center of emotional memory—are more highly activated during REM sleep than in waking, while the portions of the prefrontal cortex that direct logical thinking are nearly shut down.[128]

---

125 Andrea Rock, *The Mind at Night*, Basic Books, New York (2004), p 20

126 Andrea Rock, *The Mind at Night*, Basic Books, New York (2004), p 22

127 Andrea Rock, *The Mind at Night*, Basic Books, New York (2004), pp 149-150

128 Andrea Rock, *The Mind at Night*, Basic Books, New York (2004), p 104

Probing the Mind: How does Consciousness Work?

The psychological or psychoanalytical research on dreams by Freud and Jung and others seems to fade with the experimental research by the neurophysiologists. The theory that dreams come from the subconscious or collective unconscious is losing credibility as a result of studies of the physical phenomena such as REM or EEG, or photos of brain activation. The fact that dreaming is an activation of the brain has been supported by the evidence.

Whether a dream is experienced in color or in black and white has also been a subject of study. Most dreams are clearly experienced in color, though for some unknown reason between 20 and 30 percent play out in black and white. While reports on dreams all the way back to Aristotle included references to color, from the 1930s to 1960s the prevailing opinion among research psychologists as well as among the general public was that we dream in black and white.[129]

Animals dream, too. Koch explains that the brain basis of animals' dreaming is not that dissimilar to ours.[130] Of course we cannot rely on experiences related by animals; it is just inferred from the physical phenomena evident in REM, EEG, other studies conducted with them. We must admit though, that even in spite of all the progress which has been made on dreaming through the scientific research, there is still much to be discovered concerning the dream state.

---

129 Andrea Rock, *The Mind at Night*, Basic Books, New York (2004), pp 12-13

130 Andrea Rock, *The Mind at Night*, Basic Books, New York (2004), p 174

20

Does the Brain Dream?—A Wrong Hypothesis

Those who have believed that the brain thinks have also believed that the brain dreams. They present REM (rapid eye movement) as evidence of this. They would say that REM occurs upon the brain's command during dreaming. In brain science, medicine, neuroscience, psychology and so on, they do not challenge the belief that the brain thinks and dreams. Up to now they have believed that all information for dreaming is prepared through extremely complicated neurocircuits at the more than 10 trillion neurons and synapses in the brain so as to fabricate a story in the dream.

It is said that the most highly charged region of the brain during our most fertile dreaming periods is the limbic system—the center for generating emotion-laden action and memories. The type of memory that the brain preferentially selects for incorporation in the dreams tends to be emotionally charged.[131]

When we're awake, the disconnected dots representing the electrical activity generated by the retina are projected to a relay station

---

[131] Andrea Rock, *The Mind at Night*, Basic Books, New York (2004), p 188

in a portion of the brain called the thalamus, which in turn projects to the primary visual cortex. It then passes those signals on to various neuronal systems dedicated to specialized tasks such as face recognition or processing color or motion. Finally, all of that information flows to the highest levels of the visual system, known as the associative cortices, which store memory, direct the most abstract aspects of visual processing, and assemble the final image we see. In dreaming, however, since the retina and primary visual cortex are closed for business, the memory-rich associative cortices are actually both the starting and end points for generating visual imagery in the dreamworld. "Visual imagery is largely formed by our ideas and feelings about what things ought to look like," according to Czerner. "The eye provides information about light and dark, but it contributes nothing to meaning or perception. In both waking and dreaming, those components are supplied by the associative cortex and—to an even larger extent in dreaming than waking—by the limbic system, which regulates emotionally charged memories."[132]

Although REM has provided remarkable results in the scientific research of dreams, it is still not enough to prove the fact that the brain dreams. Science has not yet revealed the mechanism of dreaming, but REM phenomena do prove that dreaming accompanies a physiological change.

The belief that the brain dreams is analogous to the belief that the brain thinks. According to these beliefs, brain dreams and consciousness or mind activity arise as a result of the brain itself. However, even as we can establish a hypothesis that the brain will not think and that thought arising somewhere else will affect the brain, we can likewise establish a hypothesis that the brain will not dream and that the dream being processed somewhere else in consciousness will affect the brain.

According to the mechanism of consciousness in the Consciousness-Only Theory, the experimental evidences such as REM, EEG, or photos of brain activation that physiologists present may not be the right evidence that the brain dreams, but rather may be physical phenomena which result from the dreaming. In

---

132 Andrea Rock, *The Mind at Night*, Basic Books, New York (2004), p 181

Probing the Mind: How does Consciousness Work?

this Theory, consciousness is generated by contacting six objects with the corresponding six organs, and accompanies mental activities. The mental activities influence the brain, and finally the brain sends commands to the respective physical organs through the nervous system. In other words, REM may be a physical phenomenon created by consciousness generated in the dream. For example, nocturnal emission in a male is not an action that the brain has thought or made by itself, but is rather an action which has been made by the brain's command. The brain's command has been induced by mental activities and the mental activities have been made by the sixth consciousness because the first five consciousnesses are dormant during sleep. The brain cannot distinguish the sleeping state from the waking state. The brain just follows the consciousness. If the brain could think by itself and distinguish the sleeping state from the waking state, it would not deliver the command to carry out the emission during sleep.

Just as scientific evidence is not yet sufficient to prove the belief that the brain thinks by itself, so is it too early to accept the hypothesis that the brain dreams. The five sense consciousnesses are generated during the waking state, just as the sixth consciousness by the sixth organ is also generated during the waking state. In dreaming, however, only the sixth consciousness is generated since the five sense consciousnesses are dormant. The sixth consciousness is generated by contacting mind information with the mind organ. The brain is not a sense organ. The brain cannot read the mind information which is stored in Alaya just as the eye cannot read sounds, the ear cannot perceive lights, and the nose cannot perceive taste and so on. Likewise, mind information can be read only by the sixth organ; it cannot be read by the brain. The sixth consciousness or the mind organ has nothing to do with the brain.

Mental activities arise from the sixth consciousness during dreaming and affect the brain, and the brain responds to this consciousness. If the dream is perceived as threatening, the brain may command the dreamer to scream; and if the dream is in a state of tension, it may command the dreamer to emit cold sweat. The brain is a mere control tower of our body which is responding in accordance with the mental activities accompanied when the mind organ contacts mind information.

In summary, according to The Consciousness-Only Theory a dream is a matter of consciousness which is generated when the mind organ contacts mind information, but not a matter of physiology related to the brain and/or nervous system. In this regard LaBerge's researches on lucid dreams seem to be encouraging in that he added experiences on oriental meditation or awareness of consciousness to the western scientific researches. As long as we do not prove scientifically that a dream is fabricated from consciousness, the physiological research on dreams which is focused on the brain will continue.

21

How Is a Dream Made Up?—The Mechanism of Dream Consciousness

When we close our eyes and think about the Statue of Liberty we can envision the Statue in our mind. Although we do not see the Statue with our eyes, the image appears in our mind. The imagery is perceived by the sixth organ which has contacted the mind information stored in Alaya regarding the Statue. The imagery is not seen by physical eyes, but by the mind's eye of the mind organ. The imagery is a mind's eye consciousness.

When we close our eyes silently and recall the voice of our late mother or father, we can hear the voice. Although we do not hear the voice with our ears, we can remember the voice. The sound imagery is perceived by the sixth organ which has contacted the mind information regarding the voice as stored in Alaya. The sound imagery is not perceived by physical ears, but by the mind's ear of the mind organ. The sound imagery is a mind's ear consciousness.

If someone does not have any experience or knowledge about the Statue of Liberty, the mind's eye consciousness cannot arise because the information on that has not been stored in his Alaya. If someone was born after his father had died, he cannot recall the voice of his father because the information on the voice has not been stored in his Alaya.

The mechanism of a dream is quite similar to that of imagination. We perceive something in a dream and also in our imagination. In both, the five sense organs do not work, while only the sixth organ works. In both, the mind organ contacts the mind information stored in Alaya so as to give rise to visual or auditory consciousness. However, imagination is for the mind organ to contact Alaya information with intention, whereas dreaming is for the mind organ to contact it with no intention. Imagination is intentionally fabricated, while a dream is unintentionally or unwittingly fabricated. In this regard imagination is an intended association, whereas a dream is not made up by free will. Regardless of one's intention or will, a dream is dreamed based on the subconscious or unconscious desire. Accordingly, if we understand our dream we shall become aware of our subconscious or unconscious desire. Dreams delivering an important message such as a revelation seem to have a close relationship with the subconscious or unconscious desire.

A dream is an experience of consciousness in which we clearly see something through visual imagery or hear something through auditory imagery. Of course, three other sense imageries can also be perceived in a dream. Dreams are processed during sleep, which means that the consciousness is not perceived by any of the five physical organs; i.e., dreams are not made up by any of the five sense organs or the brain. Dreams are made up by the sixth organ contacting mind information. A dream is a sixth consciousness generated during sleep, and as long as a sixth consciousness is generated, the thinking cycle can work in the seventh consciousness. In the seventh, mental activities are accompanied and influence the brain and nervous system. All the consciousness generated during dreaming is stored in Alaya.

A lot of information regarding external objects is input through the five sense organs in the waking state, whereas the input of this information is almost blocked in the sleeping state. In the waking state the five sense organs are very active in the perception of the corresponding objects and the consciousness generated by the five organs activates the mind information of Alaya and results in a very active, and sometimes frenetic, thought process. In the sleeping state, however, the five organs are in a nearly comatose state. Of course they are not completely unaware, but in sleep the consciousnesses caused by the five organs are too weak to activate the mind information of Alaya and the related thought processes are greatly reduced in sleep when compared to when awake. The sixth organ alone contacts the mind information of Alaya during the sleep state, and this is without intention or free will, and not spontaneously. The sixth organ contacts Alaya by a force which is called 'subconscious or unconscious desire,' and a dream is the result of the sixth organ contacting Alaya information in accordance with this force.

The Alaya information with subconscious or unconscious desire is produced by the interest or concern of the owner. The stronger the desire is, the more forceful the information is. The forceful information hovers over the surface of the storehouse, Alaya, and has a greater possibility to contact the mind organ than less forceful information stored in the deep place of the storehouse, resulting in the make up of a dream. The forceful information produced with deep concern or interest will most likely be the most recent information, like today's information. If a person who had never worked was shoveling in the yard all day, the information on tired shoveling is around the surface of his Alaya and has a greater possibility to be contacted by the sixth organ during sleep so as to produce a dream.

Among those in the forefront of solving that mystery is Robert Stickgold, an assistant professor of psychiatry at Harvard. Stickgold came up with a novel way to try to coerce the brain into revealing its rules by examining a stage of sleep that previously had been overlooked by most researchers. As we're drifting off to sleep, we typically experience what's known as hypnagogic imagery-hallucinatory visual images and other sensations that usually aren't threaded together in narrative as most dreams are. More than a decade ago, Stickgold became fascinated by this sleep onset phenomenon while on vacation in Vermont. "After a day of hiking and rock climbing," Stickgold recalls, "as I drifted off to sleep, I immediately felt I was back on the mountain in one tricky passage where I had to cling to the rocks to pull myself up. I roused myself a couple of times, but each time I dozed off, the feeling of my hands on the rocks returned. Later in the night when I'd awake and try to get those same images back, I couldn't, but when I was first falling asleep they were unavoidable." He began taking note of other instances at sleep onset when he'd get similar strong spontaneous replays of the day's events and found that they tended to occur when his days included out-of-the-ordinary experiences, such as days spent white-water rafting or sailing in rough water.[133]

Stickgold's experience, as related above, will be one that everybody has experienced at one time or another. If we are obsessed with learning how to play billiards or golf, when lying in the bed with closed eyes, the image of billiard balls or golf balls keeps coming and fading in front of our eyes. In Alaya, all mind information is stored individually. Just like a lot of stuff is stored in a warehouse, the past information is stored at a deeper place, while the latest information is stored at a closer place for easier access. The deeper an item is stored, the more difficult it is to pick up. If an item is thought to be precious, it is stored at a particular place. Similarly, the latest information is stored at the surface of Alaya. The information on unsettled worry or major concern is repeatedly generated and stored in Alaya in layer upon layer. Very little of the information in Alaya is contacted by the sixth organ to produce dreams. Freud called dreams the royal road to the unconscious, but he insisted that we can only scratch the surface of the unconscious mind.

Many children quite often experience silly dreams because their major concern is silly things such as flying, or becoming Cinderella or the like. Such things are meaningless to adults, but they are major concerns to children. Such consciousness is stored in their Alaya and manifested in a dream. As these considerations wane in importance as we grow up, our dreams become more seri-

---

133 Andrea Rock, *The Mind at Night*, Basic Books, New York (2004), p 88

ous and realistic. Grown-ups meet deep worries or more serious or realistic matters in their dreams. Depending on the degree of fear or concern, the consciousness may be manifested in a nightmare or a revelatory dream which delivers a divine message.

As noted above, a precious item may be kept in a special place in a warehouse, and similarly, distinctive information is stored in a particular place in Alaya. Whether a piece of information is distinctive or not is proportional to the degree of recognition or awareness, the degree of importance. The stronger the degree of importance, the better the information is activated. Information concerning deep worries or other anxieties or fears is stored at a particular place and has a greater possibility of becoming a dream during sleep.

Although infrequent, some information is input through the five sense organs during sleep and result in or impact a dream. We sometimes experience that our dreaming has some relationship with the outside environmental activities. For example, we experience that the voice from a TV is material in a dream. Such experience proves that some information on external objects can be input through the physical organs during sleep; i.e., sensation through the physical organs is not completely stopped during sleep. The eyes and tongue are not open to external objects, but the ears, nose and skin are open to external objects to work to some extent even during sleep. Though the ears, nose and skin contact external objects during sleep, it is not easy to be conscious or aware of it unless the contact is strong enough. When we feel cold during sleep, we may pull up the blanket without being conscious of doing it. This means that the body (touch feeling) consciousness has arisen and stimulated the brain, and that the brain has commanded the body to pull up the blanket.

We perceive dreams mostly with visual imagery. The investigations of dream content from the 1890s and later consistently showed that nearly every dream contains visual imagery, while slightly more than half contain some auditory component. Among other sensations, touch or feelings of movement are present in less than 15 percent of dreams, while taste or smell rarely figures into dream experience at all.[134] Nocturnal emission is a representative example of touch consciousness in a dream. Although rarely, we sometimes experience smell or taste consciousness in a dream. This is because most of the Alaya information is visual information, next is auditory information, and there is very little smell, taste and touch/feeling information in Alaya. The Eye is the most important organ among the five organs in terms of consciousness. Koch says, "We are very visual creatures. One-third of the brain is given over to vision, and we have all sorts of visual experiences that can be analyzed, including vivid dreams."[135]

---

134 Andrea Rock, *The Mind at Night*, Basic Books, New York (2004), p 11

135 Andrea Rock, *The Mind at Night*, Basic Books, New York (2004), p 177

22

Why Is a Dream Illogical or Inconsistent?

The thinking cycle works during dreaming in the same manner as in the waking state, but it works very slowly due to the very small amount of input information. In the waking state a lot of information is input through the five sense organs and the thinking cycle works very rapidly and seems to be logical. When X is contacted by the eyes, A is retrieved from Alaya due to X, B is retrieved from Alaya due to A, C is retrieved due to B, D is retrieved due to C, and so on. We frequently call it 'logical thinking.' For example, when we see an apple we think about many things in series such as eating it, the sweet taste of it, apple juice, cider, cider vinegar, etc. The thinking in series is due to the fact that the mind organ contacts the mind information one by one, with each later one coming from the preceding one.

On the other hand most dreams are illogical, unlike the consciousness of the waking state; sunshine may suddenly change into a shower, or green apples may become red almost instantaneously. This is because the logical operation of the thinking cycle does not go on smoothly in dreams because the sixth object, mind information, may be almost randomly contacted by the mind organ. If the thinking cycle in the waking state is a motion picture, the thinking cycle in the dream is like a set of nearly random slides. The sunshine and shower, or the green apples and red ones in a dream are merely a few slides. If the thinking cycle is processed in the order of A, B, C, D, and so on sequentially or logically in the waking state, the thinking cycle in the dream is processed in the random order like A, X, K, B and the like. Although the random information in the dream may exhibit some relationships to each other, they seem to us to be illogical or inconsistent compared with the logical thinking process of the waking state.

A dream may sometimes seem to proceed very fast. In a dream we may experience flying through the sky from mountain to mountain, avoiding flying bullets in the battlefield, moving back and forth from past to future, etc. In fact, such dreams are fabricated with just a few cuts of the slides and we may feel that we have experienced more than in the waking state because the mind information is free from space and time constraints.

We should not dismiss all dreams as being irrational or unreasonable. We may feel that a dream is illogical or inconsistent because it is created by apparently unrelated events or thoughts, but many dreams are developed together so as to constitute a logical story which delivers some important messages.

Western scientists explain the illogical nature of dreams by relating them to physical phenomena in the brain. Because the portions of the brain that normally order our thinking are offline, what we're experiencing in a dream state can seem to be a hallucinatory world, much like what a schizophrenic experiences in waking consciousness. In fact, brain-imaging studies show that the functional anatomy of dreaming is almost identical to that of schizophrenic psychosis with the major difference being that the visuospatial system is most highly charged for dreamers, while for schizophrenics the audioverbal system is activated.[136] The fact that the visuospatial system is most highly charged means that more visual information is processed during the dream state.

---

136 Andrea Rock, *The Mind at Night*, Basic Books, New York (2004), p 96

Probing the Mind: How does Consciousness Work?

According to a paper published by Allan Hobson and his colleague David Kahn at Harvard, the story that occurs during dreaming may actually be an example of chaos theory at work in the brain. Chaos theory emerged in the 1970s as a new way for physicists, mathematicians, biologists, and other scientists to comprehend the patterns of order that exist within what appears to be disorder, allowing them to use mathematical formulas and computer modeling to examine questions ranging from how clouds form to how infectious diseases spread within a population or how galaxies are created. This way of understanding how the world works tells us that all complex systems stabilize, or self-organize, when their equilibrium is disturbed, creating a new order. Just a small change in the initial condition of a complex system can rapidly and dramatically change its eventual outcome. The concept is illustrated concretely in an example known as the butterfly effect—the proposition that the flapping of a butterfly's wing stirring the air today in California can have an effect on storm systems months later on the other side of the world.[137]

We should remind ourselves, however, that a dream is normally not a straightforward statement but is rather a metaphor. Communication in the dream state is not as free as in the waking state since dreams are made up mostly with visual imagery, with reduced auditory imagery due to the way the mind organ contacts the mind information.

Often, a creative breakthrough provided in a dream comes via a visual metaphor. For example, when Elias Howe was working on inventing the sewing machine, he was stymied by how to secure the needle to the machine in a way that allowed the needle to easily pass through the fabric, because he was still following the model of hand-held sewing needles, where the hole for the thread is located at the end opposite the needle's sharp point. The answer came to him via a dream in which he was surrounded by savages painted with war paint who were leading him to be executed. As he was being led to his death, he noticed that the warriors were carrying spears with eye-shaped holes

---

137 Andrea Rock, *The Mind at Night*, Basic Books, New York (2004), p 230

near their pointed tips. Awakening from the dream, he realized that the needle for the sewing machine should be modeled after the spears in his dreams, with the hole for the thread located near the pointed end, and that was indeed the solution that worked.[138]

As far back as we have records we can see that humans have tried to interpret dreams as messages which were given us in the form of visual metaphors. There have been lots of texts to decipher the meaning of dreams throughout human history. The Mesopotamian clay tablets included accounts of dreams and how to interpret their symbolic and metaphorical imagery, and by about 1000 B.C. texts had been written on how to decipher the meaning of dreams in both India and China. These early conceptions of the significance of dreams revolved around the notion that they were messages from the gods and could foretell the future. Due to this long history of dream interpretation, statistical analysis techniques were utilized to help develop dream interpretation systems to help capture and document these experiences. It should be noted, however, that as a dream is a matter of consciousness, the dreamer himself will be the best interpreter of his dream.

---

138 Andrea Rock, *The Mind at Night*, Basic Books, New York (2004), p 141

23

Why Is It Difficult to Remember Dreams?

It is said that an average person typically remembers his or her dream only once or twice a week. Given the fact that we all dream every night, that leaves at least ninety-five percent of our dreams forgotten. A variety of theories have suggested fanciful explanations as to why dreams are so easily forgotten ranging from Freud's belief that dreams are repressed because they contain so much taboo dream thought, to Francis Crick's view that the content of dreams is what the brain is trying to unlearn and therefore ought not to be remembered. Stephen LaBerge, a psychophysiologist, asserts that the recall of dreams probably relates to evolution. Standard memory theory explains much of what is remembered of dreams and what is not, which aspects of dream content are more readily recalled and which aspects are not, and so on. But these explanations do not answer the basic question of why it should be that dreams are so difficult to remember.[139]

When we think about it, it seems natural that it should be difficult to remember dreams. Let's consider the recall of dreams from

---

139 Stephen LaBerge, *Lucid Dreaming*, Sounds True, Colorado (2009), p 15

the perspective of consciousness. Consider consciousness during the waking hours when the six sense organs work busily during our whole waking experience. Suppose that we walked along the streets in New York all day. How many things would we remember from the myriad of things which we encountered from the time of leaving our home in the morning to when we come back home in the evening? Consider all of the buildings, shops, trees, pedestrians, cars, bikes, traffic signals, signboards, and all of the other things, and consider all of the sounds which we heard. In spite of, or maybe because of the sensory overload which we encounter during our day to day experiences we only remember a few things that were either very impressive or that caused some concern. It is also similar in our daily work life. Although we go to work every day and do many things and come back home in the evening, it is not easy to remember all the tasks that we performed or participated in during a given day. The tasks done yesterday are more difficult to remember than those done today, and those done a week ago are becoming far removed from our memory. If what we have experienced is a disastrous traffic accident or a chance meeting with a close friend of ten years ago, such things will be easily recalled in our memory for a very long time. This should remind us of the astute observation:

> *Two men looked out prison bars;*
> *One saw mud, the other stars.*
> *Anonymous*[140]

Having seen how selective our recall is during our waking hours, why should it be any better when trying to recall dreams? Dream time is the opportunity for the sixth organ to contact the sixth object, mind information, during sleep, and as we receive a lot of information through the five sense organs in the waking state, we receive a lot of information through the mind organ in dreams. It is difficult to remember all the dreams which we have

---

140 Stephen LaBerge, *Lucid Dreaming*, Sounds True, Colorado (2009), p 36

even during one night if the mind information is not special. Moreover, it may be especially difficult to recall since the dream may seem to be illogical or inconsistent. A bad dream such as a nightmare, or an auspicious dream will not be forgotten. During a nightmare we sometimes scream or produce a cold sweat, and the stronger the mind information is, the stronger the consciousness which is formed as a result of the dream. We have little choice but to remember such dreams.

Hobson or McCarley argued that the sense of judgement we need to recognize that we're dreaming, and the ability to remember exactly what we dreamed, are limited because the two neuromodulators needed for those functions are in short supply until we awaken. We therefore forget most of our dreams simply because we lack the neurochemicals needed to imprint them on memory, not because we have a Freudian censor in our mind furiously working to repress their taboo content.[141] We do not know whether the shortage of neurochemicals is a cause of forgetting dreams or a result thereof.

The dream, during which the mind organ contacts mind information to elicit a consciousness, is an expression of the subconscious or unconscious; i.e., a message received from the spiritual world. It can deliver important messages such as Mendeleev's Periodic Table, McCartney's string ensemble, Howe's sewing machine and the like, so it can be significant to recall dreams and to think about the messages. In fact, many scientists or inventors have utilized their dreams' communication including hypnagogic imagery-hallucinatory visual images in their research. We should also pay attention to our dreams even if we are not a scientist or inventor; if we have a lucky dream we should expect a good outcome, whereas if we have a bad dream we should be prudent and cautious in our daily life.

A method for recalling dreams is to try to recall them every morning when we awaken from sleep. Before getting out of the bed, recall dreams and think about what messages they may be

---

141 Andrea Rock, *The Mind at Night*, Basic Books, New York (2004), p 22

delivering. As we get out of the bed and begin to go about our daily life, dreams gradually recede from our memory as we begin to receive a lot of new information on external objects through the five sense organs. Last night's dreams will be gradually replaced by the newly encountered information from our wakened state.

So what are some concerted efforts that we could make if we wish to remember dreams? As we noted, what happens today can be best remembered today since everything recedes from memory as time passes, and the time right after awakening from dreaming is the best time to recall a dream. Building on this, it is said that one method to facilitate the recall of dreams is to drink a lot of water before going to sleep because if we drink a lot before going to sleep we awaken from sleep to urinate and tend to recall the dream during this waking time.

If we see or feel something during our daily routine which reminds us of last night's dream, we are spontaneously reminded of fragments of the dream. For example, we may recall a dream related to cars the moment we pass by the scene of a car crash. This is a kind of memory technique by association. Braun maintains that this phenomenon occurs because the dream content is actually encoded in the brain,[142] but the phenomenon is an example of the memory technique of association rather than the encoding of dreams in the brain.

The recall of dreams is a reproduction of consciousness, but the production or reproduction of consciousness is not a spontaneous occurrence but is rather a result of causes and conditions in accordance with the Nature of Dependence on Others; i.e., when we remember fragments of a dream it is initiated by something that we see or feel during our daily life. A motive functions to recall a first scene of the dream, the first scene functions to recall a second scene (a former scene), the second scene functions to recall a third scene (a second former scene) and so on. LaBerge says this is a

---

142 Andrea Rock, *The Mind at Night*, Basic Books, New York (2004), p 52

memory technique for dreams in reverse order.[143] This technique can be applied to the thinking process in waking hours. We can trace the present thinking content A as A was from B, B was from C, C was from D, and so on.

Now that we have considered how one might better recall dreams upon awakening, we should note that it is not necessary to force oneself to remember a dream which is difficult to recall. Trying to remember a 'lost' dream is similar to trying to remember what one has done in daily life. Although it is not unimportant to look back and recall what one has done in daily life, the more important thing is not to let go of the consciousness of every moment, the consciousness of the 'now' moment. We perceive a lot of information from external or internal objects and act on the perceived consciousnesses in daily life even though we are not aware of most of them. When we perceive a mind information, a consciousness is generated and the brain and nervous system respond to the consciousness even though the mind organ is not aware of the consciousness or the brain's response. If we practice to remain aware of our consciousness in daily life, we will likewise be aware of the consciousness during our dreams and will be better able to recall them.

---

143 Andrea Rock, *The Mind at Night*, Basic Books, New York (2004), p 152

24

Thinking and Judgement in a Dream—Lucid Dreaming

We do not normally recognize the dream as a dream while in the dream state; we are under the delusion that we are participating in real events. As we are not aware of the dream as a dream but rather experience it as though it were real life, we are totally immersed in the dream experience. As a result we sometimes scream, feel tormented, or break out in a cold sweat during dreaming. Such dreams are called non-lucid dreams or typical dreams. There is another category of dreams, however, called lucid dreams, and in these we recognize the dream as a dream and maintain an awareness of consciousness.

The term 'lucid dreaming' was coined in a 1913 paper written by Frederik van Eeden, a Dutch psychiatrist. A lucid dream is a dream in which one is self-aware. Even though the term is a 20th century term, the history of lucid dreaming goes to at least the 4th century B.C. when Aristotle made an apparent reference to lucid dreaming when he wrote of "something in consciousness which declares what then presents itself is but a dream." We should also note that Tibetan Buddhists have incorporated a form of lucid dreaming called dream yoga as part of their spiritual practices for more than 1,000 years.[144]

Stephen LaBerge, a U.S. neurophysiologist, has scientifically researched lucid dreaming since the 1980s, and his research has yielded many discoveries concerning lucid dreaming. Not only has his research produced much information which helps to understand the process of lucid dreaming, but it has also enabled him to invent a device which can help facilitate the practice of lucid dreaming.

Various surveys about lucid dreaming since the 1980s consistently have found that more than half of those responding (slightly exceeding 80 percent in one survey) report having had at least one dream during their lifetime in which at a minimum they became aware that they were dreaming. In some sleep lab studies, between 1 and 2 percent of awakenings during REM sleep revealed that subjects were having lucid dreams. On average, lucid dreams studied in the lab last only a couple of minutes, though some that have been verified by eye movement signals have lasted as long as fifty minutes. Frequent lucid dreamers - meaning those having such an experience at least once a month - are in the minority, ranging from less than 10 percent in one survey to slightly more than 20 percent in another. The most powerful predictor of lucidity is having good dream recall in general.[145]

Lucid dreaming is recognizing that the dream is a false image, not a real event. In the Consciousness-Only Theory, all sentient beings and all dharmas (objects or things) are deemed to be false images which are temporarily manifested by consciousness, whereas a dream is a false image temporarily fabricated by the sixth organ during sleep. Buddhism teaches that we should recognize or be aware of an arising thought in the waking state whenever it arises. If we recognize or are aware of it we are not dragged to the thought. On the other hand if we are not aware of it we are dragged to the thought or become slaves of the thought which is a false

---

144 Andrea Rock, *The Mind at Night*, Basic Books, New York (2004), p 152

145 Andrea Rock, *The Mind at Night*, Basic Books, New York (2004), p 157

image fabricated by the six sense objects. If we recognize a thought, the thought soon vanishes, and when the thought vanishes there remains only one thing: Emptiness or True-Self. If we are dragged to the thought, Emptiness or True-self never appears and thoughts arise continuously one after another. Finally, the endless thoughts culminate in an action which comes from ignorance, that we do not recognize consciousness. The ignorance is the starting point of the Twelve Links of Interdependent Co-Arising (Twelve Limbs of Dependent Origination).[146]

A dream is similar to a thought in the waking state; it is an arising of consciousness during sleep just as a thought is the same during the waking state. The thinking cycle during dreaming works similar to that during the waking state except that the thinking cycle in the waking state is triggered by the five external objects and works very rapidly, while the thinking cycle in dreaming is triggered by the sixth object only and works slowly. Even though the thinking cycle works more slowly during dreaming, it generates thinking and judgement. For example, if your friend offers you a cigarette in a dream and you have sufficient awareness you may recall that in reality you quit smoking five years ago and decline it in the dream. In Korea it is said that eating food in a dream is a symptom of illness. It is therefore recommended that you not eat food during dreaming if possible, but this is not always easy. By developing the ability of awareness we shall be aware of our dream and exhibit right thinking and right judgements in the dream state.

Contrary to this we act unconsciously in most of our waking hours. Although we swing our arms and move our legs thousands of times a day, we are not consciously aware of the individual movements. Going home from work we think about dinner; having dinner we think about a TV soap opera; watching a TV soap opera we think about tomorrow's work; and so on. Though many

---

146 Twelve Limbs of Dependent Origination is the circle of causality: ignorance, volitional action, consciousness, name and form, six organs, contact (touch), sensation, craving, grasping (clinging), becoming, birth, age and death

sages emphasized that the present moment is the most important, we do not live in the present moment but rather cling to the past or envision an uncertain future. When coming back home from work we need to be aware of the fact that we are coming back home; when having dinner we need to be aware of the fact that we are having dinner. A lot of sensations arise through the five organs and we are obsessed with the sensations, but we are not aware of the fact that we are perceiving them. However, if we try to concentrate our consciousness and enhance our awareness in our waking hours, the ability continues to function in dreaming.

In the united States, only about fifty-eight percent of people have had a lucid dream once in their lifetime. Maybe twenty-one percent have a lucid dream once or more in a month. In other words, lucidity is still rather rare. However, in another sample of people who had done either Buddhist or transcendental meditation, the average goes up to once or more a week. Here we are not talking about meditators who are specifically practicing dream yoga, but meditators in general.[147]

Buddhism teaches us to concentrate on consciousness all the time. It teaches us to be aware of any perception or discrimination through the six sense organs, cogitation or intellection in the Manas, or mental activities arising in the waking state. It teaches us that the awareness can be extended to the dreaming state. Without being aware of consciousness in the waking state it is impossible to be aware of consciousness while dreaming.

In fact, the first lucid dream he recalls in adult life occurred shortly after he returned from a workshop at the Esalen Institute, an alternative education center blending Eastern and Western philosophy located on the California coast near Big Sur. The workshop was taught by a Tibetan Buddhist, who urged participants to try to maintain consciousness throughout a twenty-four-hour period, holding on to self-reflective awareness even while dreaming.[148]

---

147 Francisco J. Varela, *Sleeping, Dreaming, and Dying*, Wisdom Publications, Boston (1997), p 103

148 Andrea Rock, *The Mind at Night*, Basic Books, New York (2004), p 151

Probing the Mind: How does Consciousness Work?

In western science they infer that the brain has a relationship with lucid dreams as well as typical dreams. Allan Rechtschaffen seems to expect some results from the imaging studies of a subject in a lucid dream:

Probably the most distinctive aspect of dreaming is its lack of reflective consciousness. While we are dreaming, we don't realize we are, which is an unusual state of consciousness. The part of the brain that informs us about our state of consciousness is not working during a typical dream, but during a lucid dream it would be. Imaging studies of a subject in a lucid dream should identify the location of the neurons that give us reflective consciousness.[149]

If we are unaware that we are dreaming we are dragged through the dream as though it were real life. We are deluded into thinking that the dream is real and we become anxious or scared in the dream. If we are aware that we are dreaming, we may hug a tiger dashing towards us without any fear, and then we shall realize that it has turned into a beautiful woman in our arms. Only when we awaken from the dream do we come to know that we were dreaming. The real life in which the six sense organs contact the corresponding six objects is the same as the dream in which the sixth organ contacts the sixth object, mind information. In our real life, we are deluded into thinking that the six objects perceived by the six organs are real or solid. Only when we see the ultimate reality of the six objects and get enlightenment shall we at last be able to realize that the real life is also a dream, and then we shall let go of the six objects. Like the dashing tiger that has turned into a beautiful woman in our arms in the dream, we shall be liberated from all attachments.

---

149 Andrea Rock, *The Mind at Night*, Basic Books, New York (2004), p 166

25

How Does Dreaming Result in Revelations?

Many people believe in revelations being disclosed in dreams. Revelations are not demonstrated scientifically but are evaluated freely. Although they are not proved in the scientific manner, there are many instances which demonstrate the efficacy of this belief in dream revelations through the many achievements which have been accomplished in accordance with revelations or information provided in dreams: the Periodic Table of the Elements was born in a dream by Russian chemist, Dmitri Mendeleev; Niels Bohr discovered the structure of the atom in a dream; Albert Einstein discovered the speed of light and the Principle of Relativity in dreams; and Paul McCartney's 'Yesterday' was composed in a dream. Accounts of such moments of inspiration or breakthroughs during dream time have been reported by other scientists, musicians, athletes, mathematicians, writers, and visual artists. Many of them have been chronicled by Harvard psychologist Deirdre Barrett in her book *The Committee of Sleep*.[150]

---

150 Andrea Rock, *The Mind at Night*, Basic Books, New York (2004), p 136

Tse Wen Chang and his wife, Nancy, moved from Taiwan to study at Harvard and in 1986 started a biotech company called Tanox. They funded the start-up themselves, with their garage serving as home for mice used in their research. An immunologist, Tse Wen was searching for a new way to treat allergies and asthma. Previous allergy drugs such as antihistamines worked by absorbing chemicals that are released in the wake of an allergy attack, but his groundbreaking notion was to use an engineered protein that would bind to substances in the body that set off allergic reactions and thereby prevent the attack from occurring in the first place. As Tanox chief executive officer Nancy Chang tells it, that out-of-the-box approach came in the dead of night. "He actually concocted that in the middle of the night in a dream, and he woke me up and told me," she recalls. "We didn't go back to sleep for the rest of the night."[151]

Donald J. Newman, mathematician at the Massachusetts Institute of Technology, solved a math problem from a dream. When he was working on a tough new theoretical math problem at MIT in the 1960s, he found that he was completely stuck. At the time he was part of a group of competitive mathematicians on campus including John Nash, whose life later became the subject of the popular book and film *A Beautiful Mind*.[152] He recalls:

"I'd been mulling over this problem for a week or so and just couldn't get anywhere with it when I had a dream that I was at a restaurant in Cambridge with Nash. I asked him about this problem in the dream and I listened to his explanation of how to do it. When I woke up, I had the solution."[153]

As shown in Newman's case, a revelation in a dream is often delivered by close friends, colleagues, neighbors and the like. Newman says that when he published a paper elucidating the problem he actually gave John Nash credit for contributing to the work

---

151 Andrea Rock, *The Mind at Night*, Basic Books, New York (2004), p 136

152 Andrea Rock, *The Mind at Night*, Basic Books, New York (2004), p 139

153 Andrea Rock, *The Mind at Night*, Basic Books, New York (2004), p 139

even though the help came via a dream. Further, he says that if he hadn't been friends with Nash, he wouldn't have solved it.[154]

New approaches to problems that materialize in dreams aren't limited to intellectual conundrums. Like the birds who improved their songs by rehearsing in their sleep, athletes sometimes find a new way to improve their performance when their logical brains are off-line.[155]

Pro golfer Jack Nicklaus was going through a period in the mid-1960s when his game was off, causing him to shoot in the high seventies. As he recounted to a reporter at the San Francisco Chronicle, he eventually had a dream about his golf swing that helped him get back in top form. "I was hitting them pretty good in the dream, and all at once I realized I wasn't holding the club the way I've actually been holding it lately," said Nicklaus. "I've been having trouble collapsing my right arm taking the club head away from the ball, but I was doing it perfectly in my sleep. So when I came to the course yesterday morning, I tried it the way I did in my dream and it worked. I shot a sixty-eight yesterday and a sixty-five today."[156]

Dreams can treat illness. The use of dreams for healing was widespread in the ancient world. The sick would sleep in the temples of Asklepios, the Greek god of healing, and during their dreams the god or his serpent familiar (hence the caduceus symbol of medicine) was said to appear, telling patients what they must do to be healed. Clearly we cannot evaluate either the effectiveness or mechanism of any resulting cures, but today we have reason to believe that dreams can indeed aid the healing process.[157]

How will dreams deliver hints or revelations on scientific ideas, compositions, gripping a club or other sports techniques, and so on? The mechanism of the revelations in dreams will not

---

154 Andrea Rock, *The Mind at Night*, Basic Books, New York (2004), pp 139-140

155 Andrea Rock, *The Mind at Night*, Basic Books, New York (2004), p 140

156 Andrea Rock, *The Mind at Night*, Basic Books, New York (2004), p 140

157 Stephen LaBerge, *Lucid Dreaming*, Sounds True, Colorado (2009), p 32

be different from in the waking state. When we get onto the No. 1 Highway in South Korea from Seoul to Busan and start to drive, we can know where we will be in five hours. Everybody can know that we are destined to arrive in Busan in five hours. Similarly, in real life we can 'foretell' the future in many circumstances by relying mainly on the five sense organs and the five consciousnesses by the organs. In a dream, however, only the sixth organ works and the sixth consciousness tells us about the future. The sixth organ might be cleverer than the five sense organs in that even though the five organs are restricted by time and space, the sixth organ transcends them.

The hints or revelations that might be obtained through dreams can be obtained in the waking state, but not without entering an alternate state of consciousness. In the waking state the five organs work in preference to the sixth organ, leaving no room for the sixth organ to work. Nonetheless, if we reach the state of deep meditation so as to quiet the five organs, the sixth organ can contact the sixth objects so as to deliver the hints or revelations while the five sense organs are in abeyance. As all are probably aware, however, it is not easy to reach the state of deep meditation while in the waking state.

Not everyone can receive hints or revelations through dreams. The Periodic Table of the Elements does not appear to just any scientist, and the gripping of a golf club is not revealed to all golfers. In order to get hints through dreams, we must concentrate on the particular matter with utmost focus day and night. The mind should be ardent and earnest like the cat's mind for catching a mouse, or the mother's mind while waiting for her son to return safely from battle. The mind must prioritize the most imperative mind information so that it will be stored at the important place of the Alaya. The surface of the Alaya will be covered with the most relevant mind information related to this focus in consciousness.

The hints or revelations are often shown after earnest prayer. Prayer is a very important means for the realization of wishes in all religions. It is taught to pray for realization of wishes in Buddhism, Christianity, Islam, etc. All religions teach "Seek and you will find."

Probing the Mind: How does Consciousness Work?

If this is not the case, it is said that the prayer lacked adequate love to power it to completion. Nobody can truly say whether or not the prayer lacked love, however, since love cannot be measured quantitatively.

Love works like this: when a mother sees her baby toddling in the tiger cage at the zoo and a tiger is approaching it she can bend the iron bars to save the baby. It is impossible for a powerful man to bend the bars in the normal state of mind. It is impossible to do that in the physical world, in the desire realm. The supernatural power does not come out in the physical world. The power does not come out without deep love. It is possible either in the form realm or in the formless realm.

The mind with deeply earnest love touches ancestors' spirits or guardian angels which exist in the three realms. Ancestors' spirits or guardian angels are about responding to the mind. The sixth organ is about contacting the infinite information of the three realms as well as the information of Alaya. It is to tune the frequencies to each other. The sixth organ receives the mind of ancestors or guardian angels. They deliver hints or revelations for the future events or deep concerns.

Tuning frequencies between sibling relationships is called synchronized tuning. In the sibling relationship, the synchronized tuning is said not to be difficult because their frequencies are the same as each other. Measuring a quality of one subatomic particle instantly affects the same quality of a synchronized particle, even if the particles are widely separated. Albert Einstein called this phenomenon 'spooky actions at a distance.' Communication between once-collocated but now widely-separated synchronized particles is instantaneous and is not affected by the illusion of time and space between them.[158] The synchronized tuning is an important theory that supports the geomantic principles in Feng Shui. In geomancy, descendants' prosperity depends on the sites of the ancestors' tombs. If they are propitious sites, the descendants are

---

158 Roberta Grimes, *Fun of Dying*, Greater Reality Publications (2010), p 29

affirmatively affected, which is explained by the synchronized tuning between sibling relationships.

When somebody has gotten a hint or revelation from a dream it means that he has concentrated or been deeply concerned about a serious problem for a long time. James Pagel, director of the Rocky Mountain Sleep Disorders Center in Pueblo, Colorado, says that in examining nondreamers to look for some common connection that might explain why they didn't report dreams, that the one difference that surfaced is that none of them had any real creative outlets or even hobbies in waking life. He says further, that perhaps people who don't have a creative drive or creative role in waking life are able to function without dreams.[159]

In western science, dreaming is explained to be connected with a neural circuitry of the brain, or a certain substance from the brain. They admit that the no-holds-barred freedom of the dreaming brain is required for the creative process, so it should not be surprising if prolific dreamers also tend toward creative pursuits in waking life. Bert States, a former professor of English and theater at both Cornell University and the University of California at Santa Barbara, speculates that people who are drawn to the arts, theoretical science, and mathematics may have neural circuitry that has "an unusual capacity to make connections that do not involve serial and analytic reasoning—the very liberty acetylcholine [the neuromodulator that is predominant during REM] apparently enables in our dreams."[160]

Western scientists developed a technique for receiving hints or revelations for insoluble problems during dreaming. The participants relied on a technique called incubation, which can be used to focus on any sort of problem prior to sleep in hopes of encouraging the brain to find an out-of-the-box solution in its chaotically creative state during the night. Deirdre Barrett suggests a set of instructions for incubation beginning with briefly describing in

---

159 Andrea Rock, *The Mind at Night*, Basic Books, New York (2004), pp 146-147

160 Andrea Rock, *The Mind at Night*, Basic Books, New York (2004), p 146

Probing the Mind: How does Consciousness Work?

writing the problem you're stuck on and taking a look at what you've written before going to bed. When you're in bed, visualize yourself dreaming about the problem and tell yourself that you will do so just as you're drifting off. Keep a pen and paper at your bedside, and upon awakening write down traces of any dream you recall. Any success you have is not likely to come through the logical, linear thinking process that you rely on in waking, because the dreaming brain generally isn't physiologically geared for that.[161]

A similar nonconventional answer that came via dream incubation is illustrated in a story Deirdre Barrett recounts about a chemist in India who was trying to develop enzymes to refine crude oil. When he set out with the intent to focus on solving the problem as he went to sleep, he proceeded to have a dream about a big truck heaped with a load of rotten cabbages. The dream seemed useless at first. But upon returning to work on his project, he suddenly realized that the dream was significant after all: decomposing cabbages would break down into exactly the type of enzyme that would work for the crude-oil refinement project he was developing. Concludes Barrett: "Dreaming is, above all, a time when the unheard parts of ourselves are allowed to speak—we would do well to listen.[162]

The mind state of dream incubation is similar to that of praying to sincerely experience a desired outcome. The mind organ will be synchronized with that of its ancestors or guardian angels, and the mind organ will contact necessary information which might be provided by them. The information will appear vividly because the dream is <u>not</u> a silly dream. (Michael, please confirm)

---

161 Andrea Rock, *The Mind at Night*, Basic Books, New York (2004), p 148

162 Andrea Rock, *The Mind at Night*, Basic Books, New York (2004), p 148

26

A Dream Is Not a Mere Dream Any More

Andrea Rock defines a dream as a mental experience during sleep that can be described during waking consciousness. Some dreams are relatively mundane, while others are hallucinatory masterpieces. Of course we're likely to be able to provide a description only if we're awakened in the midst of a dream or immediately after it ends, but even though we don't recall the majority of our dreams they're still being produced each night, and research demonstrates that they can affect the quality of our waking hours whether we remember them or not.[163]

The ultimate reality show we partake of during waking life is often—like dreaming—a con job beautifully carried out by neural circuitry of astonishing complexity. Western scientists have come to realize through their research that our real life could be a false manifestation. A half century of dream research has demonstrated that dreaming is a rich form of consciousness that we should prize

---

163 Andrea Rock, *The Mind at Night*, Basic Books, New York (2004), pp viii-ix

no less than we do our experience of the world in waking hours.[164] The scientific research is approaching Daoism in which our life is an empty dream, or the Consciousness-Only theory in which all dharmas (phenomena) are transitory and false images.

Once upon a time Zhuang Zhou dreamed he was a butterfly, a butterfly flitting about happily enjoying himself. He did not know that he was Zhou. Suddenly he awoke, and was palpably Zhou. He did not know whether he was Zhou, who had dreamed of being a butterfly, or a butterfly dreaming that he was Zhou. Zhou illustrated that the distinction between waking and dreaming is another false dichotomy. Further, Zhou taught us that there is no distinction between life and death, and that the external world perceived by the physical organs is the transformation of things.[165]

The Diamond Sutra teaches "All composed things are like a dream, a phantom, a drop of dew, or a flash of lightning. That is how to meditate on them, that is how to observe them." This is a conclusion of the Sutra. It is about teaching not to cling to the five objects, color, sound, smell, taste and tactile objects, but to see the ultimate reality through the Mind.

What we think of as solid and concrete in the material world are the external objects of color (light), sound, scents, flavor, tactile objects and dharmas. The first five objects are perceived by the corresponding five sense organs and the sixth object is viewed by the sixth organ, the mind organ. In particular, the five objects are the subject matter that human beings try to seek for their lifetime. We are trying to see more beautiful things, to hear sweeter sounds, to smell more fragrant scents, to eat more delicious food, and finally to feel tactile objects to stimulate the peripheral nerves. Sexual contact is the top of the tactile objects and fulfills the five senses. Thus, desire and passion are the most difficult cravings for a human being to be free from. Desire and passion become the most powerful karmic energy for *samsara*, death and rebirth. Next is the

---

164 Andrea Rock, *The Mind at Night*, Basic Books, New York (2004), pp 199-200

165 https://www.wikipedia.org/

appetite for food, and the next is desire for wealth. However, there is no end for the desire for the material objects. The goal is to be free from desire for anything.

Although we may be bitten by a snake in a dream, the poison does not spread throughout the body; and although we become a king in a dream, when we awaken that is nothing. We therefore believe that a dream is vain and futile since it does not affect the physical body or the real life directly. Nonetheless, during sleep we are very serious and we cling to the dream like it is a real life. We believe the dream to be solid and real without ever realizing that we are dreaming. As a result, we sometimes scream, are tormented, or break out in a cold sweat during dreaming. When a snake attacks us in a dream, we move our body to avoid it even during sleep.

On the other hand, we believe that the real life experience in which the external objects are perceived by the five sense organs is more important than the dream in which the mind objects are perceived by the sixth organ. This is logically contradictory considering that mind is more important than the material. We believe what we perceive to be material objects to be real and important, whereas what we perceive as immaterial objects are considered to be dreamlike and unimportant. This is similar to our having more concern for our body than our mind despite that we think that the mind is more important than the body. This is also similar to the fact that we go to the hospital when we contract a cold virus, but we rarely treat our mind when a virus such as greed, anger, hatred, ignorance and so on comes into our mind.

A dream is not a dream any more. If what we perceive as the five objects with the corresponding five organs is an important real world to us, then what we perceive as mind objects with the mind organ is also as important as the real world. Dreaming is a valuable opportunity which can contact the subconscious or unconscious as well as the infinite information of the three realms. We can contact more information during dreaming than during waking hours because the sixth organ is ready to do it while the five organs are all sleeping.

We are in the waking state two thirds of a day for doing something, and one third of the day sleeping. We think that doing something is more important than sleeping. We think sleeping is just for our body. However, if we concern more about the one third, our life will be extended as much as the one third which will be meaningful time.

To stand in the physical body on the Moon, or on Venus, or on any of the celestial spheres will add to human knowledge, but only to knowledge of things transitory. Humanity's ultimate goal is transcendence over the transitory. Many sages said that our real life is an empty dream. If the five objects contacted by the five corresponding organs are believed to be solidly real life, the sixth objects contacted by the sixth organ will also be solid real life. On the other hand, if the dream for the sixth organ to contact the sixth objects is believed to be just a transitory dream, the real life for the five organs to contact the five objects will also be just a transitory dream.

27

More on the Mind Organ and Mind Information

There are five ways for humans to perceive external objects. All external objects are classified into five categories: color (light), sound, scent, flavor and tactile objects. The five objects are perceived by the corresponding five organs: the eye, sight organ, perceives color (light or form) only; the ear, sound organ, perceives sound only; and so on. The eye cannot perceive sound or scent; the ear cannot perceive light or flavor, and so on. Likewise, the mind organ perceives internal objects only, mind information.

Here is one important thing. When we perceive mind information by the mind organ, we perceive it in the form of six consciousnesses. In other words, when the mind organ perceives a mind information, we perceive it as a sight consciousness, a sound, a scent, a flavor and/or a touch feeling. This means that the mind organ has an ability to convert mind information to six consciousnesses and that the mind information contains six categories of information regarding the six objects. This means that immaterial information is converted into material informations by the mind organ. This is the intrinsic capability and fantastic characteristic of the mind organ. In this regard, the mind organ is analogous to a prism.

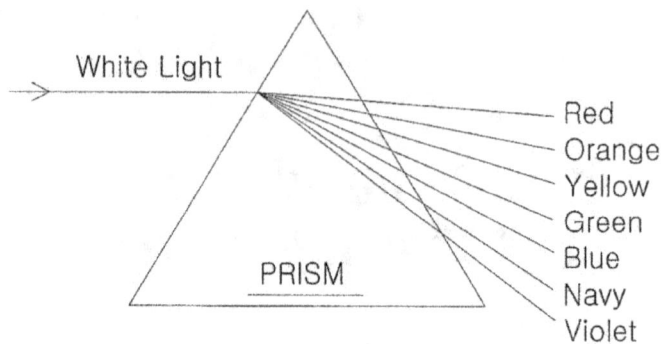

When a white light passes through a prism it is converted into rainbow colors: red, orange, yellow, green, blue, navy, and violet. Similarly, when a mind information passes through the mind organ, it is converted to six consciousnesses: sight, sound, scent, flavor, touch feeling, and dharma.

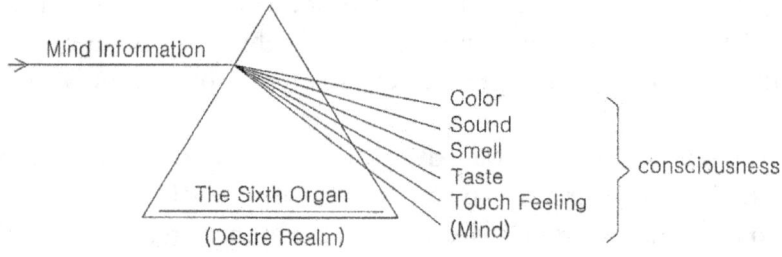

If a mind information is formed with sight information through the eyes, it will be converted to a sight consciousness; and if a mind information is formed with sound information through the ears, it will be converted to a sound consciousness. If a mind information is formed both with sight information through the eyes and sound information with the ears, it will be converted to both a sight and a sound.

Information stored in a digital camera is information on light (form), which can be converted or developed into a visual picture. Information in a digital camera cannot be reproduced into sound or smell. Information stored in an album is information on sound which can be regenerated into audio music, but information in an audio album cannot be reproduced into light or smell. On the other hand, mind information in Alaya can be converted into light (color), sound, smell, taste, or touch feeling. For example, we may easily recall the face of our late mother or father, which is a mind information of sight stored in Alaya. The mind information can be converted to light (form); i.e., a visual image by the sixth organ. Also, we may easily recall the voice of our late parents, which is a mind information of sound in Alaya. The mind information can be converted to sound; i.e., an auditory image by the sixth organ. Scent, flavor and touch feeling are similar.

In this sense, we may say that the mind organ has five inner organs. The eye in the mind organ is called mind eye or inner eye. Likewise, the mind organ has a mind ear, a mind nose, a mind tongue, and a mind body. When the mind organ reads a mind information and gives rise to a sight consciousness it is because it has an inner eye. Also, when the mind organ reads a mind information and gives rise to a sound consciousness it is because it has an inner ear.

The eye is the most important physical organ from the perspective of consciousness. As we hear that one picture is worth a thousand words, the ear is worth less than a thousandth of the eye, let alone the nose, tongue or body. The inner eye is also more important than the inner ear, the inner nose or the like. Among the Eightfold Paths,[166] the right view comes first.

---

166 The Eightfold Paths are the prescription to end suffering: right view, right intention, right speech, right action, right livelihood, right effort, right mindfulness, and right concentration.

The Buddha also regarded eyes as the most important among the physical sense organs. He explains about the five eyes: human eye, divine eye, eye of insight, eye of transcendent wisdom, and Buddha eye. The human eye is the physical eye we all have that can see flowers, the blue sky, and the white clouds. The divine eye is the eye of gods that sees very near and very far, and also sees in darkness and through obstacles. The eye of insight is the eye that can see the true nature of non-self in living beings and the impermanent nature of all objects of mind (dharmas). It is the eye of the *sravakas*[167] and *pratyeka*[168] *buddha*. The eye of transcendent wisdom is the eye of the bodhisattvas that can see the true nature of the emptiness of all objects of mind. It can see the nature of awakened mind and of the great vow. A bodhisattva with the eye of transcendent wisdom sees that he or she and all sentient beings share the same nature of emptiness, and therefore his or her liberation is one with the liberation of all sentient beings. The Buddha eye is the eye that can see clearly the past, the present, and the future, as well as the minds of all sentient beings in the past, the present, and the future.[169]

In the mind information stored in Alaya, the sight consciousness by eyes is the largest in terms of quantity. Thus, the mind information on sight is more than any other mind information on the remaining four objects, sound, scent, taste and tactile objects. Koch says, "We are very visual creatures. One-third of the brain is given over to vision, and we have all sorts of visual experiences

---

167 One who listens to the teaching of Buddha. The term originally applied to Buddha's immediate disciples, but later came to mean those who follow the teachings of Hinayana Buddhism.

168 Solitary Awakened one who due to insight into the Twelve Links of Interdependent Co-Arising has attained enlightenment on his own and only for himself.

169 Thich Nhat Hanh, *The Diamond That Cuts Through Illusion*, Parallex Press, California (1992), pp 91-92

that can be analyzed, including vivid dreams."[170] If we do not close our eyes, a lot of visual information enters into Alaya. Our eyes perceive not only all forms but all concepts by written letters. We believe that the brain will take one third for treating the large quantity of visual information. As the visual information to be processed is much more than other informations, the brain may have been developed to adapt for processing the data. Although the visual information is not stored in the brain, a larger portion of the brain will be needed for processing it. The second largest information is auditory. Our ears are open to all sounds. Our ears perceive all noises and all concepts by spoken language. As long as sounds are produced, sound consciousness is generated and the auditory information is stored in Alaya in the state of consciousness. Olfactory information or gustatory information is much less than auditory information. Both of these informations are very limited compared with the visual or auditory. The smell consciousness is generated by directly contacting particles of scents with the nose. The taste consciousness is also generated by contacting directly particles of flavor with the tongue. The sense of touch is also produced by contacting directly matter with the skin. On the other hand, the sight or sound consciousness is generated by contacting indirectly the objects with the organs through light or sound waves.

The mind information which is mainly read by the mind organ is stored in its own Alaya, but a mind organ can also read the mind information stored in others' Alaya. Thus, the mind information which can be read by the mind organ extends throughout the cosmos. In *Yogacarabhumi-sastra*, the dharmas as the sixth object are explained as both one's own objects and others' objects.[171] We believe that the former means the mind information stored in one's own Alaya, and the latter the mind information of others' Alaya which exists in the cosmos of the three realms. We call the former

---

170 Andrea Rock, *The Mind at Night*, Basic Books, New York (2004), pp 177-178

171 Hyungkeun Oh, *Study of the Sixth Consciousness in Mere-Consciousness*, Bulgyosasangsa, Seoul (1991), p 296

'Alaya information' and the latter 'infinite information of the three realms.'

In order to understand the dharmas (mind information) as the sixth object, we have to understand the Buddhist cosmology in which three realms are defined: realm of desire, realm of form, and formless realm. The realm of desire is the lowest of the three realms of existence in the Buddhist cosmology. It covers the earth and several celestial realms. Above it is the realm of form, and above these two is the formless realm. The realm of form is so called because subtle material form still exists in it. In the formless realm, beings exist without material form. The beings in the formless realm have only mind, consciousness, or mind consciousness.

In one aspect of the Consciousness-Only Theory, the cosmos is classified into eighteen boundaries from the perspective of consciousness. According to this classification, the six organs constitute six boundaries, the six objects constitute another six boundaries, and the six consciousnesses constitute a further six boundaries.

The eighteen boundaries of the cosmos have important meaning in connection with the three realms of cosmology. In *Abhidharmakosha* written by Vasubandhu, the realm of desire consists of eighteen boundaries of consciousness, the realm of form consists of fourteen boundaries of consciousness, and the formless realm consists of three boundaries of consciousness. In other words, the realm of desire has eighteen boundaries of consciousness, which are six organs, six objects and six consciousnesses; the realm of form has fourteen boundaries of consciousness (excluding smell and flavor, and their two consciousnesses), which are six organs, four objects and four consciousnesses; and the formless realm has three boundaries of consciousness, which are only the sixth organ, the sixth object and the sixth consciousness. These are represented below:

Probing the Mind: How does Consciousness Work?

Eighteen Boundaries in the Realm of Desire

(Sense Organ)	Eye	Ear	Nose	Tongue	Body	Mind
(Object)	Light (Color)	Noise	Scent	Flavor	Tactile Object	Mind Information
(Consciousness)	Sight	Sound	Smell	Taste	Touch	Sixth Consciousness

Fourteen Boundaries in the Realm of Form

(Sense Organ)	Eye	Ear	Nose	Tongue	Body	Mind
(Object)	Light (Color)	Noise	*Scent*	*Flavor*	Tactile Object	Mind Information
(Consciousness)	Sight	Sound	*Smell*	*Taste*	Touch	Sixth Consciousness

Three Boundaries in the Formless Realm

(Sense Organ)	*Eye*	*Ear*	*Nose*	*Tongue*	*Body*	Mind
(Object)	*Light (Color)*	*Noise*	*Scent*	*Flavor*	*Tactile Object*	Mind Information
(Consciousness)	*Sight*	*Sound*	*Smell*	*Taste*	*Touch*	Sixth Consciousness

As shown in the *Abhidharmakosha*'s explanation, we can easily understand eighteen boundaries of consciousness in the realm of desire since it is clear that sentient beings have six organs, there exist six objects, and there arise six consciousnesses from the six organs and the six objects. In the realm of form, however, there do not exist smell and flavor, and, as smell and flavor do not exist, smell consciousness and taste consciousness also do not exist. But, in the realm of form, nose and tongue are not non-existent because form (body) still exists in the realm of form. This is one of the striking discoveries in connection with human consciousness. In the formless realm, there exist only three boundaries of consciousness: the sixth organ, the sixth object and the sixth consciousness. In the formless realm, the physical body does not exist any more. Therefore, it's no wonder that the sixth organ and the sixth object (dharma: mind information) only exist. As long as the sixth organ and the sixth object exist, the sixth consciousness will arise.

If the sixth organ contacts an information of the form realm, it will not perceive nose consciousness and tongue consciousness, and if the sixth organ contacts an information of the formless realm, it will not perceive the first five consciousnesses, but the sixth consciousness only. During dreaming that you were eating something, if you perceived a smell or a flavor, you dreamed with the information of the desire realm, while, if you did not perceive a smell or a flavor, you dreamed with the information of the form realm.

PART III

The Mind After Death

28

The Unknown World of 'After-Death'

We do not think very much about death. Even if our parents, relatives or close friends die we regard it as inevitable, or as not directly applicable to ourselves at this time in our lives. Though we consider that our life is short, transient and impermanent, our attitude toward death is to offer condolences to the dead or to express it to the bereaved family without thinking seriously about it. As young people do not think seriously about aging and healthy people do not think seriously about illness, living people do not think seriously about death.

We are apt to consider that death or illness will occur to others but not to ourselves, at least in the near future. It seems that although others may suffer from or die of a virulent disease, we will not. Even if we believe that we shall die sometime later, it will not be in the present moment and probably not until the very far future. Furthermore, most of us do not consider after-death or the world of after-death even though we have growing concern about well-dying as well as well-being in the twenty-first century. Death is still mainly outside our concern.

The only thing uncertain in life is when we will die, whereas about the only certainty of life is that we *will* definitely die. The reason that we do not think very much about death is because life is much more important than death; we have to think about our life and do something with it before we think about death. Despite the fact that we are beings who must die someday, our focus is on pleasing the five sense organs. We do not find it necessary to think about death because we do not know anything about after death, and this prohibits us from thinking seriously about it. Furthermore, as it is assumed that we cannot fully know this domain, we are dealing with guesses, perhaps inspired, and generalities rather than final truth.[172] We therefore think that as the world of after-death is not explained with scientific knowledge, it seems right for us not to think about death very much.

Buddhism explains that when a living thing dies, the physical body is scattered into four elements: earth, water, fire and wind. If the physical body is scattered like that, does anything continue to exist? Is everything ceased? While many people are committed to the belief that death brings the total cessation of personal existence, many others claim to be agnostic, quite honestly admitting that they don't know what happens at death and therefore have no views on the matter at all. At first glance this seems quite a reasonable and intelligent position to take, for, after all, who among us really does know what happens at death?[173]

Regardless of whether we claim to be agnostic about death or not, the first question we will have concerning death is what will existence be like after death? Does something like soul or spirit exist, and if so, what will the existence be? Though we may suspect that there will exist something like a soul when a human body dies there is no scientific evidence to show it. There have been lots of attempts to prove it: some people have tried to take a picture of a soul, some have tried to record the voice of a soul, and some have tried to measure the weight of a soul. In spite of all these efforts, the life after death remains a mysterious domain to us.

---

172 Francisco J. Varela, *Sleeping, Dreaming, and Dying*, Wisdom Publications, Boston (1997), p 133

173 B. Alan Wallace, *Buddhism with an Attitude*, Snow Lion Publications, New York (2003), p 36

Probing the Mind: How does Consciousness Work?

A Gallup poll taken in 1982 showed that nearly one in four Americans believe in reincarnation. This is an astonishing statistic considering how dominant the materialist and scientific philosophy is in almost every aspect of life. However, most people still have only the most shadowy idea about life after death, and no idea of what it might be like. Again and again, people tell me they cannot bring themselves to believe in something for which there is no evidence. But that is hardly proof, is it, that it does not exist?[174]

As long as we believe in reincarnation we can say that we believe in the existence of soul, and as long as we believe in the existence of soul we may not think that the soul is without consciousness like a stone or a piece of dry wood. Despite no scientific, objective evidence, where does the belief in reincarnation or the existence of soul come from? Is it from a personal experience, a religious belief, or a simple idea? Allan Wallace advocates consciousness after death based on the experiences of meditation practitioners.

With science providing so little actual knowledge about the nature and origins of consciousness, what grounds do we have for the belief in eternal, mindless death? As soothing as this notion may be, it seems to be little more than sheer conjecture at this point. Moreover, it simply ignores the experiences of countless contemplatives throughout the world who have achieved deep states of meditative concentration and claim to have seen for themselves the existence of their own past lives. Buddhist contemplatives do not regard themselves in 'terrible muddle' with regard to consciousness. Perhaps that's because they are part of a rigorous heritage that has taken the experiential investigation of consciousness very seriously for over two millennia, whereas modern science largely overlooked consciousness until the last decade of the twentieth century. And it still has no rigorous means of investigating consciousness firsthand, which is the only way we even know that consciousness exists. No wonder science is still so much in the dark in this regard![175]

---

174 Sogyal Rinpoche, *The Tibetan Book of Living and Dying*, Harper One, New York (2002), p87

175 B. Alan Wallace, *Buddhism with an Attitude*, Snow Lion Publications, New York (2003), p 38

In the scientific world, the brain is dead when the physical body dies, consciousness is dead when the brain is dead, and consciousness after death does not exist. They think that the death of the physical body is the final endpoint. They do not think that the life after death; i.e., the consciousness after death, is worth striving to discover. On the one hand, though many people believe that something like a soul exists after death, on the other hand, many people still believe that nothing exists after death or take the position that they do not have any idea.

Religious Sages said "The consciousness does not die. It's only the body that dies."[176] Westerners limit the human life cycle to a short span between birth and death; Easterners see an eternal cycle of birth, death, and rebirth. Westerners argue over whether the afterlife could be as real as the physical world; Easterners declare that both are mental projections.[177]

What kind of consciousness does the afterlife have? Is the consciousness of the afterlife similar to that of the sleeping state? The five sense organs do not work any more in either sleep or in death, but while the five organs cease working temporarily in sleep, they cease working permanently in death. If we awaken from sleep they begin to operate again, but in death they do not. This is the only difference between sleep and death, or between dream and death. If the consciousness of the afterlife is similar to that of the dreaming state, will the afterlife also entail suffering, screaming or sweating as in dreams?

---

[176] Ani Tenzin Palmo, Reflections on a Mountain Lake, Snow Lion Publications, New York (2002), p 154

[177] Deepak Chopra, *Life After Death*, Three Rivers Press, New York (2006), p 41

29

What Is Soul?

I knew an L.A. woman who as a child had come home from school, and as she entered the door she saw her young cousin from Chicago standing in the corner waiting for her. Both were about eight at the time. The cousin didn't speak, and the girl ran to tell her mother that they had a visitor. When she entered the kitchen her mother was crying. The little girl asked why, and her mother said that there had been a sudden death in the family. It was the cousin from Chicago, who had died that morning. Did the girl see her cousin as a vision, a premonition, or merely as a coincidental act of imagination? As she tells the story, she saw her cousin 'for real.' Yet what do we mean by 'for real' except that something is convincing? This encounter with a departed relative can be judged as either hallucinatory or deeply spiritual depending not on the event itself but on who is looking at it.[178]

Besides the L.A. girl's story there are numerous real life experiences about ghosts or phantoms. We cannot see a ghost or phantom with our physical eyes—the ghost or phantom can be seen with the sixth organ, in particular, with the mind's eye (inner eye) of the sixth organ. As such experience is not in the domain of the

---

178 Deepak Chopra, Life After Death, Three Rivers Press, New York (2006), pp 87-88

material world it has not been proven in a scientific manner. Up to now, science has been limited to the five sense objects and has not been extended to the sixth object or the sixth organ.

Because the dominant western scientific view equates the mind with the brain, and the person with the mind, the objective of modern medicine has been to keep the brain alive, sometimes at the expense of other organ systems.[179] If the brain is dead, western science seems not to consider it as worthy of additional research. Although experimental researches such as near-death studies have been carried out, the fundamental research on consciousness or mind seems not to have been carried out totally separated from the brain in western science.

Unlike traditional scientists, psychologists and psychoanalysts predominantly believe in the existence of soul or spirit. C. G. Jung said, "All science (Wissenschaft) is a function of the soul, in which all knowledge is rooted. The soul is the greatest of all cosmic miracles, it is the condition sine qua non of the world as an object. It is exceedingly astonishing that the Western world (apart from very rare exceptions) seems to have so little appreciation of this being so."[180]

However, Jung asserted that the soul is a transcendent consciousness which descendants inherit from their ancestors, or universally as a member of the human race, but this does not directly mean that the soul exists after death. The concept of transcendent consciousness offered by Jung is not to explain something existing after death, but rather he asserted that there is some information in the human consciousness which is not acquired during a given lifetime. Jung did not uncover how the transcendent consciousness is inherited by descendants or by every member of the human race,

---

179 Francisco J. Varela, *Sleeping, Dreaming, and Dying*, Wisdom Publications, Boston (1997), p 141

180 Erwin Schrodinger, *What is Life? with Mind and Matter and Autobiographical Sketches*, Cambridge University press, Cambridge (2008), p 119-120

but, if it is done, many things about the soul or spirit after death will be revealed.

Each of the four major religions affirms that there is a subtle and death-surviving element—vital and psychical—in the physical body of flesh and blood. It may be a permanent entity or Self such as the Brahmanic *Atma*, the Islamic *Ruh*, and the Christian *Soul*, or it may be only a complex of activities (or *Skandha*), psychical and physical, with life as their function to the Buddhists. These *Skandha* do not constitute a simple Being or state of existence, but rather are a complex in continual change, and therefore, a series of physical and psychical momentary states successively generated the one from the other, a continuous transformation. Thus to none of these Faiths is death an absolute ending, but to all it is only the separation of the *Psyche* from the gross body.[181]

All religions, including these four religions, admit the existence of soul or spirit. Though there are differences in detailed descriptions from religion to religion, they admit that something exists as psychical or physical (or consciousness) after death. On the other hand, all religions traditionally persuade people to lead a life of virtue due to fear of not only death, but also unknowns of the next life. When they assert the existence of soul or spirit after death it seems to be regarded not as a means for achieving the objective of religion by introducing the next life, but rather a result of insights and intuitions by the saints of each religion.

If something exists after death, what will it be? As it is not a material existence such as the five objects, color (light), sound, smell, taste, or tactile object, it must be immaterial and intangible. On the other hand if the existence does not have consciousness or mind, such as stones at the side of a road or fallen leaves in the woods, it will not be important or worth much for us and it will never be in the region of our concern, and will never be regarded as an object of the unknown. However, although we do not know about the existence after death, it seems to us that we have no

---

181 W.Y. Evans-Wentz, *The Tibetan Book of The Dead*, Oxford University Press, New York (1960), p lxviii

choice but to believe that something like consciousness or mind must be present and active in this existence.

Buddhists take the position that consciousness remains after death. Although the existence is not called a soul or a ghost in Buddhism, Buddhists are certain of a continuum of consciousness as an existence working and changing endlessly after death. The basis of the Buddhist assertion of the conservation of consciousness is the experience of the Buddha himself, corroborated by countless Buddhist contemplatives after him. The insights from such direct experience were then formalized within the context of a coherent, rational account of the nature and causes of consciousness. Many Buddhists and other contemplatives have claimed to know that consciousness continues on after death, and many have given clear instructions on how to discover this truth for oneself.[182]

Tibetan Buddhism explains very specifically about the continuum of consciousness of after-death. The book, *The Tibetan Book of The Dead*, which the founder of Tibetan Buddhism, Padma Sambhava, wrote, explains about the continuum of consciousness. The book maintains, not in virtue of tradition or belief, but on the sound basis of the unequivocal testimony of yogins who claim to have died and re-entered the human womb consciously.[183] According to the Tibetan theory of the book, the culminating process of death ends only upon the complete separation of the Bardo body from its earth-plane counterpart.[184] The Bardo body means a continuum of consciousness at death. It is also called the Intermediary Being or the the Middle Existence or frequently the Soul.

Bardo literally means 'between *Bar* and *do*;' i.e., 'between two states'—the state between death and rebirth—and, therefore,

---

[182] B. Alan Wallace, *Buddhism with an Attitude*, Snow Lion Publications, New York (2003), p 37

[183] W.Y. Evans-Wentz, *The Tibetan Book of The Dead*, Oxford University Press, New York (1960), p v

[184] W.Y. Evans-Wentz, *The Tibetan Book of The Dead*, Oxford University Press, New York (1960), p 18

Probing the Mind: How does Consciousness Work?

'Intermediate' or 'Transitional' State.[185] The different *bardos*, therefore, represent different states of consciousness of our life: the state of waking consciousness, the normal consciousness of a being born into our human world, known in Tibetan as the *skyes-nas bardo*; the state of dream consciousness (*rmi-lam bardo*); the state of *dhyana*, or trance consciousness, in profound meditation (*bsam-gtan bardo*); the state of the experiencing of death (*hchhi-kha bardo*); the state of experiencing of Reality (*chhos-nyid bardo*); the state of rebirth consciousness (*srid-pa bardo*).[186]

Many cognitive scientists claim to know that consciousness ceases at death. They believe that despite the fact that modern science has no means of objectively detecting the presence or absence of consciousness in anything—human, animal, plant, or

---

185 W.Y. Evans-Wentz, *The Tibetan Book of The Dead*, Oxford University Press, New York (1960), p 28

186 W.Y. Evans-Wentz, *The Tibetan Book of The Dead*, Oxford University Press, New York (1960), p lxi
"In other words, the six *bardos* are: the natural state of Bardo while in the womb (*Skye-gnas Bardo* (pron. *Kye-nay Bardo*): 'Intermediate State', or 'State of Uncertainty, of the place of birth (or while in the womb)); the Bardo of the dream-state (*Rmi-lam Bardo* (pron. *Mi-lam Bardo*): 'Intermediate State', or 'State of Uncertainty, during the experiencing of the dream-state); the Bardo of ecstatic equilibrium, while in deep meditation (*Ting-nge-hzin Bsam-gtam Bardo* (pron. *Tin-ge-zin Sam-tam Bardo*): 'Intermediate state', or 'State of Uncertainty, during the experiencing of *Dyhana* (Meditation) in *Samadhi* (Ecstatic equilibrium))'; the Bardo of the moment of death (*Hchi-khahi Bardo* (pron. *Chi-khai Bardo*): 'Intermediate State', or 'State of Uncertainty, of the dying moment (or moment of death)); the Bardo during the experiencing of Reality (*Chos-nyid Bardo* (pron. *Cho-nyid Bardo*): 'Intermediate State', or 'State of Uncertainty, during the experiencing of Reality); the Bardo of the inverse process of sangsaric existence (*Lugs-hbyung Srid-pahi Bardo* (pron. *Lu-jung Sid-pai Bardo*): 'Intermediate State', or 'State of Uncertainty, in the inverse process of sangsaric (worldly) existence'—the state wherein the Knower is seeking rebirth)." (W.Y. Evans-Wentz, *The Tibetan Book of The Dead*, Oxford University Press, New York (1960), p 102)

mineral.[187] Their argument that the teachings are untrue merely because the scientist himself has no conscious memory of his many births and deaths is scientifically untenable. The field of the normal man's sense perceptions is, as can be demonstrated, narrowly circumscribed and extremely limited. There are objects and colors he cannot see, sounds he cannot hear, odors he cannot smell, tastes he cannot taste, and feelings he cannot feel. And beyond his work-a-day consciousness, which he assumes to be his only consciousness, there are other consciousnesses of which yogins and saints have cognizance, and of which psychologists are beginning to glean some, but as yet very little, understanding.[188]

Near death experience is one approach for studying the consciousness of after-death. Dr. van Lommel, who conducted the Dutch study of near-death experiences, screened 344 patients whose heart had gone into chaotic twitching instead of a normal regular heartbeat in the hospital. Talking to them within days of being revived, van Lommel discovered that anesthesia or medications didn't affect their experience. What he marvels most at, however, are those reports of consciousness in the absence of brain activity.[189]

At that moment these people are not only conscious; their consciousness is even more expansive than ever. They can think extremely clearly, have memories going back to their earliest childhood and experience an intense connection with everything and everyone around them. And yet the brain shows no activity at all![190]

Lommel's observations undercut the dying-brain theory of materialism, since the brain has stopped functioning before the

---

187 B. Alan Wallace, *Buddhism with an Attitude,* Snow Lion Publications, New York (2003), p 37

188 W.Y. Evans-Wentz, *The Tibetan Book of The Dead*, Oxford University Press, New York (1960), p viii

189 Deepak Chopra, *Life After Death*, Three Rivers Press, New York (2006), p 43

190 Deepak Chopra, *Life After Death*, Three Rivers Press, New York (2006), p 43

near death experience begins. Now it is certain that consciousness does neither exist in nor come from the brain. In the Consciousness Only Theory, the world of after-death as well as the real life is regarded as a projection of consciousness. We do not know whether the projection of consciousness after death is manifested by the consciousness which had been experienced during lifetimes, or if it is manifested by the conscious activities after death, but we can hardly deny that consciousness remains after death.

In order to understand the consciousness of after-death, we have to understand that of the waking life. In the waking state, the six organs work so as to give rise to six consciousnesses, but we do not concern ourselves very much with the sixth. The consciousness after death has nothing to do with the five organs, so it should be approached from understanding of the sixth consciousness (mind), the Manas (seventh) and the Alaya (eighth).

What is left losing breath, body, and mind is what the Buddhists call 'unborn awareness,' or 'the clear light of death.' Unborn awareness is awareness in its primordial state, unstructured by experience or by a human brain and nervous system. The primordial nature of awareness is not structured by a sense of subject versus object. Unborn awareness is also not conditioned by being a good or bad person or even by being human. For centuries, contemplatives who have maintained continuity of awareness throughout death and subsequent reincarnation have described the details of the death experience, including the nature of unborn awareness. All of us will have the same opportunity as contemplatives to experience primordial awareness at death. We have no choice. We will lose our breath, our bodies, and our minds, and primordial awareness is what will be left. We will have an opportunity to ascertain the unobscured, unborn nature of awareness when we die; but whether we will be able to make use of this opportunity is another question. If we are offered a meal but don't know how to open our mouth, we cannot eat. Death offers us primordial awareness on a plate. Will we be prepared to take the opportunity of ascertaining it, tapping into this wellspring of wisdom, compassion, and power? Whether or not unborn awareness is ascertained during death is contingent upon whether it has been ascertained during life. The way to ascertain unborn awareness during life is to practice.[191]

---

[191] B. Alan Wallace, *Buddhism with an Attitude,* Snow Lion Publications, New York (2003), pp 111-112

30

Mechanism of After-Death Consciousness

In order to understand consciousness of the after-death state, we have to understand that of the waking life. In the waking state the six organs work so as to give rise to the six consciousnesses, but we understand only the five consciousnesses. As discussed before, we do not concern ourselves very much about the sixth (mind), since we do not truly comprehend the mind and mind information. In 'mind' as a general term, we believe that the mind is generated in the brain, and we believe that the brain produces thinking.

Buddhism defines the sixth organ as a mind organ, and the corresponding object as mind information, like the relation of the five sense organs and the corresponding five objects. It teaches that the sixth consciousness is generated when the mind organ contacts a mind information. Further, it defines a seventh as thinking consciousness (Manas) and an eighth as storehouse consciousness (Alaya). The consciousness after death has nothing to do with the five organs. It should be approached from understanding of the sixth consciousness, Manas and Alaya. In other words, even after we die, the sixth consciousness is generated by the mind organ and the mind information, thinking is processed in the seventh, and the arising consciousness by the sixth and seventh is stored in the eighth. These three consciousnesses constitute after-death consciousness.

Death is quite similar to sleep in that the five organs do not work. During sleep, they almost cease working, but not completely. The only difference between sleep and death is that the five organs resume working when we awaken from sleep, but they do not return to the functioning state after death. Anytime we awaken from sleep we can revitalize our memory as well as all consciousnesses, but in death the five organs cannot be reawakened. In this sense, death looks like 'eternal sleep'.

In the mechanism of after-death consciousness, the first five consciousnesses through the five sense organs are cut off. The information on the five sense objects is no longer input into the sixth organ. In death, only the sixth organ remains, and it contacts mind information from Alaya. When the sixth organ contacts the mind information a series of thinking is generated and constitutes the seventh consciousness. Mental activities also arise in this thinking cycle, and the seventh consciousness and mental activities are stored in Alaya.

In the waking state a tremendous amount of information on sense objects is input through the five sense organs, and this information activates the mind information stored in Alaya. The activated information results in further associations and related thinking processes so that the mind seems to run away on its own in the 'drunken monkey' effect. On the other hand, in sleep or death the mind information is not activated as much as in the waking state since the sixth organ only sporadically contacts the mind information in these states. If the consciousness in the waking state is like a motion picture, that in sleep or death is like a few snapshots or slides. In sleep or death, the thinking process operates very slowly, sometimes appearing to be stopped. The intermittent contacts of mind information constitute dreams during sleep or consciousness in death. Of course, the mind information which is contacted

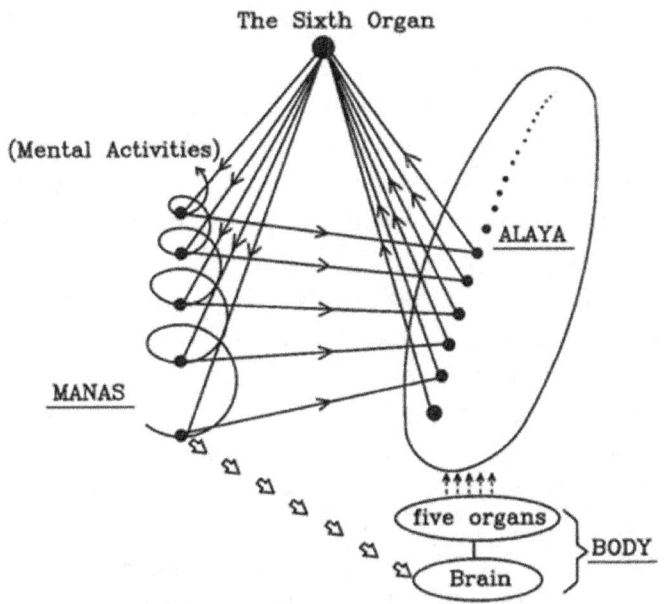

Mechanism of Consciousness During a Dream

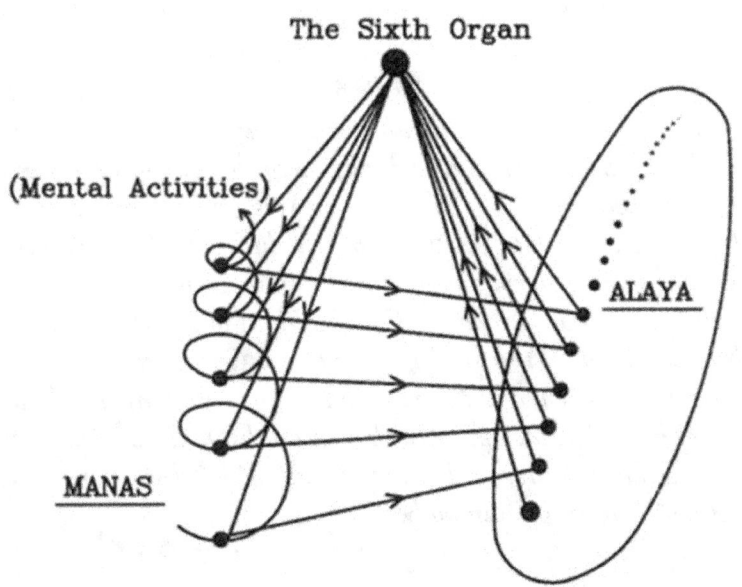

Mechanism of Consciousness After-Death

by the mind organ is not limited to its own Alaya. The mind organ contacts the infinite information of the three realms which is stored not only in its own Alaya, but also in others.

We might ask how the sixth organ will contact the mind information after death, and which information among the tremendous amount of mind information stored in all Alaya can be contacted by the sixth organ in death? Information that the deceased cared deeply about during his lifetime will be easily contacted by the sixth organ, and the information of concern at the time of death will also be more readily available. Needless to say, most of the information stored in Alaya through a lifetime is about the five sense objects, and mostly about desire, anger and ignorance. All of our goals during a lifetime are to go a good school, to be well educated, to marry a good spouse, to get a higher position, to make more money, to live happily, and so forth. They are materialistic desires, sexual desires, passion, appetite desires, desire for honor, desire for sleep, and so on. Besides these, thoughts, beliefs, teachings, and the like will also be reflected through the sixth organ.

As a man is taught, so he believes. Thoughts being things, they may be planted like seeds in the mind of the child and completely dominate his mental content. Given the favourable soil of the will to believe, whether the seed-thoughts be sound or unsound, whether they be of pure superstition or of realizable truth, they take root and flourish, and make the man what he is mentally. Accordingly, for a Buddhist of some other School, as for a Hindu, or a Moslem, or a Christian, the Bardo experiences would be appropriately different: the Buddhist's or the Hindu's thought-forms, as in a dream state, would give rise to corresponding visions of the deities of the Buddhist or Hindu pantheon; a Moslem's to visions of the Moslem Paradise; a Christian's, to visions of the Christian Heaven, or an American Indian's to visions of the Happy Hunting Ground. And, similarly, the materialist will experience after-death visions as negative and as empty and as deityless as any he ever dreamt while in the human body.[192]

---

192 W.Y. Evans-Wentz, *The Tibetan Book of The Dead*, Oxford University Press, New York (1960), pp 33-34

Probing the Mind: How does Consciousness Work?

The world of consciousness in death is similar to that of a dream. In Greek mythology, sleep and death are brothers, Morpheus and Thanatos. The world of after-death consciousness is similar to that of dream consciousness. Dream consciousness returns to real life consciousness everyday when awakened from sleep, but after-death consciousness does not return to real life consciousness for a very long time, until reborn. Just as we feel happy or suffering in a dream, a similar consciousness occurs after death. The after-death consciousness is generated on the basis of the mind information that has been stored in a person's Alaya during their lifetime. If they have stored a lot of information on Buddha in their Alaya, the information on Buddha will be reflected; and if a lot of information on Jesus Christ had been stored, the information on Jesus Christ will be reflected.

This phenomenon appears in near death experiences. These people in a near death experience see Christ, or the saints, or their relatives; something that is familiar to them, obviously. When one reads the bardo descriptions one sees descriptions of peaceful and wrathful appearances wearing Indian clothes and adornments. It is true that in fact everyone will have their own cultural projections on the experience. The whole presentation of deities within mandalas comes from India, and it thus draws upon Indian culture. It's very likely that a person from another culture would have different experiences. A recent, extraordinary Tibetan scholar by the name Geshe Gendun Choephel said that since Buddhism came from India, the Sambhogakaya, the very subtle body of a Buddha, is depicted as wearing a crown and ornaments of an Indian king. Whereas, he said, if Buddhism had originated in Tibet, then maybe the headdress would be of a Tibetan style. And if Buddhism had originated in China, then the Sambhogakaya might be depicted with a long beard.[193]

The apparitional visions seen by the deceased in the Intermediate State are not visions of reality, but nothing more than

---

[193] Francisco J. Varela, *Sleeping, Dreaming, and Dying*, Wisdom Publications, Boston (1997), p 211

the hallucinatory embodiments of the thought-forms born of the mental-content of the percipient; or, in other words, they are the intellectual impulses which have assumed personified form in the after-death dream-state.[194] None of all these deities or spiritual beings has any real individual existence any more than have human beings.[195]

Rationally considered, each person's after-death experiences are entirely dependent upon his or her own mental content. The after-death state is very much like a dream state. What one dreams depends on what mental content one has. What the deceased on the Bardo plane sees is due entirely to his own mental content. There are no visions of gods or of demons, of heavens or of hells, other than those born of the hallucinatory karmic thought-forms constituting his personality, which is an impermanent product arising from the thirst for existence and from the will to live and to believe.[196] Every vision in which spiritual beings, gods or demons, or paradises or places of torment and purgation play a part, in a Bardo or any Bardo-like dream or ecstasy, is purely illusionary—being based upon sangsaric phenomena.[197]

---

194 W.Y. Evans-Wentz, *The Tibetan Book of The Dead*, Oxford University Press, New York (1960), p 31

195 W.Y. Evans-Wentz, *The Tibetan Book of The Dead*, Oxford University Press, New York (1960), p 32

196 W.Y. Evans-Wentz, *The Tibetan Book of The Dead*, Oxford University Press, New York (1960), p 34

197 W.Y. Evans-Wentz, *The Tibetan Book of The Dead*, Oxford University Press, New York (1960), p 35

31

Communication with the Dead

In connection with the continuum of consciousness from birth to death to rebirth, the Tibetan Buddhism explains six Bardos. Among them, the last three Bardos relate to the death to rebirth. The Bardo of the moment of death is Hchi-khahi Bardo (pron. Chi-khai Bardo) which means 'Intermediate State' or 'State of Uncertainty, of the dying moment (or moment of death). The next Bardo is Chos-nyid Bardo (pron. Cho-nyid Bardo) which experiences Reality. The last Bardo is Lugs-hbyung Srid-pahi Bardo (pron. Lu-jung Sid-pai Bardo) which is 'Intermediate State' or 'State of Uncertainty, in the inverse process of sangsaric (worldly) existence—the state wherein the Knower (the deceased) is seeking rebirth.[198]

In Tibet, the *hpho-bo* (pron. *pho-o*) performance is carried out for a dying person when the death-symptoms are completed. The priest called *hpho-bo* or 'extractor of the consciousness-principle' is about extracting consciousness from the dying person. In the performance, the priest reads *The Tibetan Book of The Dead* for Chi-khai Bardo of the dying moment and Cho-nyid Bardo experi-

---

[198] W.Y. Evans-Wentz, *The Tibetan Book of The Dead*, Oxford University Press, New York (1960), p 102

encing Reality. By doing so, the dying person or the deceased can understand what stage he is in, in the dying process, and get some inspiration or guidance he will need.[199]

O nobly-born (so-and-so), listen. Now thou art experiencing the Radiance of the Clear Light of Pure Reality. Recognize it. O nobly-born, the present intellect, in real nature void, not formed into anything as regards characteristics or colour, naturally void, is the very Reality, the All-Good.

Thine own intellect, which is now voidness, yet not to be regarded as of the voidness of nothingness, but as being the intellect itself, unobstructed, shining, thrilling, and blissful, is the very consciousness, the All-good Buddha.

Thine own consciousness, not formed into anything, in reality void, and the intellect, shining and blissful,—these two—are inseparable. The union of them is the Dharmakaya state of Perfect Enlightenment.

Thine own consciousness, shining, void, and inseparable from the Great Body of Radiance, hath no birth, nor death, and is the Immutable Light—Buddha Amitabha.

Knowing this is sufficient. Recognizing the voidness of thine own intellect to be Buddhahood, and looking upon it as being thine own consciousness, is to keep thyself in the [state of the] divine mind of the Buddha.[200]

If the deceased has learned, as the Bardo Thoedol (*The Tibetan Book of The Dead*) directs, to identify himself with the Eternal, the Dharma, the Imperishable Light of Buddhahood within, then the fears of death are dissipated like a cloud before the rising sun. Then he knows that whatever he may see, hear, or feel, in the hour of his departure from this life, is but a reflection of his own conscious and subconscious mental content; and no mind-created illusion

---

199 W.Y. Evans-Wentz, *The Tibetan Book of The Dead*, Oxford University Press, New York (1960), p 102

200 W.Y. Evans-Wentz, *The Tibetan Book of The Dead*, Oxford University Press, New York (1960), pp 95-96

can then have power over him if he knows its origin and is able to recognize it.[201]

Westerners have a doubt on the religious performance. How can a dead person hear *The Tibetan Book of The Dead*? Sogyal Rinpoche responds to the question: "The simple reply is that the consciousness of the dead person, when it is invoked by the power of prayer, is able to read our minds and can feel exactly whatever we may be thinking or meditating on. That is why there is no obstacle to the dead person's understanding *The Tibetan Book of The Dead* or practices done on their behalf, even though they may be recited in Tibetan. For the dead person, language is no barrier at all, for the essential meaning of the text can be understood fully and directly by his or her mind."[202] Although they may have been, when living, blind of the eye, or deaf, or lame, yet on this After-Death Plane thine eyes will see forms, and thine ears will hear sounds, and all other sense-organs of thine will be unimpaired and very keen and complete.[203] That is, the mind organ reads the mind information. When dead, the five sense organs are dead, but the mind organ is developed to read mind information. This is analogous to, when living, if somebody loses sight and becomes blind, his hearing faculty or tactile sensation becomes better developed.

According to Tibetan Buddhism, it is impossible that they should not liberate people of the highest, the average, and the lowest intellectual capacity. The reasons are because, firstly, the consciousness in the Bardo possesses supernormal power of perception of a limited kind, whatever is spoken to one then is apprehended. Secondly, because—although [formerly] deaf or blind—here, at this time, all one's faculties are perfect, and one can hear whatever is addressed to one. Thirdly, being continually pursued by awe and

---

201 W.Y. Evans-Wentz, *The Tibetan Book of The Dead*, Oxford University Press, New York (1960), p lxii

202 Sogyal Rinpoche, *The Tibetan Book of Living and Dying*, Harper One, New York (2002), p 309

203 W.Y. Evans-Wentz, *The Tibetan Book of The Dead*, Oxford University Press, New York (1960), p 158

terror, one thinketh, 'What is best?' and, being alertly conscious, one is always coming to hear whatever may be told to one. Since the consciousness is without a prop (without the human-plane body to depend upon), it immediately goeth to whatever place the mind directeth. Fourthly, it is easy to direct it. The memory is ninefold more lucid than before. Even though stupid [before], at this time, by the workings of Karma, the intellect becometh exceedingly clear and capable of meditating whatever is taught to it. Hence the answer is because it [i.e. the Knower] possesseth these virtues.[204]

If the religious performance for the deceased in Tibet is effective to the continuum of consciousness thereof, it seems that the living people's mind can be transmitted to the deceased. If so, why is the deceased's mind not transmitted to the living people? Will it be impossible? If free communication is possible between the living people and the deceased, the concept of death will be redefined.

The mind organ should be trained in order for a living person to read the mind of a deceased. It is analogous to the fact that a sight organ should be trained for a while in order to read written letters, or that a sound organ should be trained for a long time in order to learn a language. Even though we have never trained our mind organ to read mind information, after death the mind organ will at last resume the capability to read mind information since the five organs can no longer function. If we did not train our own mind organ as long as we were alive, however, it will be very difficult for the mind organ to read mind information after-death.

We might ask ourselves if the sixth organ of the deceased can read the mind information, why can that of the living person not read the mind information of the deceased? This is because—to the living person—the five consciousnesses by the five sense organs always precede the sixth consciousness by the sixth organ. As long as the five consciousnesses remain aware, the sixth organ by itself cannot read the mind information, so the five consciousnesses must be stopped in order for the sixth organ to read the mind

---

[204] W.Y. Evans-Wentz, *The Tibetan Book of The Dead*, Oxford University Press, New York (1960), pp 182-183

Probing the Mind: How does Consciousness Work?

information. In order to stop the five consciousnesses we should be in a clear, transcendental state of consciousness which is called *samadhi*. This is a built-in self protective feature in that if the sixth organ of the living person were to work at the non-*samadhi* state he could see a ghost or a phantom and could become so focused on the ghost or phantom, which is called possession, that it would cause a physical or mental disorder. In this 'out of mind' state he blocks awareness of the five consciousnesses, but his sixth organ can work and he honors the ghost or phantom and the associated sounds as his reality. On the other hand, in the state of 'sound of mind,' he can be aware of the five consciousnesses correctly, and, as a result, he can neither see a ghost or phantom nor listen to a sound. It is absolutely true that a ghost or phantom does not exist to people who are 'sound of mind.'

In the clear, transcendental state of consciousness like the state of *samadhi*, he can see a ghost or phantom through his mind organ. In the L.A. girl's story, when she saw her young cousin from Chicago in her room it was because her sixth organ worked. The girl had seen a phantom of her cousin in the state of being aware of consciousness. A guru can also see a ghost or phantom through his mind organ in the state of *samadhi*.

32

Reincarnation and Samsara

William George I was an excellent fisherman. He was an American Indian and believed in reincarnation like others of his tribe. He eagerly sought a rebirth as he was getting old, so he told his third son and daughter-in-law that if he gets a rebirth after death he wishes to be born as their son. He then showed them two spots on his body and told them that when they had a new son he would have the two spots on his body, indicating that the son is a reincarnation of him. One of the spots was on his left shoulder; the other was on his left elbow. He gave his third son a watch that was inherited from his mother, and told him to keep it safe for it would become evidence for his reincarnation later. Several weeks after that he went missing from the fishing boat he had worked. This was in August of 1949. Not long thereafter the third daughter-in-law became pregnant and had a baby on May 5, 1950. This was nine months since George I had gone missing. The daughter-in-law had a dream while she was in labor and was told by George I that he wished to see her son. She was surprisingly awakened from the dream and looked around because it seemed to her that George I was there. In the dream she saw George I just the same as the last image when he was alive.

The new baby was born with spots on his left shoulder and left elbow just as his grandfather, and due to this the baby was named George II. Growing up, it became certain that he was a reincarnation *of his grandfather. He looked like his grandfather in his face, gait, character, etc. It seemed to them that he had a lot of knowledge on fishing and boats, and that he knew where the best bay for fishing was. One day he saw the watch in his mother's jewelry box and he told her "That is mine." His memory of the previous life faded out around ten.*[205]

The story above is one of twenty examples showing that a human being gets a rebirth as a human being after death which were recorded in the book *Eternal Freedom* of Zen Master *Seong Chul*. Besides them, there are numerous examples about reincarnation of human beings after death. These have just not been proved scientifically.

A lot of saints and sages who attained the highest enlightenment taught us that there are many previous lives as human beings, and reincarnation repeatedly happens. Such return to the earth plane takes place after release of the guilt of his sins in a state of 'Hell,' or the expiration of the term of enjoyment in 'Heaven' as he knows it, which his Karma has gained for him. However, most of the deceased take immediate rebirth on earth when they see visions of mating men and women. When they, at this final stage towards the awakening to earth-life, now know that they do not have a gross body of flesh and blood, they urgently desire to have one in order that they may again enjoy physical life on the earth world. Reincarnation is also recognized in psychology. The Freudian psychoanalyst will find herein a remarkable passage supporting his doctrine of the aversion of the son for the father. The passage says that if the deceased is to be born as a male, the feeling of its being a male comes upon the knower, and a feeling of intense aversion for the father and attraction for the mother is begotten, and vice versa as regards birth as a female. This is, however, an old Buddhist doctrine found elsewhere.[206]

---

205 Zen Master Seong Chul, *Eternal Freedom*, Changkyungkak, Korea, Gyungnam (1999), pp 281-282

206 W.Y. Evans-Wentz, *The Tibetan Book of The Dead*, Oxford University Press, New York (1960), pp lxxix-lxxx

Probing the Mind: How does Consciousness Work?

In Buddhism, when the world of after-death ends, the existence gets a rebirth into a new world. The new world is one of the six realms: human realm, animal realm, hell realm, hungry ghost realm, Asuras realm, and God realm. Among them the human realm and animal realm are physical worlds where a physical body accompanies and where the five organs work again. The hell realm, hungry ghost realm, Asuras realm, and God realm are not physical worlds, but are worlds of consciousness. Although these are worlds of consciousness, the existence again undergoes a rebirth after passing death in these worlds and a rebirth again takes place in one of the six realms.

In the *Chi-khai Bardo*, the deceased is, unless otherwise enlightened, more or less under the delusion that although he is deceased he still possesses a body like the body of flesh and blood. When he comes to realize that really he has no such body, he begins to develop an overwhelming desire to possess one; and, seeking for one, the *karmic* predilection for *sangsaric* existence naturally becoming all-determining, he enters into the *Sid-pai Bardo* of seeking Rebirth, and eventually, with his rebirth in this or some other world, the after-death state comes to an end.[207]

If it is true for the continuum of consciousness to be reborn, what will be the nature of rebirth? Is rebirth random? Why is someone born in wealth, while someone else is born in poverty? Does nature play roulette so that in one life you are human but in the next, for no reason at all, you are a frog? If there is coherence to rebirth, what is the nature of that coherence? The Buddha's claim was that, from the perspective of an awakened awareness, there is coherence—certain types of actions give rise to certain types of consequences. The coherence is called karma.[208]

The continuum of consciousness of a deceased selects a family where it will be reborn depending on its karma. It selects one

---

[207] W.Y. Evans-Wentz, *The Tibetan Book of The Dead*, Oxford University Press, New York (1960), pp 29-30

[208] B. Alan Wallace, *Buddhism with an Attitude*, Snow Lion Publications, New York (2003), p 52

family which, it thinks, is the best among all available families, and the family it selects becomes its biological parents. The selection of a family in the process of rebirth is analogous to the selection of a spouse in the process of marriage. At the marriageable age, young men and women meet many admirers. However, each selects the best one among them. At the time of rebirth, the continuum of consciousness of a deceased meets many families, but selects only one, the best among them.

As The Tibetan Book of the Dead teaches, the dying should face death not only calmly and clear-mindedly and heroically, but with an intellect rightly trained and rightly directed, mentally transcending, if need be, bodily suffering and infirmities, as they would be able to do had they practiced efficiently during their active lifetime the Art of Living, and, when about to die, the Art of Dying.[209] Buddhists and Hindus alike believe that the last thought at the moment of death determines the character of the next incarnation. As the Bardo thodol teaches, so have the Sages of India long taught, that the thought-process of a dying person should be rightly directed, preferably by the dying person if he or she has been initiated or psychically trained to meet death, or, otherwise, by a guru or a friend or relative versed in the science of death. Sri Krishna, in the Bhagavad Gita (viii, 6), says to Arjuna, "One attaineth whatever state <of being> one thinketh about at the last when relinquishing the body, being ever absorbed in the thought thereof."[210]

When we believe in rebirth, what will be reborn? As the physical body scatters into four elements (earth, water, fire and wind) it is not to be reborn. If so, we can say soul or spirit is to be reborn. However, if the soul or spirit does not have any consciousness, i.e., any information about the previous life, the rebirth of it is worthless for us. In order for the rebirth of soul to be meaningful, the

---

[209] W.Y. Evans-Wentz, *The Tibetan Book of The Dead*, Oxford University Press, New York (1960), pp xiv-xv

[210] W.Y. Evans-Wentz, *The Tibetan Book of The Dead*, Oxford University Press, New York (1960), pp xviii

reborn soul should have information about the previous life. In other words, the reborn soul is a consciousness itself, a continuum of consciousness, or a complex of the sixth, seventh, and eighth consciousnesses. All information of consciousness about all previous lives as well as the present life is stored in Alaya. When a rebirth occurs, the Alaya is about updating the information of the present life. That's why the Alaya is said neither to be identical nor to be different. The information becomes meaningful when it is retrieved and read by the mind organ. In consequence, the soul is a continuum of consciousness in which the sixth organ (mind organ) contacts and reads the eighth consciousness (mind information: Alaya) and the seventh consciousness (thinking process) is generated between them.

The King asked Nagasena: "When someone is reborn, is he the same as the one who just died, or is he different?"

Nagasena replied: "He is neither the same, nor different... Tell me, if a man were to light a lamp, could it provide light the whole night long?"

"Yes."

"Is the flame then which burns in the first watch of the light the same as the one that burns in the second... or the last?"

"No."

"Does that mean there is one lamp in the first watch of the light, another in the second, and another in the third?"

"No, it's because of that one lamp that the light shines all night."

"Rebirth is much the same: one phenomenon arises and another stops, simultaneously. So the first act of consciousness in the new existence is neither the same as the last act of consciousness in the previous existence, nor is it different."[211]

In Buddhism, the soul hypothesis is denied in view of the fact that the soul is not a solid identity. In denying the soul hypothesis, Buddhism of all Schools maintains that personal immortality is impossible, because all personal existence is but a mere flux

---

211 Sogyal Rinpoche, *The Tibetan Book of Living and Dying*, Harper One, New York (2002), p 95

of instability and continual change, karmically dependent upon the false concept that phenomena, or phenomenal appearances, or phenomenal states and beings, are real. Thus, Buddhism holds that individualized mind or consciousness cannot realize Reality.[212] The right doctrine appears to be that as man has evolved through the lowest forms of being (Hinduism speaks of 8,400,000 graded kinds of births culminating in man), so by misconduct and neglect to use the opportunity of manhood there can, equally, be a descent along the 'downward path' to the same low forms of being from which humanity has, with difficulty, emerged.[213] And retrogression and progression alike are time-processes: ages pass ere the fire-mist becomes the solidified planet; an Enlightened One is the rare fruit of unknown myriads of embodiments; and man, the highest of the animal-beings, cannot become the lowest of the animal-beings, no matter how heinous his sins, at one bound.[214] Progression or retrogression—never an unchanging neutral state of inactivity—are the alternatives within the Sangsara; and the one or the other, within any of the mansions of existence, cannot lead the life-flux to the threshold of that mansion—neither the sub-human to the human, nor the human to the sub-human—save step by step.[215]

Samsara never runs down. The cycle of existence from rebirth to rebirth is like being a ball in a perpetual motion pinball machine. Merely wishing "I have been in samsara for countless eons and have had enough" won't get you out. Samsara runs of its own momentum as long as it is fueled by the same habitual patterns. The Buddhist hypoth-

---

212 W.Y. Evans-Wentz, *The Tibetan Book of The Dead*, Oxford University Press, New York (1960), pp 224-225

213 W.Y. Evans-Wentz, *The Tibetan Book of The Dead*, Oxford University Press, New York (1960), p. lxxxii

214 W.Y. Evans-Wentz, *The Tibetan Book of The Dead*, Oxford University Press, New York (1960), pp 43-44

215 W.Y. Evans-Wentz, *The Tibetan Book of The Dead*, Oxford University Press, New York (1960), p 43

esis is that samsara stops only when we take radical measures and break through the habitual patterns of delusion.[216]

To be born as a human being is a privilege, according to the Buddha's teaching, because it offers the rare opportunity of liberation through one's own decisive effort, through a 'turning-about in the deepest seat of consciousness,' as the Lankavatara Sutra puts it.[217] Apart from liberation by gaining Nirvana after death—thus cutting asunder forever the karmic bonds of worldly or sangsaric existence in an illusionary body of propensities—the only hope for the ordinary person of reaching Buddhahood lies in being reborn as a human being; for birth in any other than the human world causes delay for one desirous of reaching the Final Goal.[218]

The quality of life in the realm of the gods may look superior to our own, yet the masters tell us that human life is infinitely more valuable. Why? Because... we have the awareness and intelligence that are the raw materials for enlightenment, and because the very suffering that pervades this human realm is itself the spur to spiritual transformation. Pain, grief, loss, and ceaseless frustration of every kind are there for a real and dramatic purpose: to wake us up, to enable and almost to force us to break out of the cycle of samsara and so release our imprisoned splendor. Every spiritual tradition has stressed that this human life is unique, and has a potential that ordinarily we hardly even begin to imagine. If we miss the opportunity this life offers us for transforming ourselves, they say, it may well be an extremely long time before we have another. Imagine a blind turtle, roaming the depths of an ocean the size of the universe. Up above floats a wooden ring, tossed to and fro on the waves. Every hundred years the turtle comes, once, to the surface. To be born a human being is said by Buddhists to be more difficult than for that turtle to surface accidentally with its head

---

216 B. Alan Wallace, *Buddhism with an Attitude,* Snow Lion Publications, New York (2003), p 48

217 W.Y. Evans-Wentz, *The Tibetan Book of The Dead,* Oxford University Press, New York (1960), p lxi

218 W.Y. Evans-Wentz, *The Tibetan Book of The Dead,* Oxford University Press, New York (1960), p 30

poking through the wooden ring. And even among those who have a human birth, it is said, those who have the great good fortune to make a connection with the teachings are rare; and those who really take them to heart and embody them in their actions even rarer, as rare, in fact, "as stars in broad daylight."[219]

The profound doctrine of pre-existence and rebirth, which many of the most enlightened men in all known epochs have taught as being realizable, is now under investigation by our own scientists of the West. And some of these scientists seem to be approaching that place on the path of scientific progress where, as with respect also to other findings by the Sages of Asia long before the rise of Western Science, East and West appear to be destined to meet in mutual understanding.[220]

---

[219] Sogyal Rinpoche, *The Tibetan Book of Living and Dying*, Harper One, New York (2002), pp 117-118

[220] W.Y. Evans-Wentz, *The Tibetan Book of The Dead*, Oxford University Press, New York (1960), p ix

33

Why Don't We Remember Previous Lives?

Reincarnation has not yet been proven scientifically. Although many exemplary cases on reincarnation are reported, it cannot be proved because the continuum of consciousness of after-death is not revealed. If everybody could remember their previous lives, reincarnation would be unquestionably recognized. Leaving the scientific proof on the existence of reincarnation aside, we will be able to investigate from the Consciousness Only point of view the reason why we do not remember our previous lives.

"If we have lived before," I'm often asked, "why don't we remember it?" But why should the fact that we cannot remember our past lives mean that we have never lived before? After all, experiences of our childhood, or of yesterday, or even of what we were thinking an hour ago were vivid as they occurred, but the memory of them has almost totally eroded, as though they had never taken place. If we cannot remember what we were doing or thinking last Monday, how on earth do we imagine it would be easy, or normal, to remember what we were doing in a previous lifetime?[221]

---

221 Sogyal Rinpoche, *The Tibetan Book of Living and Dying*, Harper One, New York (2002), p 87

However, what we remember of our previous lives is not just a matter of our memory. What we remember of our previous lives means that the information on the previous lives should exist somewhere and be read by some means. Where does the information exist or where is it stored? And also, what organ can read the information? According to the Consciousness Only Theory, the information is stored in the eighth consciousness, Alaya, and is read by the mind organ. For the psychologists who believe in rebirth, it is stored in unconsciousness. We therefore say that the information on the previous lives exists in Alaya or unconsciousness, in completeness, in a potentially realizable consciousness.

When one reads the information on the previous lives which is stored in Alaya, it is remembering the previous lives. Such phenomena sometimes happen to children of ages one to three. When they begin to learn some words, they sometimes tend to talk about something in their previous lives. They say "I am such and such a person who lived at such and such a place before."[222]

Hypnotists say that hypnosis is one of the methods which can contact unconsciousness so that it might read the information of previous lives. However, although somebody has read the information of his previous life, there is no scientific evidence that he has read it. Dreaming is another method which can read the previous lives that are stored in Alaya or unconsciousness. As the five organs stop contacting the corresponding objects during sleep, sleep is the only time that the sixth organ can work. It is therefore during sleep that the sixth organ contacts Alaya so as to produce dreams, and if the sixth organ contacts information about a previous lifetime during a dream, the dreamer is able to recall this previous life.

Meditation is another method for recollecting previous lives. As a result of intensive practice in long, meditative retreats, some experience of deeper clarity occurs, and at that moment people recall their past life. Some of them have been able to recall twenty or thirty lifetimes, some even during the Buddha's time. That

---

[222] Zen Master Seong Chul, *Eternal Freedom*, Changkyungkak, Korea, Gyungnam (1999), p105

means the power of memory is increasing, so automatically the memory of the previous lives would also increase.[223]

The sixth organ is the only means or program which can read the past-life information, but we have never operated this program, never tried to access it during our lifetime. We contact the five objects and operate the five organs so as to stimulate the thinking cycle from birth—our life is heavily oriented toward seeking the five objects in order to satisfy the five organs. Although the sixth organ has the ability to read mind information including previous lives, the sixth is not trained to do it, but is trained by our intellect to read the information which is generated by the five organs. We are not trained to stop the random thinking process so as to read the information of previous lives which is stored in Alaya. Just as we cannot read without learning letters and we cannot speak without learning spoken words, it is impossible to read the information of Alaya without learning how to do it.

When awakened from sleep we resume consciousness of the present life, retaining the identity of the physical body. However, when reborn from death, we get a rebirth with a new physical body. When we get a rebirth, the former consciousness before the rebirth has already become a consciousness of the previous life and a new consciousness for the present life begins to form. The consciousness of the previous life is stored in Alaya. There is sleep as a gap between yesterday and today, but it is not difficult to recall the consciousness of yesterday. There is death as a gap between the previous life and the present life, so it is much more difficult to remember the previous life. Why?

If all consciousnesses are stored in Alaya, Alaya has no difference between sleep and death. Regardless of whether awakened from sleep or reborn from death, Alaya is the same. The only difference between sleep and death is that the means for expressing the consciousness are different from each other. When awakened from sleep we do not forget both spoken language and written letters

---

[223] Francisco J. Varela, *Sleeping, Dreaming, and Dying*, Wisdom Publications, Boston (1997), p 210

that we have learned during the present life. However, when we get a rebirth, we totally forget both spoken language and written letters that we had learned during the previous life. Sleep does not affect the continuity of the spoken language and written letters, whereas death totally cuts off the continuity. On being born, nobody can speak a word, nobody can read a letter. This is an absolute truth and an unalterable law of the universe. Although we recall the previous life when reborn, there is no means to express it. It takes quite a long time to learn spoken language and written letters. It shouldn't be surprising that children of ages one to three who begin to learn some words sometimes talk about things concerning their previous lives. A lot of information on the previous life may remain at the surface of Alaya and be easy to recall, and a lot of new information has not yet been input through the five organs. They, of course, begin to learn a spoken language and written letters from birth and this begins to input new information in their Alaya. In fact, the previous life is not an important concern for them; their major concern is about the five sense objects. The imminent things for them at the 'now' moment are to fill their hungry stomach and to avoid the hot or cold. As they grow and learn a spoken language and written letters, a lot of new information on the sense objects are input through the corresponding five organs and stored in Alaya. The information on the previous life is covered with the new information and stored more deeply in Alaya, and is therefore getting more difficult to recall. As the recall of previous lives is exhausted, the recall of the succeeding life is created. In other words, the karma of previous lives is exhausted, and the karma of the succeeding (current) life is produced.[224]

---

224 The Nineteenth Stanza of The Thirty Stanzas

34

Impetus for Reincarnation—Karma

I was recently reminded of just how uncanny this transformation is. I know a couple from Italy who suffered a terrible family tragedy two years ago when their teenage son, Enrico, killed himself. He had gotten drunk with some friends, one of whom started playing with his father's handgun. It went off and Enrico was killed. His family was devastated, all the more when it was suggested but never proved that their son had shot himself playing Russian roulette. A week after he died his mother went into his bedroom. She had the impulse to pray for her son, and as she knelt by his bed she heard a noise. A remote-control toy car of Enrico's had fallen off the shelf for no apparent reason. It began to run around the floor, and the mother removed its batteries. Still it continued to run. This strange phenomenon lasted three days, she told me. It was witnessed by the entire family, and Enrico's older sister, the one he was closest to, insisted that her brother was operating the car. She asked it questions, as one would a Ouija board, and the car would go left or right to signal yes or no.

Months later Enrico's father happened to be in India, and he went to a **jyotishi**, or astrologer. Certain jyotishis do not cast your chart but consult already written charts, many dating back centuries, that apply to the person who comes for a reading. (This decision is made according to the time a person appears and by matching certain personal data with charts that the astrologer has on hand.) This was *true of my friend, who was told the following story: In his previous lifetime he had lived on the west coast of India. He was desperate to have a son, but unfortunately his wife was barren. The couple adopted a baby boy when suddenly she became pregnant and in time delivered a boy of their own. After the biological son's birth, the father began to ignore the adopted boy and abuse him. Tormented by this the boy committed suicide at exactly the same age as Enrico. The astrologer told my friend that there was a connection here. The former son was reborn as Enrico, and he committed suicide again to show his father what it was like to lose a real son. Naturally, my friend was quite shaken to hear this, but when he met me some months later, he said that the final result was a sense of peace. He had come to terms with Enrico's tragic death and understood the karma behind it.*[225]

The samsara of birth, death and rebirth is fashioned by the conditions and causes resulting from our previous lives. The reincarnation is a fruit obtained by a special force which is called *karma*. 'Karma' is the Sanskrit word for 'action' or 'deed.' In anthropological terminology, 'karma' is a thick, theory-laden term. Karma refers to the nature of actions and how their long-term consequences play out over time.[226]

According to the Consciousness Only Theory, *Bijas*, which means mind information stored in Alaya (the mind information is called 'seed of mind'), has a certain amount of energy or driving force which is called karma or karmic energy. Just as the mind information cannot be materialized, the karmic energy cannot be transformed into a physical amount. The karmic energy is a spiritual force or spiritual energy but not a physical energy, but the karmic energy is strong enough to produce a physical result or a physical fruit.

The samsara of birth, death and rebirth is explained by the law of causality in Buddhism. The law of causality is based on the

---

[225] Deepak Chopra, *Life After Death*, Three Rivers Press, New York (2006), pp 239-240

[226] B. Alan Wallace, *Buddhism with an Attitude,* Snow Lion Publications, New York (2003), p 50

Probing the Mind: How does Consciousness Work?

principle that a fruit, or a result, is produced when a cause meets a proper condition. According to the Theory, there are four conditions and ten causes, and five fruits are produced by the conditions and causes.[227] Reincarnation is one of the five fruits. Four conditions are prepared by the eighth consciousnesses. Ten causes are prepared by fifteen supporting bases which are from 'actions' or 'motives'.[228] The causality is analogous to a seed maturing into a fruit under a proper condition. A seed is a cause. In order for the seed to sprout and grow it should meet a proper condition such as soil, moisture, temperature, sunshine and the like. The seed breaks the shell and the soil. In other words, strong energy exists in the seed. Likewise, the causes and conditions prepared by the eight consciousnesses have strong energy so as to produce a fruit of reincarnation. Thus, the seed of mind information has the karmic energy, karma, or habit energy.

Karma is created by duhkha. Karma may be duhkha itself. The duhkha is sorrow and suffering. It includes vexing passions. It has a close relationship with deeds and cannot be separated from deeds. Sorrow and suffering means all the suffering that is projected and engendered by deeds. Deeds mean all the acts that bring about reincarnation. Vexing passions mean all the afflictions which give rise to deeds and which engender birth. The more the duhkha is, the stronger the karmic energy is. To be killed produces the hardest duhkha among all deeds. Suicide is an action which gives himself or herself the hardest duhkha so as to produce the strongest karma.

---

227 Four conditions are condition qua cause (causative condition), condition qua antecedent (antecedent condition), condition of perceived object (perceived condition), and condition of contributory factor (contributory condition); ten causes are speech cause, observation-dependence cause, projecting cause, producing cause, complementary cause, adductive cause, special cause, combining cause, impeding cause, and non-impeding cause; and five fruits are fruit of retribution, similar fruit (fruit of the same order), fruit of disentanglement, fruit of virile activity, and fruit of contributory causes.

228 Dukkyu Choi, *Mechanism of Consciousness during Life, Dream and After-death*, Authorhouse, Bloomington (2011), pp 164-169

Suicide cannot be a means which can stop the duhkha. The next life should be reborn with the strongest karma.

The karma by deeds is tenfold; three unwholesome deeds of the body, four of speech, and three of the mind. The three of the body are intentional killing, stealing and sexual misconduct. The four of speech are harsh and abusive speech, lying, slander and idle gossip. The three of the mind are avarice, anger and ignorance. The fundamental karmic framework of Buddhism is the ten virtues and ten non-virtues. These do's and do not's cover the most common problems in life. Committing a non-virtuous deed plants a seed that can potentially produce a negative impact as it matures in the mind-stream in this lifetime and the ones to follow. Once karma is imbedded in a stream of consciousness, it is carried from one lifetime to another until it is catalyzed. Just as a plant seed can remain dormant in the desert for decades and sprout to life at the first contact with water, a karmic seed can lie dormant for a long time, from lifetime to lifetime, before a catalyst triggers its ripening.[229] The karma by deeds has habit energy which will cause the continuous procession of births and deaths.

Karma is created by *Bijas* (seeds of mind information) which are stored in Alaya. There are three *Bijas*; *Bijas* by names and concepts, *Bijas* by Atman-adhesion, and *Bijas* by deeds. The continuous procession of births and deaths is due to the operation of the three *Bijas*. The *Bijas* by names and concepts are the immediate *Bijas* of each of the conditioned dharmas, which create habit energy. These *Bijas* express the meaning and make it known to others, and reveal or cause the object to be present. The *Bijas* by Atman-adhesion proceed from the false concept of 'I-and-mine.' There are two kinds of Atman-adhesion: one is innate Atman-adhesion which belongs to the sixth and seventh consciousnesses, and the other is Atman-adhesion of discrimination or speculation, which belongs to the sixth consciousness. The former is to be cut off by the 'path of meditation and self-cultivation,' while the latter

---

229 B. Alan Wallace, *Buddhism with an Attitude*, Snow Lion Publications, New York (2003), pp 56-57

Probing the Mind: How does Consciousness Work?

is abandoned or cut off by the 'path of insight into Transcendent Truth.' The *Bijas* created and invoked by the two Atman-adhesions are karmic energies which manifest as habitual ways of responding to events or actions in the perceived world. These 'karmic habits' solidify the distinction between the self and the non-self in relation to sentient beings, etc.; i.e., maintain a 'self-image.' The *Bijas* by deeds bring about consequence in the three realms. There are two kinds of deeds. One is impure-good deeds which produce agreeable fruits, the other is bad deeds which produce disagreeable fruits. The consequences of the *Bijas* created and invoked by the two deeds can therefore result in either good or bad destinies.[230]

Buddhists regard ignorance as the root of suffering, and ignorance has two parts. One type of ignorance is failure to attend to our actual nature, the nature of our own awareness. Not attending to who we actually are is a form of ignorance. A second kind of ignorance is identifying with things that we are not. We mistake as 'I' and 'mine' things that in fact do not have a self in them, cannot be an 'I' or 'mine.' These two errors are the essence of ignorance, the root of samsara, the source of suffering. The myriad of thoughts and emotions that arise in the mind, the entire array of mental phenomena that we habitually identify with so strongly, is not our true identity. Identifying with these phenomena is what is meant by ignorance.[231] Ignorance is the first link in the chain of causation.

The karma theory becomes a basis of the Twelve Links in the Chain of Dependent Origination which is explained as a principle of samsara. The Twelve Links are the best-known application of the Buddhist concept of dependent origination, identifying the origins of suffering to be in craving and ignorance. The Twelve Links reveal the origins of phenomena, and the feedback loop of conditioning and causation that leads to suffering in current and future

---

230 Wei Tat, *CH'ENG WEI-SHIH LUN*, The Ch'eng Wei-shih Lun Publication Committee, Hong Kong (1973), p 583

231 B. Alan Wallace, *Buddhism with an Attitude,* Snow Lion Publications, New York (2003), p 91

lives.[232] The Twelve Links start from ignorance and end at death, promulgating samsara: (1) all deeds or predispositions originate from ignorance; (2) consciousness is originated from predispositions; (3) name and form is originated from consciousness; (4) six sense-organs are originated from name and form; (5) touch (contact) is originated from six sense-organs; (6) sensation is originated from touch; (7) desire is originated from sensation; (8) grasping is originated from desire; (9) existence is originated from grasping; (10) birth is originated from existence; and (11 & 12) old age and death are originated from birth.

In order to cut off the loop of samsara (birth-old age-death), existence should be cut off; in order to cut off the existence, grasping should be cut off; in order to cut off the grasping, desire should be cut off; in order to cut off the desire, sensation should be cut off; in order to cut off the sensation, contact should be cut off; in order to cut off the contact, the six sense-organs should be cut off; in order to cut off the six sense-organs, names and forms should be cut off; in order to cut off the names and forms, consciousness should be cut off; in order to cut off the consciousness, deeds should be cut off; and in order to cut off the deeds, ignorance should be cut off. In order to cut off the ignorance, Wisdom (*Prajna*) should be developed.

How we obtain Wisdom depends on the individual practice. This is a distinction of Buddhism unlike other religions. Whereas a religion based on theism teaches how to reach the ultimate goal of salvation through the Absolute God, Buddhists can reach the ultimate Wisdom only through the individual practice. It depends on the individual's consciousness whether he will die with the belief that happiness by the five objects in the present life is the highest because he believes nothing exists after death or doesn't know about the world, whether he will die storing in Alaya the belief that, when he dies, the Absolute God will save his after-death life, or whether he will try to empty Alaya so as to reach the Wisdom

---

232 http://en.wikipedia.org/wiki/Twelve Links

Probing the Mind: How does Consciousness Work?

through the awareness that there exists merely Consciousness regardless of life and death, and that all dharmas are manifested by the Consciousness. We will meet the right one depending on the individual's karma.

35

Nirvana—Eternal Life

The Buddha saw that all who are born become old, and sick, and finally die. A life cannot avoid such sufferings. Lord Buddha determined to seek out a life with no suffering, a life with not getting old, not sick and not dying, and he finally realized that there is such a life with no sufferings—a life which is 'not born.' If a life is not born it will not die, so in order not to die, it should not be born. As we have seen in chapter 32, a life is reincarnated in one of the six realms: human realm, animal realm, hell realm, hungry ghost realm, Asuras realm, and God realm. But Buddhism says that there is another world beyond the six worlds. In the six realms, birth and death and rebirth repeat endlessly, but there is another world in which life is eternal; this is the world called nirvana, the world that the Buddha experienced. He who realized nirvana, the Buddha, has spoken of it to His own disciples as follows:

There is, disciples, a Realm devoid of earth, water, fire and air. It is not endless space, nor infinite thought, nor nothingness, neither ideas nor non-ideas. Not this world nor that is it. I call it neither a coming nor a departing, nor a standing still, nor death, nor birth; it is without a basis, progress, or a stay; it is the ending of sorrow.

For that which clingeth to another thing there is a fall; but unto that which clingeth not no fall can come. Where no fall cometh, there is rest, and where rest is, there is no keen desire. Where keen desire is not, naught cometh or goeth; and where naught cometh or goeth there is no death, no birth. Where there is neither death nor birth, there neither is this world nor that, nor in between—it is the ending of sorrow.

There is, disciples, an Unbecome, Unborn, Unmade, Unformed; if there were not this Unbecome, Unborn, Unmade, Unformed, there would be no way out for that which is become, born, made, and formed; but since there is an Unbecome, Unborn, Unmade, Unformed, there is escape for that which is become, born, made, and formed.[233]

The Consciousness Only Theory provides us with solutions on fundamentals of human being. The Theory explains that all sentient beings and their birth and death are fabricated by mind or consciousness only, therefore nothing permanent or eternal does exist, only consciousness exists. All sentient beings are temporary incarnations which are manifested by consciousness. Thus, the Theory explains about the mechanism of consciousness and the principles of samsara, birth, death and rebirth. The Theory was originated from the Buddha and theoretically systemized by Maitreya (A.D 270-350). Following thereafter, Asanga (A.D 300-389) and his brother, Vasubandhu (A.D 320-400) completed the philosophy. Vasubandhu wrote two books, Vijnaptimatratasiddhi-trimsika (Trimsika: Thirthy Stanzas on Mere-Consciousness) and *Wei-shih Erh Shih Lun* (Vimsatika: Twenty Treatises on Mere-Consciouness). The Thirty Stanzas are very brief like a poem with no annotation. Therefore, a lot of sastra-masters wrote commentaries on the Thirty Stanzas so as to further develop the Theory. Hsuan Tsang (A.D 602-664) studied the Consciousness Only Theory in India. He wrote the *Ch'eng Wei-shih-Lun* (Treatise on the Doctrine of Consciouness Only) which annotated the Thirty Stanzas.

---

233 W.Y. Evans-Wentz, *The Tibetan Book of The Dead*, Oxford University Press, New York (1960), p 68

Probing the Mind: How does Consciousness Work?

The Consciousness Only Theory— Mechanism of Consciousness

The Consciousness Only Theory may explain about the mechanism of consciousness. The Theory can give us solutions on any questions which have not been addressed yet in psychology, psychoanalysis or any other modern sciences. The Theory is not a religious construct, but a systematically coherent science.

The origin of the Theory, Abhidharmakosha ('Treasure Chamber of the Abhidharna'), defines the phenomenal world comprised of material and mind as '5 classes 100 species'.

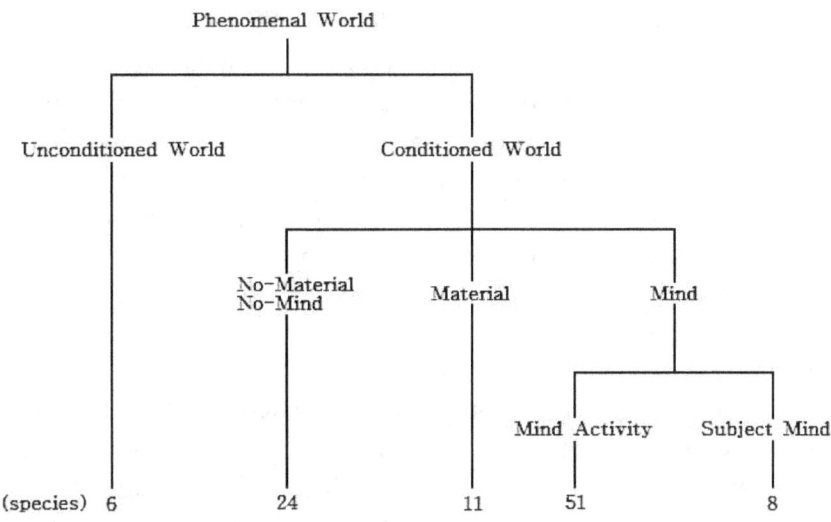

The phenomenal world, cosmos, is classified into Unconditioned world and Conditioned world. The Unconditioned world is the ultimate truth world, the world of the highest reality, the world of no birth and no death, Nirvana. The Unconditioned world is explained with six species.

The Conditioned world is further classified into three categories: mind, material, and no-mind and no-material. The no-mind and no-material category has 24 species. Time, numerals and directions are among the 24 species. It was really astonishing to define 'time, numerals, directions, etc,' as 'no-mind and no-material' about 2,500 years ago. The material category has eleven species; five physical objects (color, sound, scent, flavor and tactile objects), five physical organs (eye, ear, nose, tongue and body) and dharma color. The dharma color cannot be perceived by human eyes. It is again classified into five subspecies. For example, there are infinitesimal materials like atoms or molecules, and ideational material like rabbit's horns or turtle's hair. Among the five subspecies, it is said that there is a substantial material which can be seen by a higher Bodhisattva but not by an ordinary layman. The mind category is again classified into subject mind and phenomenal mind (mind activity). There are eight species in the subject mind, which means the eight consciousnesses. There are fifty one species in the phenomenal mind, which means fifty one mental activities. The Unconditioned world, no-mind and no-material, material, subject mind, and phenomenal mind are called '5 classes.' Six species in the Unconditioned world, 24 species in the no-mind and no-material, 11 species in the material, 8 species in the subject mind, and 51 species in the phenomenal mind (mind activity) constitutes '100 species.' It was an amazing thing to establish the systematic classification of the phenomenal world comprising material and mind as '5 classes 100 species' about 2,500 years ago.

The first five consciousnesses associated with the physical organs cease to exist when the physical body dies. If so, when does the sixth consciousness become extinct? According to the Thirty Stanzas, the sixth consciousness manifests itself at all times, except for being born into the 'heavenly world without thought (*Asannasatta*),'[234] except also for those in the two mindless

---

[234] According to the Buddhist cosmology, there are three realms: realm of desire, realm of form, and formless realm. The realm of desire is the lowest of the three realms of existence. It has six different worlds. The realm of form is so called because subtle material form still exists in it. It has eighteen different worlds. The *Asannasatta* is one of them as the thirteenth. The formless realm is the uppermost of the three consecutive vertical realms, where beings are without material form. It has four different worlds.

Probing the Mind: How does Consciousness Work?

Samapattis (two forms of meditation in which there is no more activity of thought) and those who are in states of sleep and stupor or unconsciousness.[235] The sleep means a state of deep sleep with no dreaming. If a being is born in a world other than the *Asannasatta*, the sixth consciousness will manifest at all times. If so, the sixth consciousness has nothing to do with death. Despite death of the physical body, the sixth consciousness will continue, and the sixth cannot continue without mind information which is stored in Alaya. As long as the sixth consciousness arises, the seventh will definitely arise. If this is so, the sixth, seventh and eighth have a common denominator in that the three will exist after death of the physical body. In this view, the three are called the 'post three consciousnesses' compared to the first five consciousnesses. The sixth consciousness also has a common denominator with the first five in that it has its own organ and the corresponding object like the first five. The seventh or eighth do not have their own organs or a corresponding object.

When does the Manas (seventh consciousness) cease? According to the Thirty Stanzas the Manas ceases to exist at the stage of Arhatship, in the meditation of annihilation and on the supramundane path.[236] Arhatship means to be in a state of complete extinction of thought and other mental activities. That Manas ceases to exist means that the seventh consciousness, cogitation or intellection, stops or vanishes. That does not mean becoming a fool. When the cogitation or intellection in the Manas stops, a transcendental wisdom appears. This wisdom is called the Universal Equality Wisdom. The Mind associated with the Universal Equality Wisdom sees the identity of all dharmas, and the complete equality between its own self and other sentient beings.

The Alaya consciousness (eighth consciousness) is also said to cease at the stage of Arhatship, the state of the saint who enters

---

235 The 16th Stanza of the Thirty Stanzas: Wei Tat, *CH'ENG WEI-SHIH LUN*, The Ch'eng Wei-shihLunPublication Committee, Hong Kong (1973), p477

236 The seventh stanza of the Thirty Stanzas

Nirvana. In this state, the obscuring barrier of vexing passions has been completely cut off.[237] In the Diamond Sutra, the state of the saint is explained as fourfold: Stream-Enterer, Once-Return, No-Return, and Arhatship. When the Alaya consciousness ceases, the cycle of death and rebirth is stopped. The death of the physical body does not extinguish Alaya consciousness, but Alaya consciousness is believed to be a determinant of the cycle of death and rebirth. If physical death allows the Alaya to be stopped, the cycle of death and rebirth will not be repeated. In the state of Arhatship, all discrimination, thought, and mental activities are stopped. New seeds of mind are neither produced nor stored in Alaya, and old seeds of mind which had been stored in Alaya are released. Finally, the storehouse will be empty and the Alaya consciousness will not arise any more, and no more rebirths will occur.

The Consciousness Only Theory was established on the basis of Vijnaptimatratasiddhi-trimsika (Trimsika: Thirthy Stanzas on Mere-Consciousness) by Vasubandhu (A.D 320-400) and *Ch'eng Wei-shih-Lun* (Treatise on the Doctrine of Consciouness Only) by Hsuan Tsang (A.D 602-664). Before that, the Buddha had preached the Diamond Sutra (Vajraccedika Prajnaparamita Sutra), which seems to be 'practical principles on mind'.

The Diamond Sutra—'Practical Principles on Mind'

The Diamond Sutra is the most fundamental sutra among eighty thousand sutras in Korean and Chinese Buddhism. The Diamond Sutra is composed of only 5,149 Chinese letters in a total 32 chapters. This Sutra teaches the Consciousness Only philosophy. In particular, the Sutra teaches practical guidance on mind. It does not teach us about the Five Precepts, the Four Noble Truths, or the Noble Eightfold Paths. The Consciousness Only Theory explains the mechanism of consciousness, while the Diamond Sutra teaches practical principles on mind or consciousness. The Theory teaches us how the mind works, and the Sutra teaches us how we generate

---

237 The fourth stanza of the Thirty Stanzas

the mind. The Sutra teaches us that our mind is vulnerable to be deceived by the name and form of things, and therefore teaches us to see reality, and finally to reach the True Nature.

The first teaching of the Sutra is to throw away self-view. It teaches us not to attach to the self-view because the self-view is a false image with no true self. As long as the self-view, person-view, living being-view, and life span-view are not thrown away, it is impossible to be a Bodhisattva (Buddhist saint). Walking in the woods at night, if we see a snake we will probably feel very frightened. But if we shine our flashlight on it and see that it is just a rope, we will feel a great relief. Seeing the snake was an erroneous perception, and the Sutra teaches us that the four erroneous perceptions—views of a self, a person, a living being and a life span—are the root of our suffering. A bodhisattva is someone who is free from all of these wrong views.

Therefore, the Buddha taught in the Sutra "In a place where there is something that can be distinguished by objects, in that place there is deception. If you can see the objectless nature of objects, then you can see the Tathagata."[238] This means that since the concepts, ideas, images, or mental phenomena of the objects could deceive you, do not be deceived by them. We may be deceived by the drunken appearance of a person and we cannot see the true nature of him or her. If you are not deceived, you can see the reality or true nature of the objects, and further, the Tathagata, the Buddha nature.

In the Sutra the Buddha said that He had not taught about self-view, even though he had. Why? Because the self-view is not self-view, but the name of it. Likewise, the mind is not mind, but the name of it. Such teachings repeat thirty times in the Sutra. The reason for such repeating is not to attach to the concepts, ideas, images, or mental phenomena of the objects, but to see the reality or true nature of them. Thus, the Buddha said "Someone who

---

238 The Diamond Sutra (*The Vajrachedika Prajnaparamita Sutra*), Chapter 5

looks for me in form or seeks me in sound is on a mistaken path and cannot see the Tathagata."[239]

In the Sutra, the Buddha teaches "Someone who accepts the Buddha's teachings and puts them into practice, even if only a gatha (an abridged verse of the Buddha's teaching) of four lines, and explains them to someone else brings more happiness than someone who fills the 3,000 chiliocosms [worlds] with the seven precious treasures as an act of generosity."[240] If you do not understand the importance of the Alaya consciousness, you will regard this teaching as an exaggerated metaphor; but, if you understand the importance of the Alaya consciousness as the basis of the Manas consciousness, you will understand that this teaching is not an exaggeration. The seven precious treasures amounting to the number of sands in the Ganges does not contribute any help to the production of a pure mind. Instead they contribute to produce a pure mind or a pure thinking, they will contribute to produce a desire or a craving. The information that should be stored in Alaya in order to produce a pure mind is the Buddha's teachings such as the gathas instead of the precious treasures.

To give rise to a pure and clear mind (mental activity) not relying on color (form), sound, smell, taste, tactile object, or dharma is not easy to understand or even to practice. How can we produce a pure mind? How can we control the free association and jumping intellect in the frenetic 'monkey-mind' thinking cycle, or the mental activities arising therefrom?

In the Sutra, the Buddha teaches "All the bodhisattvas should give rise to a pure and clear mind (mental activity). In order to give rise to such mind, they should not rely on forms (colors), sounds, smells, tastes, tactile objects, or dharmas (objects of mind: mind information). They should give rise to the mind without relying on

---

[239] The Diamond Sutra (*The Vajrachedika Prajnaparamita Sutra*), Chapter 26

[240] The Diamond Sutra (*The Vajrachedika Prajnaparamita Sutra*), Chapters 8, 11, 13 and 24

any of the objects."[241] This teaching is the heart of the Diamond Sutra. This teaching means "Do not attach to the six objects, and do not follow a preconception which is formed from the polluted mind information stored in Alaya." Although you see a person with a faint whiff of wine, the Buddha teaches us not to cause a violent reaction and generate considerable stress. The Buddha teaches us that the violent reaction and considerable stress are formed in accordance with the mind information stored in Alaya, but they are not the true nature of the person we see.

Buddhism teaches us not to produce a discriminating mind. That we should not produce a discriminating mind does not mean to sit like a fool without thinking, since a discriminating mind is a kind of mental activity which arises in the thinking process along with the four vexing passions. As long as the vexing passions intervene, a pure mind cannot be produced. When a pure mind is produced, a pure seed of mind is stored in Alaya and the seed of mind can again produce another pure mind through the fully controlled thinking cycle.

In conclusion, the Sutra teaches "All composed things are like a dream, a phantom, a drop of dew, or a flash of lightning. That is how to meditate on them, that is how to observe them."[242] This is not to cling to the six objects, colors, sounds, smells, tastes, tactile objects and objects of mind, but to see the ultimate reality through the Mind.

No Birth and No Death World of Nirvana—The Prajnaparamita Sutra

The Prajnaparamita Sutra is the core among the Buddhist sutras. The Sutra shall be recited in every Buddhist ceremony or dharma talk. The Sutra is the shortest, consisiting of 260 Chinese characters. This Sutra is the flower of all sutras and the essence of

---

241 The Diamond Sutra (*The Vajrachedika Prajnaparamita Sutra*), Chapter 10
242 The Diamond Sutra (*The Vajrachedika Prajnaparamita Sutra*), Chapter 32

Buddhism, the one that preached about the Ultimate Truth after Nirvana has been reached.

The Prajnaparamita Sutra[243]

When Avalokiteshvara Bodhisattva was practicing the profound prajna paramita, he illuminated the five skandhas and saw that they are all empty, and he crossed beyond all suffering and difficulty.

Shariputra, form does not differ from emptiness; emptiness does not differ from form. Form itself is emptiness; emptiness itself is form. So, too, are feeling, cognition, formation, and consciousness.

Shariputra, all dharmas are empty of characteristics. They are not produced, not destroyed, not defiled, not pure, and they neither increase nor diminish.

Therefore, in emptiness there is no form, feeling, cognition, formation, or consciousness; no eyes, ears, nose, tongue, body, or mind; no sights, sounds, smells, tastes, objects of touch, or dharmas; no field of the eyes, up to and including no field of mind-consciousness; and no ignorance or ending of ignorance, up to and including no old age and death or ending of old age and death. There is no suffering, no accumulating, no extinction, no way, and no understanding and no attaining.

Because nothing is attained, the Bodhisattva, through reliance on prajna paramita, is unimpeded in his mind. Because there is no impediment, he is not afraid, and he leaves distorted dream-thinking far behind. Ultimately Nirvana!

All Buddhas of the three periods of time attain Anuttarasamyaksambodhi through reliance on prajna paramita. Therefore, know that prajna paramita is a great spiritual mantra, a great bright mantra, a supreme mantra, an unequalled mantra. It can remove all suffering; it is gen-

---

243 http://www.cttbusa.org/heartsutra/heartsutra.htm

uine and not false. That is why the mantra of prajna paramita was spoken. Recite it like this:

'Gate gate paragate parasamgate bodhi svaha!'

The Heart Sutra preaches that all things are emptiness. The five skandhas and the six objects are all empty. Form itself is emptiness; emptiness itself is form. All dharmas are empty of characteristics. Thus, they are not produced, not destroyed, not defiled, not pure, and they neither increase nor diminish. Such preaching cannot be understood in the Conditioned world of material. First, the nature of Emptiness should be understood. The nature is not 'nothing' like '0' in '000' or '0000', but 'emptiness' like '0' in '1000' or '10000'.

Further, the Buddha says, "In emptiness there is no form, feeling, cognition, formation, or consciousness; no eyes, ears, nose, tongue, body, or mind; no sights, sounds, smells, tastes, objects of touch, or dharmas; no field of the eyes, up to and including no field of mind-consciousness; and no ignorance or ending of ignorance, up to and including no old age and death or ending of old age and death. There is no suffering, no accumulating, no extinction, no way, and no understanding and no attaining." The Buddha had taught for forty-five years since He got enlightenment about six organs, six objects, six consciousnesses, further two more consciousnesses, ignorance, how to overcome ignorance, wisdom, samsara, cycle of birth and rebirth and more. However, in the Sutra, the Buddha strongly denied all the things that he had taught for forty five years. Why? This means that we should throw away the raft after we go across the river. Our final goal is to go across the river but not the raft. Once we cross the river the raft is not needed any more. Our final goal is to reach the Ultimate Reality of Nirvana but not the mind, consciousness, mechanism of consciousness, wisdom and others. Once we reach Nirvana there is nothing that we attach to.

Because nothing is attained, the Bodhisattva, through reliance on prajna paramita, is unimpeded in his mind. Because there is no impediment he is not afraid, and he leaves distorted dream-thinking far behind. Ultimately Nirvana! All Buddhas of the three periods of time attain Anuttarasamyaksambodhi through reliance on prajna paramita. Therefore, know that prajna paramita is a great spiritual mantra, a great bright mantra, a supreme mantra, an unequalled mantra. It can remove all suffering; it is genuine and not false. That is why the mantra of prajna paramita was spoken. Thus, the Sutra suggests us to recite the song:

Gate gate paragate parasamgate bodhi svaha!
Gate gate paragate parasamgate bodhi svaha!
Gate gate paragate parasamgate bodhi svaha!

Let'go, let's go, hurry up, to the state of enlightenment, to the Nirvana!
Let'go, let's go, hurry up, to the state of enlightenment, to the Nirvana!
Let'go, let's go, hurry up, to the state of enlightenment, to the Nirvana!

Appendix—Summary of the Consciousness Only Theory

Buddhism is more concerned about mind than is any other religion. If we can say that Christianity is a religion of belief, we can say Buddhism is a religion of mind. Of course, Christianity does have significant doctrines related to the mind, and Buddhism does not exist without belief, but we can make that generalization. Among the doctrines of Buddhism, the Consciousness Only philosophy emphasizes mind. It states that all sentient beings and their birth and death are products of the mind, or consciousness, and therefore nothing permanent or eternal exists. Only consciousness exists.

The No-Self doctrine is another important doctrine in Buddhism. It explains that there is no true self (inherent existence) in you or in me, or in any sentient being or in dharma. This doctrine is one of the most difficult doctrines to understand. Clearly we see that we are here, all sentient beings also exist, and all dharmas exist too. Despite this, if a true self of me or you, or of any sentient being does not exist, who am I and what are all sentient beings? The No-Self doctrine appears to us like a sophism. The doctrine is the same as the 'Emptiness doctrine'. In early Buddhism, it was called 'No-Self doctrine,' and later in Mahayana Buddhism, it was called 'Emptiness doctrine.'

Various aspects of Mahayana Buddhist philosophy are often used as the basis of insight meditation. There are two major schools in Mahayana Buddhism: one is Madhyamaka, the School of the Middle Way, and the other is called Yogachara or Chittamatra, the School of the Mere-Consciousness.[244]

Madhyamaka philosophy uses the concept of emptiness as a therapeutic remedy for these ills of samsaric creatures. Emptiness, or *sunyata*, in Madhyamaka philosophy does not mean that things do not exist. It does not mean that our everyday experience of the world is somehow completely erroneous, that it is all a dream. Many people in the West think this is exactly what the Mahayana tradition is saying, but just because things lack inherent existence or a permanent enduring essence does not mean they don't exist. Mountains, chairs, tables, houses, people, cars, and televisions all exist, but they do not have inherent existence. Realizing that no essences inhere in empirical objects diminishes our tendency to cling to things. Understanding emptiness allows us to see the world as it is and not believe the world as it appears to our deluded mind.[245]

Madhyamaka introduced the causality doctrine to prove that all sentient beings do not have inherent existence. The founder of Madhyamaka, Nagarjuna, said "There is no being that can exist on its own without depending on anything else; no self-sufficient being. Everything is interdependent. Everything that exists on both the physical and mental plane involves the idea of interdependence, or pratityasamutpada." All sentient beings come into being because of what is called interdependent origination, or pratitya-samutpada—that is, due to causes and conditions. This implies that nothing has inherent existence, because if they had any kind of essence

---

[244] Traleg Kyabgon, *The Essence of Buddhism*, Shambhala Publications, INC., Boston (2001), p71

[245] Traleg Kyabgon, *The Essence of Buddhism*, Shambhala Publications, INC., Boston (2001), p 72

or independent existence there would be no need for the whole idea of causality.[246] Both the Buddha and Nagarjuna have said that the idea of interdependent origination is identical with the concept of emptiness. Nagarjuna has said that emptiness is interdependent origination, and interdependent origination is emptiness. So when we say that things are interdependently produced, or that things come into being through the interdependence of causes and conditions, it is the same as saying things are empty by nature. Through the understanding of emptiness based upon interdependent origination, we are able to form the right view, which voids these two extremes of eternalism and nihilism. In Madhyamaka philosophy, ultimate reality is not seen as something that exists outside of or above the empirical reality with which we are confronted every day. Rather, emptiness is the nature of the very world that we live in, so the nature of the empirical world is ultimate reality.[247]

On the other hand, the Mere-Consciousness doctrine of Yogachara is that only consciousness exists. Yoga in this context means 'meditation,' while chara means 'practice,' so Yogachara has been translated as 'the school of meditation,' emphasizing the primacy of meditation in understanding ultimate reality (not that the Madhyamaka school doesn't do this also). This school is also called Chittamatra—a term that has given rise to much confusion in the West, where it has usually been translated as 'mind only.' This has led many interpreters of Mahayana Buddhism to think that this particular school denies the existence of the external world, positing that everything exists only in the mind, and they therefore consider Mahayana Buddhism to be the same as the Western theory known as idealism. British idealists such as Bishop Berkeley assert that only ideas in the mind are real, and that apart from ideas, nothing exists. This is not what the Chittamatrins mean when they say that everything is 'mind only.' What they mean is

---

246 Traleg Kyabgon, *The Essence of Buddhism*, Shambhala Publications, INC., Boston (2001), pp 73-74

247 Traleg Kyabgon, *The Essence of Buddhism*, Shambhala Publications, INC., Boston (2001), p75

that our perception of external reality is mind-dependent. In other words, we can only have access to the external world through our mind.[248] The Yogacharins say that when we look at things on all different levels—on the sensory level, the conceptual level, or the moral level—we can see that what we experience is colored by our presuppositions, prejudices, and predilections. This means that there is no such thing as objective reality in the ultimate sense. On a sensory level, for example, we perceive a tree or car with our visual sense, but there is no tree or car existing of its own accord independently of the mind. Insects would not perceive a tree or a car in the way we would, because they lack our concepts relating to trees and cars.[249] Another contribution that the Yogachara school has made to the general Mahayana tradition and philosophy is the notion of Buddha-nature, or tathagatha-garbha. Madhyamaka philosophers talk about absolute and relative bodhichitta, but they do not talk about Buddha-nature as such. Relying on certain authoritative Mahayana sutras, the Yogacharins formulated this concept by saying that all sentient beings have the seed or potential to obtain enlightenment.[250]

While Madhyamaka emphasizes emptiness, Yogachara emphasizes consciousness. These two philosophies of Mahayana look different from each other, but they are not. According to their doctrines it is said that emptiness can be understood by understanding the relation of consciousness on outside objects with mind. In the Mere-Consciousness doctrine of Yogachara, not only the Middle Way doctrine of consciousness is introduced as an important conclusion, but interdependence of mind and causality of death and rebirth are also importantly dealt with. Mere-Consciousness is sometimes said to be a doctrine that has been

---

248 Traleg Kyabgon, *The Essence of Buddhism*, Shambhala Publications, INC., Boston (2001), p 79

249 Traleg Kyabgon, *The Essence of Buddhism*, Shambhala Publications, INC., Boston (2001), p 80

250 Traleg Kyabgon, *The Essence of Buddhism*, Shambhala Publications, INC., Boston (2001), pp 82-83

completed to understand the No-Self and the Emptiness doctrines. According to *Ch'eng Wei-shih-Lun* (Treatise on the Doctrine of Mere-Consciousness), by concluding that Atman (self) and dharmas are non-existent, Emptiness and consciousness are not nonexistent and the Mere-Consciousness doctrine of Yogachara complies with the Middle Way doctrine of Madhyamaka.

The Mere-Consciousness Doctrine was originated by the Buddha, and theoretically systemized by Maitreya (A.D 270-350). Following thereafter, Asanga (A.D 300-389) and his brother, Vasubandhu (A.D 320-400) completed the philosophy.[251]

The Mere-Consciousness of Mahayana is analogous to the Abhidharmakosa-sastra of Hinayana. Mahayana is usually distinguished from early Buddhism, or Hinayana, which literally means 'small vehicle.' Mahayana is 'large vehicle.' The Abhidharmakosa-sastra is a philosophy regarding the phenomenal world based on objects and mind, whereas Mere-Consciousness is a philosophy regarding consciousness based on mind (*citta*), intellection (*manas*) and consciousness (*vijnana*). While the Abhidharmakosa-sastra is a basic philosophy of Hinayana, the Mere-Consciousness is a basic philosophy of Mahayana.

Asanga, who was born in Gandhara, Northern India, began as a Hinayana Buddhist but later became a Mahayanan. He wrote two major books. One is Samdhinirmocana Sutra which annotated Madhyamaka Sutra of Nagarjuna, the other is Mahynasamgraha in which the Mere-Consciousness doctrine is organized based on the Mahayana Abhidharma Sutra.[252]

Vasubandhu, like his elder brother, Asanga, began as a Hinayana Buddhist but also later became a Mahayanan. He made remarkable achievement on the Mere-Consciousness philosophy and wrote two books: Vijnaptimatratasiddhi-trimsika (Trimsika: Thirthy Stanzas on Mere-Consciousness) and *Wei-shih Erh Shih Lun*

---

251 Zen Master Seong Chul, One Hundred Discourses I, Changkyungkak, Korea, Kyngnam (1987), p 195

252 Zen Master Seong Chul, One Hundred Discourses I, Changkyungkak, Korea, Kyngnam (1987), p 196

(Vimsatika: Twenty Treatises on Mere-Consciouness). The Thirty Stanzas are very brief, like a poem with no annotation. Therefore, a lot of sastra-masters wrote commentaries on the Thirty Stanzas so as to further develop the Mere-Consciousness philosophy. The Thirty Stanzas later became the basis of Hsuan Tsang's masterpiece, *Ch'eng Wei-shih-Lun*.[253]

The Mere-Consciousness philosophy was spread into China to found the Fa-hsiang (Dharmalaksana: Vijinaptimatrata) school. The Fa-hsiang school originated from Hsuan Tsang (A.D 602~664) who studied the Mere-Consciousness philosophy in India. He wrote *Ch'eng Wei-shih-Lun* (Treatise on the Doctrine of Mere-Consciousness) which annotated the Thirty Stanzas and became the cornerstone of the Fa-hsiang school. In fact it was Hsuan Tsang's most eminent disciple, Kuei Chi, who wrote a Commentay on *Ch'eng Wei-shih-Lun* (a work of outstanding excellence) and became the founder of the Fa-hsiang school. As the Fa-hsiang school emphasized the Middle Way of No-existence and No-emptiness, it was called a Middle Way school. The philosophy of Fa-hsiang adopted many doctrines of the Mere-Consciousness philosophy of India, including among them the eight consciousnesses doctrine including Alaya consciousness (Alayavijnana).[254]

The Thirty Stanzas by Vasubandhu is a foundation of the Mere-Consciousness philosophy. The framework of the Mere-Consciousness was made by Maitreya and Asanga, and the systematic completion was achieved in the Thirty Stanzas by Vasubandhu. The translation of the Thirty Stanzas into Chinese by Hsuan Tsang is composed of only thirty songs like poems. Each song has only twenty Chinese letters in four phrases. The Thirty Stanzas consists of only 600 Chinese letters.

The Thirty Stanzas contain the essence about consciousness. Realizing that the Thirty Stanzas was replete with intricate and

---

253 Zen Master Seong Chul, One Hundred Discourses I, Changkyungkak, Korea, Kyngnam (1987), pp 196-197

254 Zen Master Seong Chul, One Hundred Discourses I, Changkyungkak, Korea, Kyngnam (1987), pp 198-199

profound meanings, Vasubandhu had intended to write his own commentary on it but he died before doing so. Subsequently, the task of expounding the philosophy underlying the Thirty Stanzas fell to ten sastra-masters, each of whom composed a commentary on them. These ten sastra-masters are Bandhusri, Cittrabhanu, Gunamati, Sthiramati, Nanda, Shuddhacandra, Dharmapala, Jnamitra, Jinapura and Jnanacandra. Hsuan Tsang authored *Ch'eng Wei-shih-Lun* based on the Thirty Stanzas, a creative and elaborate exposition of the Thirty Stanzas and a synthesis of the ten commentaries.

Ch'eng Wei-shih-Lun represents the power of Hsuan Tsang and his disciple Kuei Chi's literary and spiritual genius. This work is enormous compared with the Thirty Stanzas, as it consists of ten Chinese volumes. As the book was synthesized with the ten commentaries, various different views were also introduced. According to the book there are many agreeable aspects, but there are also many different views on the consciousness doctrines. For example, according to Mere-Consciousness, each sentient being has a fundamental consciousness (Alayvijnana: Storehouse Consciousness), which evolves in a homogeneous and continuous series and carries within it the 'seeds' (Bijas) of all dharmas. In regard to the origin of Bijas, one theory asserts that they are all inborn and natural; i.e., innately existing in Alaya consciousness, and none of them come into being as a result of causality. However, another theory explains that Bijas are all born as a result of causation. A third theory is that there are actually two kinds of Bijas. Some Bijas are natural or inborn, other Bijas are those whose existence has had a beginning and come into being as a result of being caused by actual dharmas.[255] As shown in the example above, different views in many aspects remain unchanged with not much progress for more than 1,000 years.

The Thirty Stanzas consists of three parts, a first part from the first stanza to the nineteenth, a second from the twentieth to the

---

[255] Wei Tat, *CH'ENG WEI-SHIH LUN*, THE CH'ENG WEI-SHIH LUN PUBLICATION COMMITTEE, Hong Kong (1973), pp LXI-LXI

twenty-fifth, and a third from the twenty-sixth to the thirtieth. The first part explains the principles and mechanism of eight consciousnesses, the second part explains the natures of consciousness, and the third part explains the holy path of attainment in which five stages for obtaining Buddhahood through the Mere-Consciousness doctrine are explained.

According to this philosophy there are eight consciousnesses, which are the first six consciousnesses by the six organs, Manas consciousness as the seventh, and Alaya consciousness as the eighth. The eight consciousnesses are grouped into the first five consciousnesses by the five physical organs, and the post three consciousnesses of the sixth, Manas and Alaya. As the sixth organ is Mind, the sixth consciousness is called 'Mind consciousness.' Also, as the sixth object is dharmas, the sixth consciousness is called 'consciousness of dharmas.' The first six consciousnesses have a function of perception or discrimination of the respective object, the seventh functions as cogitation or intellection, and the eighth is for storing all seven consciousnesses.

The Buddha, in many passages of His Sutras, teaches that Citta (seed of mind), Manas (intellection) and Vijnana (consciousness) have different meanings: that which accumulates and produces (all things) is called Citta (seed of mind), that which reasons and cogitates is called Manas (intellection), and that which discriminates is called Vijnana (consciousness). In connection with the eight consciousnesses, the eighth is called *citta*, the seventh is called *manas*, and the remaining six are called *vijnana*. Among the three, citta is regarded as the most important because it is deemed to be seeds of consciousness

The Mere-Consciousness Doctrine was developed on the basis of the eighth consciousness, Alaya Vijnana. It is not clear when the term 'alaya' was used. Although it is said that the term was used in Mahayana Buddhism, needless to say, it must have been used since Early Buddhism by the Buddha Himself. The meaning of the term in Early Buddhism is not identical with that in Yogachara in Mahayana Buddhism. Despite this, the term was not made after the Buddha. The terms, citta, manas, and vijnana were used in Early Buddhism prior to Hinayana Buddhism.[256]

The first important characteristic of the Mere-Consciousness Doctrine is in the eighth consciousness, Alaya, which is a storehouse for storage of all consciousnesses. All the six consciousnesses and the seventh, including mental activities, are stored in Alaya without exception. Strictly speaking, Alaya is not a kind of consciousness. Just as sound or smell is not a truly a kind of consciousness, so neither is Alaya. Alaya is deemed as a storehouse of all consciousnesses which we perceived, thought and felt. Alaya is like a database in which all data are saved. Alaya contains all the seven consciousnesses. It does not matter whether the consciousness has been acknowledged or not. Further, Alaya contains not only all consciousnesses of the present life, but also of all the previous lives. Alaya is a formative element in birth and rebirth. Alaya in Buddhism corresponds to the unconscious or subconscious in psychology or psychoanalysis.

The second important characteristic of Mere-Consciousness is in the seventh consciousness, Manas. It has the nature and character of cogitation or intellection, and is called 'cogitation consciousness.' According to *Ch'eng Wei-shih-Lun*, Manas consciousness manifests itself with Alayavijnana as its basis and support, and takes Alayavijnana as its object. The Mere-Consciousness philosophy separates cogitation consciousness from the six sense consciousnesses by introducing Manas. It has not been introduced either in psychology or psychoanalysis, though thinking or thought consciousness is not denied. Western science in particular believes that the process of thinking is carried out in the brain, and they cannot imagine the process of cogitation without the brain. In Mere-Consciousness, however, Manas is not explained as correlating with either the brain or any other physical organ. Mere-Consciousness defines the seventh consciousness as Manas, which is different from the first six and the eighth, Alaya consciousness.

---

256 Zen Master Seong Chul, One Hundred Discourses I, Changkyungkak, Korea, Kyngnam (1987), p 208

The third important characteristic of the Mere-Consciousness Doctrine is in the sixth consciousness, Manovijnana. There is no doubt about the first five consciousnesses, but the sixth is not straight forward. The first five consciousness are called 'sense consciousnesses,' while the sixth 'sense-centre consciousness.' The sixth consciousness is generated by the sixth organ which is explained as 'organ of Mind' or 'root of Mind.' It is clear that the sixth organ is not the brain. It must be a non-physical and immaterial organ, but it is capable of reading mind information, resulting in generating a sixth consciousness, Manovijnana.

The second part of The Thirty Stanzas, from the twentieth to the twenty-fifth, explains about the natures of consciousness. They are nature of mere-imagination, nature of dependence on others, and ultimate reality. The nature of mere-imagination of consciousness means that the reality of things is assumed by imagination. This is an illusion, for things are imagined to really exist where in fact there are none. It is like seeing a mirage which vanishes as one approaches it. Imagined objects have, therefore, no objective reality. However, the first five and the eighth consciousnesses do not have the nature of mere-imagination. Only the sixth and the seventh are possessed of the faculty of imagination. The nature of dependence on others means that all discriminations by consciousness are produced by causes and conditions. There is nothing self-existing in the world, everything depends for its existence on something else, things are universally mutually conditioned, endlessly related one to another. The ultimate reality, as the third nature, means the genuine nature of consciousness thus revealed by the Emptiness or Voidness (*sunyata*) of Atman and dharma. The ultimate reality is the complete and perfect 'real nature' of all dharmas.

Buddhism describes the transformation of the Eight Consciousnesses into the Four Wisdoms. The Consciousness-Only philosophy explains that four transcendental wisdoms are attained by transformation of the mental attributes of consciousness. The Four Wisdoms are the Perfect Achievement Wisdom, the Profound Contemplation Wisdom, the Universal Equality Wisdom, and the Great Mirror Wisdom. The Perfect Achievement Wisdom is attained by virtue of the transformation of the five sense consciousnesses, the Profound Contemplation Wisdom by the transformation of the sixth, the Universal Equality Wisdom by the transformation of the seventh, and the Great Mirror Wisdom by the transformation of the eighth. The welfare and happiness of all sentient beings are promoted through the Perfect Achievement Wisdom. The mind associated with the Perfect Achievement Wisdom manifests itself through the desire to promote the welfare and happiness of all sentient beings in a diversity of consciously-realized actions of the body, the voice, and the mind. The Perfect Achievement Wisdom must be attained through living in the material world which obeys the laws of nature; i.e., water always flows to a lower level, the law of gravity applies to all objects, an onion will not produce a rose, and as one sows so shall he reap, etc. The Profound Contemplation Wisdom is attained by the transformation of the sixth consciousness. With this Wisdom the sixth organ (mind) perceives the sixth objects (mind information) with profound clarity and without hindrance. This is the spiritual world where the mind organ experiences wonderful observations. If the Profound Contemplation Wisdom is attained the mind organ can see unseeable objects, hear soundless sounds, smell scentless scents, taste food without flavor, and be free from space and time. The Universal Equality Wisdom is attained by the transformation of the seventh consciousness. The mind associated with this Wisdom sees the identity of all dharmas, and the complete equality between its own self and other sentient beings. This Wisdom is always united with great benevolence, great compassion, etc., and is the special supporting basis for the Profound Contemplation Wisdom. The Great Mirror Wisdom is attained by the transformation of the eighth consciousness. The mind associated with this Wisdom is entirely dissociated from all mental discriminations. The Great Mirror is free from errors in its perception of all objects. Like a big mirror reflects all objects as they are, this Wisdom reflects the absolute reality of all things as they are.

According to the Consciousness-Only Theory, there are five stages of progress or development towards enlightenment: the stage of moral provisioning (the path of preparation), the stage of intensified effort (the path of application), the stage of unimpeded penetrating understanding (the path of seeing), the stage of exercising cultivation (the path of meditation), and the stage of final attainment or ultimate realization (the path of no more learning). The five stages are the steps to reach the holy path of attainment. The first two, the path of preparation and the path of application, are normally referred to as worldly paths, whereas the last three are known as supramundane paths. On the last three paths there is a greater development of wisdom. From the Buddhist perspective, without wisdom we operate on the level of a worldly person. No matter how kindhearted we are, or how well behaved we may be, if we are devoid of wisdom we are still operating within the context of this world and not the world of spirituality. Wisdom does not necessarily mean being clever. Wisdom in Buddhism has more to do with having a real understanding of ourselves and the phenomenal world. On the *Shravaka* level it means understanding impermanence, and on the level of the *Bodhisattva* it means understanding emptiness. A really spiritual person must possess the qualities of compassion and love as well as wisdom. Even if compassion and love are present in the mind-stream of a particular individual, if that person is lacking in wisdom he or she is still not a fully developed person.[257]

---

257 Traleg Kyabgon, *The Essence of Buddhism*, Shambhala Publications, INC., Boston (2001), pp. 97-98

Bibliography

Merriam-Webster's Collegiate Dictionary, Eleventh Edition. (2003). (F. C. Mish Ed. 11th ed.). Springfield, MA: Merriam Webster, Inc.

Amen, D. G. (1998). *Change your brain, change your life : the breakthrough program for conquering anxiety, depression, obsessiveness, anger, and impulsiveness* (1st ed.). New York: Times Books.

Atkins, P. W. (2003). *Galileo's Finger: the Ten Great Ideas of Science.* Oxford; New York: Oxford University Press.

Brockman, J., & OverDrive Inc. (2013). *Thinking the new science of decision-making, problem-solving, and prediction* (pp. 1 online resource). Retrieved from http://princeton.lib.overdrive.com/ContentDetails.htm?ID=8BE117A2-7BB6-4097-97B2-A5364EFD181A

Bstan 'dzin rgya, m., Varela, F. J., & Engel, J. (1997). *Sleeping, dreaming, and dying : an exploration of consciousness with the Dalai Lama ; foreword by H.H. the Fourteenth Dalai Lama ; narrated and edited by Francisco J. Varela ; with contributions by Jerome Engel, Jr. ... [et al.] ; translations by B. Alan Wallace and Thupten Jinpa.* Boston: Wisdom Publications.

Capra, F. (2010). *The tao of physics : an exploration of the parallels between modern physics and Eastern mysticism* (5th ed.). Boston: Shambhala.

Choi, D. (2011). *Mechanism of consciousness during life, dream and after-death*. Bloomington, IN: AuthorHouse.

Choi, Y. (2004). *Possession, The Homeless of Soul*. Seoul: Inwha.

Chopra, D. (2006). *Life after death : the burden of proof* (1st ed.). New York: Harmony Books.

Chul, S. (1987). *One Hundred Discourses I (Available only in Korean)*. Changkyungkak, Korea: Kyngnam.

Chul, S. (1999). *Eternal Freedom (Available only in Korean)*. Changkyungkak, Korea.

Conze, E. (2001). *Buddhist wisdom : containing the Diamond Sutra and the Heart Sutra* (1st ed.). New York: Vintage Books.

Cook, F. H., Xuanzang, Vasubandhu, Xuanzang, Vasubandhu, & Numata Center for Buddhist Translation and Research. (1999). *Three texts on Consciousness Only : Demonstration of Consciousness Only*. Berkeley, Calif.: Numata Center for Buddhist Translation and Research.

Doidge, N. (2007). *The brain that changes itself : stories of personal triumph from the frontiers of brain science*. New York: Viking.

Dossey, L. (2013). *One Mind: How Our Individual Mind is Part of a Greater Consciousness and Why It Matters* (1st edition. ed.) Hay House, Inc.

Evans-Wentz, W. Y., Karma gliṅ, p., & Zla ba bsam, g. (1960). *The Tibetan book of the dead; or, The after-death experiences on the Bardo plane, according to Lāma Kazi Dawa-Samdup's English rendering* (3d ed.). New York,: Oxford University Press.

Gelernter, D. (2014, January 2014). *The Closing of the Scientific Mind*. Commentary Magazine.

Goldstein, J. (1976). *The experience of insight : a natural unfolding*. Santa Cruz: Unity Press.

Goswami, A. (2007). *Mind Before Matter: Visions of a New Science of Consciousness* (J. E. M. a. P. D. Trish Pfeiffer Ed.). New Alresford, Hampshire, UK: IFF Books.

Goswami, A., Reed, R. E., & Goswami, M. (1993). *The self-aware universe: how consciousness creates the material world*. New York: Putnam's Sons.

Grimes, R. (2010). *The Fun of Dying: Find Out What Really Happens Next!* (1st ed.): Greater Reality Publications.

Hanh, T. N., Laity, A., & Nguyen, A. H. (2010). *The diamond that cuts through illusion commentaries on the Prajñaparamita Diamond Sutra* (pp. 1 online resource (150 p.)). Retrieved from http://libproxy.lib.unc.edu/login?url=http://site.ebrary.com/lib/uncch/Doc?id=10469185

Hart, W. (1987). *The art of living : Vipassana meditation as taught by S.N. Goenka* (1st ed.). San Francisco: Harper & Row.

Ickes, W. J. (2003). *Everyday mind reading : understanding what other people think and feel*. Amherst, N.Y.: Prometheus Books.

Jotika, U. (2008). *Geography of Mind* (E. Park, Trans.). Seoul, S. Korea: Yonbangjuk.

Jung, C. G. (1966). *Two essays on analytical psychology* (2d ed.). New York: Pantheon.

Kim, M. (2008). *East and West*. Seoul: Yedam.

Kim, S. (2014). *Watching*. Seoul: Jungshinsegyesa.

Koch, C. (2004). *The Quest for consciousness : a neurobiological approach*. Englewood, CO: Roberts and Company Publishers.

Kyabgon, T. (2001). *The essence of Buddhism : an introduction to its philosophy and practice*. Boston: Shambhala.

LaBerge, S. (2009). *Lucid dreaming : a concise guide to awakening in your dreams and in your life*. Boulder, Colo.: Sounds True.

Mahesh, Y. (2001). *Science of being and art of living : transcendental meditation* (Newly rev. & updated. ed.). New York, N.Y.: Plume.

Nagasawa, Y. (2008). *God and phenomenal consciousness: a novel approach to knowledge arguments.* Cambridge; New York: Cambridge University Press.

Nagel, T. (2012). *Mind and Cosmos: Why the Materialist Neo-Darwinian Conception of Nature Is Almost Certainly False.* New York: Oxford University Press.

Nhất, H. n., Laity, A., & Nguyen, A. H. (2010). *The diamond that cuts through illusion : commentaries on the Prajñaparamita Diamond Sutra* (Rev. ed.). Berkeley, Calif.: Parallax Press.

Nisargadatta. (1973). *I am that.* Bombay: Chetana.

Nisbett, R. E. (2003). *The geography of thought : how Asians and westerners think differently-- and why.* New York: Free Press.

Oh, H. (1991). *Study of the Sixth Consciousness in Mere-Consciousness.* Seoul: Bulgyosasangsa.

Pearce, J. C. (1992). *Evolution's end: claiming the potential of our intelligence* (1st ed.). San Francisco: HarperSanFrancisco.

Pinker, S. (1997, 2009). *How the mind works* (Norton pbk. ed.). New York: Norton.

Poppe, N. (1971). *The Diamond Sutra; three Mongolian versions of the Vajracchedikā Prajñāpāramitā.* Wiesbaden,: Harrassowitz.

Radin, D. I. (2013). *Supernormal: science, yoga, and the path to extraordinary psychic abilities* (First edition. ed.) New York, Random House, Inc, Deepak Chopra Books

Radin, D. I. (1997). *The conscious universe: the scientific truth of psychic phenomena* (1st. ed.). New York, N.Y.: HarperEdge.

Rock, A. (2004). *The mind at night : the new science of how and why we dream* (1st ed.). New York: Basic Books.

Schrœdinger, E., & Schrœdinger, E. (2012). *What is life? : the physical aspect of the living cell ; with, Mind and matter ; & Autobiographical sketches* (Canto ed.). Cambridge ; New York: Cambridge University Press.

Sharma, R. S. (1998). *The monk who sold his Ferrari : a fable about fulfilling your dreams and reaching your destiny* (1st ed.). San Francisco: HarperSanFrancisco.

Sheldrake, R. (2012). *Science set free: 10 paths to new discovery.* New York: Deepak Chopra Books.

Sogyal, R., Gaffney, P. D., & Harvey, A. (2002). *The Tibetan book of living and dying* (10th anniversary ed.). London: Rider.

Stanford University., & Center for the Study of Language and Information (U.S.). (1997 (with quarterly updates)). *Stanford encyclopedia of philosophy* Retrieved from http://openurl.cdlib.org/?sid=UCB:CAT&genre=article&issn=1095-5054

Tenzin, P. (2002). *Reflections on a mountain lake : teachings on practical Buddhism.* Ithaca, N.Y.: Snow Lion Publications.

Tucker, J. B. (2013). *Return to life: extraordinary cases of children who remember past lives* (First Edition. ed.). New York: St. Martin's Griffin.

Varela, F. J., Bstan 'dzin rgya, m., & Engel, J. (1997). *Sleeping, dreaming, and dying : an exploration of consciousness with the Dalai Lama ; foreword by H.H. the Fourteenth Dalai Lama ; narrated and edited by Francisco J. Varela ; with contributions by Jerome Engel, Jr. ... [et al.] ; translations by B. Alan Wallace and Thupten Jinpa.* Boston: Wisdom Publications.

Vasubandhu, & Anacker, S. (1984). *Seven works of Vasubandhu, the Buddhist psychological doctor.* Delhi: Motilal Banarsidass.

Velmans, M. N., Yujin. (2012). *Introduction to Monist Alternatives to Physicalism.* Journal of Consciousness Studies: Special Issue on Monist Alternatives to Physicalism, 19 (Number 9-10).

Wallace, B. A., Quirolo, L., & Ye śes rdo, r. (2003). *Buddhism with an attitude : the Tibetan seven-point mind-training* (2nd ed.). Ithaca, NY: Snow Lion Publications.

Xuanzang, Vasubandhu, & Wei, T. (1973). *Ch'eng wei-shih lun; the doctrine of mere-consciousness.* Hong Kong,: Ch'eng Wei-shih Lun Publication Committee.

Xuanzang, Vasubandhu, Xuanzang, Vasubandhu, Cook, F. H., & Numata Center for Buddhist Translation and Research. (1999). *Three texts on Consciousness Only : Demonstration of Consciousness Only.* Berkeley, Calif.: Numata Center for Buddhist Translation and Research.